Disciplines in Art Education: Contexts of Understanding
General Series Editor, Ralph A. Smith

Art History and Education

ART HISTORY
AND
EDUCATION

Stephen Addiss and
Mary Erickson

UNIVERSITY OF ILLINOIS PRESS
Urbana and Chicago

This volume and the others in the series Disciplines in Art Education: Contexts of Understanding are made possible by a grant from the Getty Center for Education in the Arts. The J. Paul Getty Trust retains all publishing rights to the individual essays in the series. The views expressed in the volumes are those of the authors and not necessarily those of the J. Paul Getty Trust.

Library of Congress Cataloging-in-Publication Data

Addiss, Stephen.
    Art history and education / Stephen Addiss and Mary Erickson.
       p.   cm. — (Disciplines in art education)
    Includes bibliographical references and index.
    ISBN 0-252-01970-9 (cl). — ISBN 0-252-06273-6 (pb)
    1. Art—Historiography. I. Erickson, Mary. II. Title.
III. Series.
N380.A33   1993
707'.2—dc20   92-24034
                                      CIP

Contents

General Series Preface

Since the early 1980s, the Getty Center for Education in the Arts, which is an operating entity of the J. Paul Getty Trust, has been committed to improving the quality of aesthetic learning in our nation's schools and museums. According to the organizing idea of the center's educational policy, teaching about the visual arts can be rendered more effective through the incorporation of concepts and activities from a number of interrelated disciplines, namely, artistic creation, art history, art criticism, and aesthetics.

The resultant discipline-based approach to art education does not, however, mandate that these four disciplines be taught separately; rather, the disciplines are to provide justifications, subject matter, and methods as well as exemplify attitudes that are relevant to the cultivation of percipience in matters of art. They offer different analytic contexts to aid our understanding and aesthetic enjoyment, contexts such as the making of unique objects of visual interest (artistic creation), the apprehension of art under the aspects of time, tradition, and style (art history), the reasoned judgment of artistic merit (art criticism), and the critical analysis of basic aesthetic concepts and puzzling issues (aesthetics). Discipline-based art education thus assumes that our ability to engage works of art intelligently requires not only our having attempted to produce artworks and gained some awareness of the mysteries and difficulties of artistic creation in the process but also our having acquired familiarity with art's history, its principles of judgment, and its conundrums. All are prerequisite to building a sense of art in the young, which is the overarching objective of aesthetic learning.

Although no consensus exists on precisely how the various components of aesthetic learning should be orchestrated to accomplish the goals of discipline-based art education, progress toward these objectives will require that those charged with designing art education programs bring an adequate understanding of the four disciplines to bear on their work. It is toward generating such needed understanding that a five-volume series was conceived as part of the Getty Center's publication program. To narrow the distance separating the disciplines from classroom teaching, each book following the introductory volume will be coauthored by a scholar or practitioner in one of the disciplines (an artist, an art historian, an art critic, and a philosopher of art) and an educational specialist with an interest or competence in a given art discipline. The introductory volume provides a philosophical rationale for the idea of discipline-based art education. It is hoped that the series, which is intended primarily for art teachers in elementary and secondary education, for those who prepare these teachers, and for museum educators, will make a significant contribution to the literature of art education.

Ralph A. Smith
General Series Editor

General Editor's Introduction

The present volume was prepared by an art historian and an art educator. Stephen Addiss is Tucker-Boatright Professor of Art and Humanities at the University of Richmond and adjunct curator of Oriental art at the New Orleans Museum of Art. A performer of international traditional music as well as an artist who exhibits paintings and calligraphy, Addiss is the author and narrator of a number of music programs devoted to contemporary and Asian music, and he has represented the United States in numerous concerts and workshops abroad. While teaching at the University of Kansas, he also served as codirector of a humanities program for gifted high school students in eastern Kansas. Some of his recent publications are *One Thousand Years of Art in Japan* (editor and coauthor, 1981), *Samurai Painters* (1983), *Tall Mountains and Flowing Waters: The Arts of Uragami Gyokudo* (1987), and *The Art of Zen: Japanese Painting and Calligraphy, 1600–1925* (1989), and *Narrow Road to the Interior* (illustrator, 1991). Addiss's multiple interests make him uncommonly qualified to address the role of art history in a program of discipline-based art education.

Mary Erickson is a professor of art education in the School of Art at Arizona State University, Tempe. She has taught in the public school and community college systems of Illinois and Indiana and was for a number of years a faculty member of the Department of Art Education at Kutztown University in Pennsylvania. Her interests encompass all areas of art education, and she has conducted numerous in-service workshops for teachers on planning and curriculum development. She has also developed learning resources and created pedagogical games for the teaching of art. For her indefatigable efforts on behalf of art education, Erickson was elected Pennslvania art educator of the year for 1990–91. Because of her longtime interest in art, aesthetic education, and the history of art and her involvement with the practical aspects of art education, she brings to the idea and implementation of discipline-based art education a perspective that is humane, enlightened, and relevant.

Art History and Art Education is noteworthy for the closeness of the collaboration that is possible between a subject-matter specialist and a specialist in the education of teachers. In this volume, two scholars jointly introduce the discipline of art history in a manner that is suitable as a foundation for the development and planning of education programs for young people. The writers' cooperation is abundantly in evidence: they coauthored the preface as well as the epilogue, and Erickson makes repeated illuminating references to the chapters written by Addiss. The latter, for his part, obviously remains aware throughout that he is primarily addressing neither professional colleagues nor a general public with an interest in art but, specifically, teachers of art. Addiss has written as an educator, that is, as a person concerned with opening minds and promoting independent thought. Art history may be uniquely suited to such a pedagogical purpose, for it is, as Addiss points out, a field in which final answers are seldom possible and which, consequently, offers opportunities for free inquiry and independent conclusions. It is probably to stimulate such inquiry that Addiss has generously interspersed his text with questions to the reader, questions that teachers may also profitably ask their students.

Open-mindedness and fairness of spirit pervade Addiss's presentation of Western as well as non-Western cultures and of traditional as well as contemporary methodologies in art history. He is, on the whole, very grateful for the most recent developments in his specialty. "The new social approach to art history," Addiss writes, "has added a great deal to our field, and few current scholars have not widened their range of study as a result"—or, as feminist art historians have done, moved to redress old biases. But he also notes that, to present their case, too many scholars formulate theories with the intention of demolishing their rivals. If art educators were to adopt such a strategy, they would be committing themselves to the mistaken belief that one, and only one, methodology constitutes a valid approach to art history.

Perhaps Addiss puts the issue of contending art-historical viewpoints into proper perspective when he says that "art history always starts with the image itself, and words are secondary." As if in further affirmation of the primacy of the image, he notes that "there is something magical and primordial in artistic creation that can cut through time and space to reach our inner spirit. The study of art history by itself cannot make this happen, but it can increase and inform our responses, adding greatly to our understanding and delight."

If a willingness to let the discipline of art history expand into some hitherto alien territories and a hospitable attitude toward new ideas are distinctive of Addiss's chapters, they likewise characterize Erickson's. She takes a panoramic view of art history when she asserts that "art history learning for all students in elementary and secondary schools should include an introduction to art from around the world, an overview of Western art history, and an introduction to art-historical inquiry processes." She also pleads for the historical study of a wide range of handcrafted as well as mass-produced objects and believes that a multicultural stance is appropriate for a multiethnic democratic society. Educators contemplating the teaching of art history must thus face the problem of a superabundance of content deemed appropriate for such instruction.

Erickson, however, provides a firm scaffolding upon which to construct an art history program and takes due notice of the restrictions that limit, often severely, what teachers can hope to accomplish. There are first the practical constraints of student readiness. Although art history may be made comprehensible to elementary school children, the nature of their comprehension will be vastly different from the understanding achieved by more mature students. Erickson gives useful advice on what may be appropriate for different age levels. Then there are the professional and ethical constraints imposed by the demands of sound curriculum planning. Scope and sequence as well as lesson and unit planning require scrupulous attention, lest the result be what she calls a "smattering of isolated learning."

Integration is really less a theoretical choice of the discipline-based approach than it is a practical necessity for art educators: there simply is not enough instructional time to teach the four disciplines separately— nor was that ever envisioned. Students should certainly learn something about art history (and art criticism, aesthetics, and artistic creation), but primarily they should be taught how to use the disciplines to deepen and inform their aesthetic responses. "It may not be important that primary school children be able to distinguish one art discipline from another," says Erickson, "but those who develop the curriculum should be able to do so." To help teachers make these distinctions, she frames short definitions and thoughtful suggestions about how art history can inform instruction in each of the other disciplines.

Erickson's chapters derive particular strength from her own experience in the teaching of art history and her intimate knowledge of what teachers find most useful. She provides not only several practical examples of lesson plans but also concepts and categories that can help art teachers organize their thinking and teaching. She discusses, for example, three ways of teaching art history, three categories of art-historical inquiry, two types of art-historical research, four phases of artistic production, and five areas of aesthetics. But she is also familiar with the ways in which art history teaching can go wrong. One is the practice of simply attaching the label "art history" to things that have traditionally been done in art programs and in other parts of the curriculum. Another is a willingness to allow content to be dictated exclusively by student preferences (although Erickson does tolerate, and even recommends, some concessions to student interests at the expense of historical significance and aesthetic value). Neither approach, however, will ensure the building of an effective sense of art history.

A subsidiary goal of the teaching of art history is the engendering in students of an appreciation of the discipline itself. Some appreciation will accrue as part of students' being familiarized with rudiments of the skills and attitudes of art-historical inquiry. But just as discipline-based art education as a whole envisions acquainting learners with some of the finest masterpieces of the visual arts from around the world, so art history instruction should include at least one exemplar of actual scholarly practice. Addiss supplies one in his "Study of a Single Project," a report on a phase of his own work. One hopes teachers will pay special attention to and make use of Addiss's discussion, for it will give students some idea of the extent of the skills professional art historians must possess and the kinds of attitudes they must have cultivated. In Addiss's case, these include fluency in at least two other languages and the ability to read and translate a variety of even more difficult scripts, as well as magnitudes of patience, persistence, and attention to detail that may tax the comprehension of young minds.

Ralph A. Smith

Preface

This book begins with three simple questions: Why should we study and teach art history? Is art history necessary or useful for the education of our children? Can't we leave this field to "experts"?

These questions offer us a challenge and an opportunity. As we shall see, art history can offer many different approaches and methods, but above all it inspires direct participation. By becoming involved in studying and teaching the history of art, we explore the nature of the world and of ourselves through the expression of the human spirit in every time and culture, including our own.

We live in a visual age. Not only are we bombarded with images from the media, but we are all constantly making artistic decisions for ourselves. Choosing a suit, a shirt, a dress, a coat; buying a painting, a photograph, or a poster to put up on the wall; picking out a greeting card; finding the appropriate earrings; selecting a tie, a carpet, housepaint, bedspreads, or a new car—all these require decisions about form, color, and design. Just as we reveal ourselves by what we say and do, we all make personal statements visually by the way we dress, cut our hair, and decorate our rooms. Yet we are seldom conscious about the artistic decisions in our life or the origin of our tastes and standards. Instead, we tend to think of art primarily as objects in museums.

In the past ten years, museums have experienced an unprecedented surge of popularity. Attendance at special exhibitions in large cities sometimes exceeds a million people, and more school buses lumber through museum parking lots than ever before. Americans are eager to learn about art and to have their children encounter the masterpieces of the past. Nevertheless, much of our visual culture comes from books, magazines, television, and films. Even in these cases, works of art from the past have left their imprint. Sometimes the image of a painting, sculpture, or building will be shown directly in the media. At other times, the visual influence appears in a disguised form. The conceptions of color, space, and form developed by major artists of the past have been internalized by commercial artists, photographers, and film directors, reaching us secondhand. Nothing is totally new; we are bombarded with visual stimuli that have their roots in the past.

It is amazing, under these circumstances, how different our tastes can be. A great deal still depends upon whatever influences we have absorbed from family and friends. Yet children in the same family, receiving similar visual stimuli over the years, may develop extremely different artistic interests. Various visual signals trigger different reactions, although we ourselves may not be aware of the origins of or reasons for our responses.

How much of our visual decision making is related to "art"? Philosophers and aestheticians have devoted many volumes to trying to define this elusive word, but perhaps the painter Marcel Duchamp gave the most interesting suggestion when he said, "Art is continuous, only seeing is intermittent." He implies that there are constant opportunities for artistic vision, but we only rarely take advantage of them. He also suggests something more daring: whatever we can see as art becomes art. It may be paintings in a museum, the architecture of some buildings in our town, or the fortuitous combinations of colors when children's raincoats hang on a wall. In this sense, art becomes an activity rather than merely a thing. It can be both the action of creating and the responsive activity of the viewer.

Each work of art is a potential stimulus, and the works we consider the greatest are those that give rise to the deepest human experiences. Art is a kind of vision, innate in everyone and able to be developed into a richly rewarding part of our lives. Although we all make artistic choices, we are largely unconscious of our own sense of visual culture. One major purpose of art education is to develop that sense, in terms of creativity and appreciation, so that we more fully experience the multicultural world around us and also come to a better understanding of ourselves.

"A work of art is only worthy of the name if it offers the beholder the chance of uniting with the creator." The French movie director Jean Renoir, the son of the famous Impressionist painter Auguste Renoir, wrote these words in *My Life and My Films.* Unifying ourselves with great works of art is surely an exciting prospect. But how can we, living in late twentieth-century America, unite with Renoir, Michelangelo, a Japanese Zen artist, or the anonymous architects and sculptors of Chartres Cathedral? Can art history, as an integral part of art education, help us?

Art comes alive only when we become part of it. In the same way, art history is alive only when we become part of its process. It is not enough to memorize images or to learn the names and dates of famous masters. Art history offers us much more—the chance to participate in the entire world of artistic expression: from prehistoric times to the present day, and from Africa, Asia, and Europe to our own towns, schools, and homes. In the process we will also discover that art history can be one of the most exciting ways to investigate the cultures of the world and their histories. Like every other activity, the more of ourselves we put into it, the more we will gain in return, ultimately leading to sharing the vision of artists of the past—and perhaps finding the artist in ourselves.

How much does the art we learn in school help us toward this goal? According to some observers, precollege art education has long been at a low ebb in the United States. In the last decade, the stress upon "basic learning"—math, science, and English—has hindered the development of art classes in the schools. By the early 1990s, more than half the students in the United States were taught art by classroom teachers with little or no professional preparation in art rather than by art specialists. Furthermore, the fact that art classes seem to have little relevance to other studies has made them easy targets for time and budget cuts. Many schools now allocate one hour or less each week for art; some have eliminated art altogether.

To counter this depressing picture, there has recently been an emphasis upon the importance of art education. This movement, spearheaded by a number of art educators and supported by the Getty Center for Education in the Arts, has fostered the concept of discipline-based art education (DBAE). From this viewpoint, art teaching in the schools is enhanced by combining the creation of artworks with criticism, aesthetics, and art history. This broader approach is designed to become part of the general education of American students and therefore enables art to be understood by all as well as coordinated with other subjects in the curriculum. It is important, for example, to study European and Japanese cultures to appreciate European and Japanese art and, conversely, to study the art to understand the cultures. This wider conception of art instruction, including art history, has already begun to increase the support for art classes in some school systems where DBAE has taken root.

What of higher education? Art historians have long lamented that students entering college have almost never heard of art history and do not realize that courses in art history might interest them. All too often art history majors themselves come to the field very late in their college careers. Even beginning graduate students frequently do not have enough undergraduate credits to enter an art history program without a series of make-up classes. Unfortunately, art historians complain that their field is not known to precollege students but do almost nothing to change the situation. In particular, they have not worked with art educators in cooperative ventures to make the process of studying world art available to students of all ages. Above all, art historians have not fully shared the excitement and joy of studying the most creative achievements of every age and every culture. There is no reason for this excitement to be reserved for college students; it can be shared with students at all levels of development.

This pioneering volume is an effort first to show how art history functions and second to demonstrate how effectively it can be utilized in elementary and secondary school classes. Making art part of our understanding of ourselves and of the world is a major challenge. Art history can be approached and used for many different purposes, and it provides many new opportunities within the field of education. This book is about these opportunities. As such, it will stress participation at all educational levels.

This volume is organized into two parts. The first, by Stephen Addiss, introduces and raises issues about the discipline of art history; and the second, by Mary Erickson, examines and makes proposals about how art history can be made a part of the general education of young people in America.

Readers with different backgrounds will find some chapters more directly related to their interests than others. Both parts of the book, however, are essential to significant improvement in art history education in elementary and secondary schools. The disciplines of art history and art education have changed significantly in recent years. Those interested in the realities of educational change who fail to take a new look at the broadened range of art-historical inquiry presented here may close off important options or may build campaigns for change on unsound foundations. Likewise, proposals for change rooted in the discipline of art history but inattentive to the realities of education are unlikely to find acceptance or successful implementation in schools across the country.

Mindful of the interdependence of the two parts of this book, readers may benefit from introductory comments about what they can expect to find in the various chapters. In an attempt to be "user friendly," a menu of approaches is outlined below, with a description of the chapters in order and suggestions for readers of different backgrounds.

Chapter 1 focuses upon art before there was art history. How can we deal with the paintings, sculptures, and ceramics created in neolithic and paleolithic eras before there were systems of writing? Instead of studying history and culture to understand art, we now must use art as one of the major clues to help us understand human society. Included are discussions of the four basic viewpoints toward art history: studying the work, the artist, the audience, and the culture. What can we learn from each of these approaches? With no written evidence, we must sometimes speculate, and it can be a challenge to use our own empathy and creativity to explore the world of culture and art.

The second chapter deals with traditional views of art history, including approaches taken in ancient Greece, China, India, and Europe up to the early twentieth century. Because we now have access to historical documents, including some about art theory, we have another element to add to our understanding: How can we best correlate art, cultural history, and theory? This chapter explores mimetic theories of art (does it copy nature?) and compares the art theories of civilizations that had very different views about the purpose of art. It also discusses more briefly the arts of tribal societies, folk arts, and the arts of popular culture.

Chapter 3 presents some of the new methodologies in recent art history. Beginning with fresh variants of the basic approaches, it examines questions of style, iconography, and iconology. It then reviews the study of periodization by considering the question: How useful is it to divide art into historical eras such as ancient, medieval, Renaissance, and baroque? This chapter also presents some new approaches that emphasize social history, feminism, semiotics, and post-Marxist views of art. Although some of these methodologies are very controversial, they offer new windows into an understanding of our past as well as our contemporary culture.

The fourth chapter discusses more specifically the activities and functions of art historians. What exactly do art historians do? In what way is technology (such as the use of computers) useful, and how is it changing the field? What is the role of cultural studies for art historians? In what specific ways might an art-historical project be accomplished? How do scholars approach art writing? What kinds of reference materials are available and how can they help in the process of inquiry? This chapter combines the excitement and nitty-gritty details of art-historical scholarship.

Chapters 5 through 9 discuss how these art historical processes can be related to education and how they can come alive for students of all ages. The central problem for our schools is how to establish and build the teaching of art history in elementary and secondary classes. This problem is approached from a different direction in each of the five remaining chapters of the book. Although these chapters specifically address teaching art history at the elementary and secondary levels, college professors of art history may be interested in how their students have been educated traditionally and in the proposals now being advanced that could change significantly how incoming students understand art history. Any art historians involved in course preparation or art education program revision should find these issues stimulating to consider as they apply to higher education.

Chapter 5 considers traditions in the history of art education that might influence possibilities for change today. It discusses how art was once considered part of moral education, but fifty years ago a broader base of study was advocated. This historical background can help us to understand how the current momentum for change is affected by traditional realities and resources. If art educators examine the traditions within which they have been educated, they will recognize why they, or some of their colleagues, may be reluctant to acknowledge the necessity for change and growth.

The sixth chapter focuses upon the importance of teaching art history within the general education curriculum for elementary and secondary students. Many individuals are responsible for the education that young people receive in our schools. School board members, superintendents, principals, supervisors, and other professional educators work together to make the hard choices about what will be taught, to whom, and how. This chapter addresses these issues. The importance of art history is discussed and justifications are found from within the field, from aesthetic and humanities education, and from fundamental educational needs. Chapter 6 affirms that the discipline of art history is a rich source of educational content and concludes with definitions of three methods of teaching: art history as artworks, art history as information, and art history as the process of inquiry.

Chapter 7 suggests adaptations and choices for teaching art history in light of both educational levels and students' different developmental characteristics. How might art history teaching in the elementary grades be implemented? What are the potentials for art history in secondary grades? To help in planning developmentally appropriate instruction, Michael Parsons's five stages of art understanding are reviewed.

Chapter 8 examines the organization and teaching of art history within the school curriculum. What goals are appropriate and how can learning be achieved at different levels? This chapter includes a discussion of the scope and sequence of art-historical inquiry and a sample lesson plan on the Chinese landscape painting tradition. The chapter concludes with some suggestions for unit planning.

The final chapter looks at the issue of art history within the larger structure of elementary and secondary art curriculum. Where and how can art history make a contribution to the total art program? In particular, how can art history be integrated with the creation of art, with aesthetics, and with art criticism?

The epilogue offers readers a challenge regarding the uses of art history, not only in art education but in life. There are also four appendixes, a bibliographic essay containing suggestions (chapter by chapter) for future readings, and an index.

This book has been written primarily for art educators. However, other readers, including parents, community members, and students, are also welcome. They all have an opportunity in chapters 1 through 4 to encounter a fascinating discipline that offers a unique orientation to the visual world. They can also discover in chapters 5 through 9 some of the complexity and reality that educators face as they attempt to offer the young people of this country the most worthwhile and effective education possible.

One way to understand the opportunities in teaching art history is by analogy to computers. Some of us are old enough to remember a time before computers existed, a time when we never imagined that we would be using them at work and in our homes. How did we respond when they appeared? Many of us realized that there was a lot to learn about them and how they work, but we weren't sure we wanted to spend the time necessary to introduce ourselves to this new domain. Others of us loved everything about computers from our first exposure; we couldn't get enough equipment, knowledge, and experience in this exciting new world. Perhaps most of us have overcome our initial reluctance to enter the new territory and have come to value the extended options that computers provide. Now there are many who were born and educated in the age of computers, who are fluent in their use and can't imagine surviving without them.

So it is with art history. Many people know little about the discipline and have a hard time imagining why we think it's important enough to be part of every American's general education. Some people have enough understanding of the field to realize how much more there is to know, and they are concerned about gaining access to what's really important in the field. Others have a powerful interest in art history and have devoted their lives to sharing its excitement with others. Perhaps most art educators have accepted the importance of art history in art education and are exploring ways of introducing, refining, and extending our ideas about how it can be effectively taught. The day may come when all young people, and eventually all Americans, will have the opportunity to learn about art around the globe and through time and will know how to inquire into their own visual heritage.

The full implementation of art history into our educational system is a demanding and difficult task. What it offers in return is an understanding of our own visual age, a viable approach to cultures of all times and places, and above all the opportunity to enrich our lives through exploring the profound manifestations of the human spirit that art has provided—and continues to provide—to us all.

Acknowledgments

I would like to express my appreciation to Anne El-Omami for introducing me to the world of art education, to the Getty Center for Education in the Arts, and to Ralph A. Smith of the University of Illinois at Urbana-Champaign for inviting me to undertake this project. Mary Erickson was the most delightful, insightful, and cooperative co-author that any writer could wish for, while Susan Craig gave extremely helpful advice for the section on art history resources. Patricia Fister, H. S. Lita, and Denise Stone were kind enough to read my manuscript and make excellent suggestions. Stephen Goddard and Jon Blumb of the Spencer Museum of Art assisted me in selecting and providing photographs for the first four chapters. Neva Entrikin and Carol Anderson, along with the staff of the art history department at the University of Kansas, provided splendid support, as always.

Before completing my section of this book, I found it very helpful to lead a graduate class in art history methodology during the spring term of 1990. I would like to thank each of the students in that class because they were also my teachers: Tracey Cady, Thomas Dedoncker, Carole Firnhaber, Grant Haden, Robert Hickerson, Anselm Huelsbergen, Jenyi Lai, Jan March, Rachel Melton, William North, Jacqueline Reed, Helen Seymour, Raechell Smith, Margaret Stenz, Sarah Thompson, Kimberley Wagoner, and Stephanie Weldon.

Stephen Addiss

My interest in the subject of this book is as old as my career in art education is long. Many people and institutions have influenced and inspired that interest. I am grateful to Kutztown University for providing release time for the preparation of the manuscript and for its support of travel and editorial assistance. I was fortunate to have been a member of an art education department with a strong commitment to serving teachers and of a sufficient size to allow specialization. I would like to express my appreciation to my colleagues, specifically to Tom Schantz for his unwavering loyalty, to Marilyn Stewart for her challenges, and to Eldon Katter for his creative and caring partnership through the years. In classes, and in many cases years after graduation, students have been a continuous source of inspiration. Thank you.

I am grateful to the National Art Education Association for providing the meeting ground where people interested in teaching art history have been able to find stimulation and an opportunity to exchange ideas. I am also grateful to the Getty Center for Education in the Arts, which has supported reflection on the teaching of art history as a significant component of discipline-based art education and which, together with Ralph A. Smith, has given me the opportunity to work with Stephen Addiss, who has been an exciting and supportive partner in this undertaking.

I would like to thank Brendan Strasser for his editorial diligence, insightful challenges, and assistance in drafting chapters 5 through 9 of the bibliographic essay. In addition I would like to thank Georgia Chamley-Brevik for reviewing my manuscript and offering her valuable suggestions and Nicholas Bowen for his photographic work. Material from the appendixes is used by permission of the managing director of CRIZMAC. Finally I would like to thank my mother and father for forty-five years of support and encouragement and Claire Andrews for her patience and willingness to listen.

Mary Erickson

Art History and Education

1

Art before Art History

Paleolithic Art

In 1879, a young girl in Altamira, Spain, wriggled through a small opening in the ground and found herself in a cave covered with huge paintings of animals. She came out and told her father, who crawled in to see for himself. As he moved deeper into the cave he discovered small engraved areas as well as more and more mammals, mostly bison, painted in blacks, reds, oranges, and browns on the rippling ceiling among the stalactites. He was astonished. The animals, often painted to conform to the natural shape of the rock, were large, three or four feet long, and they seemed to walk, lie down, crouch, curl up, stand, and bellow. He decided that these paintings must be prehistoric, the first discovery of the oldest extant artworks created by human beings (fig. 1).

Experts scoffed: the paintings at Altamira were simply too good to have been done by "primitive" people and must be fakes, or at least the work of more recent painters. One artist declared: "By their composition, strength of line and proportions, they show that their author was not uneducated; and, though he was not a Raphael, he must have studied Nature at least in pictures or well-made drawings, as is seen by the abandoned mannerism of their execution. Such paintings are simply the expression of a mediocre student of the modern school."[1]

Soon more caves with wall paintings were discovered, mostly in northern Spain and southern France. It became undeniable that prehistoric hunter-gatherers, living thousands of years before the invention of writing, had created some of the most beautiful and exciting artworks ever seen.

This story offers many lessons. One is never to believe experts without thinking for yourself. Another is that art, unlike science, does not really "progress," it only changes, with something lost and something gained at every step of the way. Finally, each opinion as to what is meaningful is important. Art is many things to many people, and the finest works, like the best literature and music, communicate directly to receptive individ-

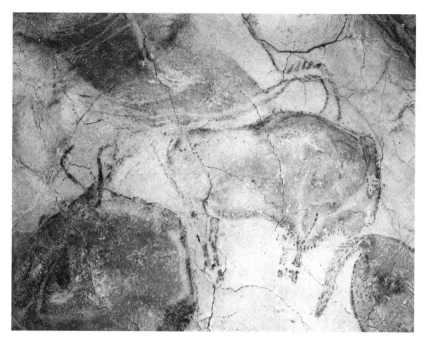

Fig. 1. Prehistoric art, painting from the "Hall of the Bisons," Altamira Caves, Spain. Photo: Giraudon/Art Resource, New York, N.Y.

uals through the ages—this is one of the reasons we study art history. But do these works of art always communicate the same thing?

There is an anecdote about a maharaja from India who visited London and was taken to hear an orchestral concert. Mozart and Beethoven symphonies were performed to great applause. When the maharaja was asked what he liked best, he replied, "the part before the man with the stick came in." When we stop to think about it, an orchestra tuning up sounds a bit like Indian music, which has a single drone note (like the orchestra's tuning note A) while other notes depart from it and then return. This anecdote illustrates that we do not all listen the same way, for the maharaja found music in exactly the part of the concert we ignore.

Reading a favorite novel again after some years we may think, My, how that author has changed. Likewise, we do not see the same painting the same way twice, much less the way anyone else sees it. The experience of the arts is not universal or timeless but instead is active, individual, and constantly changing. Shakespeare is reinterpreted anew every decade, if not in every performance. A building looks different in every light, and a sculpture changes when viewed from different angles. Most of all, our own perceptions change, so we should not expect art to be static any more than a human is always the same.

The field of art history, like that of art itself, is constantly metamorphosing. As we change and our society changes, our views of the art of the past will change. What is remarkable is that the creative expressions of people living completely different lives, many thousands of years ago, should still be able to fascinate our minds and move our emotions. There is something magical and primordial in artistic creation that can cut through time and space to reach our inner spirit. The study of art history by itself cannot make this happen, but it can increase and inform our responses, adding greatly to our understanding and delight. Practical suggestions for the study of art history in primary and secondary education are offered in later chapters, and a sample lesson plan covering Paleolithic art is offered in appendix 2. But first we can explore how art history works and how it has evolved over time to deal with the art of every period of human existence.

Judging from the cave paintings and other early artworks, visual expression was very important to peoples of the "prehistoric" era. More than two hundred caves have now been discovered containing well over ten thousand paintings. In part because there are no written documents from the Paleolithic age (35,000 to 9,000 B.C.), the study of the art of the hunting and gathering peoples involves a lot of guesswork. Why were large animals painted so often and so realistically? Why are humans shown simply as stick figures? Why are some paintings found in huge chambers while others are hidden in little nooks and crannies? Why were some paintings done on top of others when there was enough empty space on the walls for them all? Why are there similar styles and subject matter over such a wide territory, from Russia to India to the famous caves of southern France and northern Spain? And even more basically, why were the caves painted at all?

Many theories—and many objections to them—have been offered in response. One of the earliest theories was that cave paintings were done as personal artistic expression. This is a popular rationale for creating art today, and the cave paintings seem so bold and dramatic that we can imagine the excitement that motivated the artists. The criticism of this theory is that art as a form of self-expression is a rather recent concept, only existing in very sophisticated societies. Although it is dangerous to draw exact parallels, hunter-gatherers today do not seem interested in the concept of art as personal expression.

A second theory is that the paintings were done as tributes to the animals that were killed for food. Painting animal forms to gain power over animals or to placate their spirits has been called "sympathetic magic." It is true that some modern hunting societies have such tributes, but an analysis of the animal bones found in ancient caves shows that Paleolithic people ate mostly small animals. Why, then, are the paintings primarily of larger mammals? If this is "sympathetic magic," why the discrepancy?

A third theory is that the paintings were educational, made to show younger members of the group what the large mammals looked like and how to hunt them. Prehistoric footprints of adults and children remain around painted areas in a few of the ancient caves. Was this the beginning of art education? The objection to this theory is that although some paintings are visible in large cave chambers, others are so hard to reach that they could not have been used for teaching. Were they, or at least some of them, not meant to be viewed at all, like much funerary art of later periods?

A fourth theory is that the paintings were part of ceremonies and were used in symbolic, perhaps even religious, ways. Certainly, seeing them today in their dramatic cave settings arouses a feeling of awe in many viewers: how thrilling they must have seemed thousands of years ago with only the flickering light from torches and oil lamps. However, the previous objection still holds: Why were some paintings done in such small nooks and crannies?

Another theory involves totemism, where an animal represents a particular group of people. Not only was this common among American Indians, but a form of totemism still exists today in our names for sports teams (Detroit Lions, St. Louis and Phoenix Cardinals). However, since most caves have depictions of several large mammals, it seems unlikely that one kind of animal represented any particular group of people.

A few scholars have suggested that the paintings of animals represent male and female principles and therefore celebrated fertility. But this remains speculative since there is no corroborating evidence.

Finally, some have thought that the paintings were simply decorations. After all, most humans in various societies have wished to decorate their surroundings in some manner. However, the paintings have such narrative scope and emotional power for modern viewers that this seems unlikely. Furthermore, this theory does not address the questions of why the animals were portrayed so realistically while humans were shown as stick figures, or why some paintings were done on top of others.

Why were the caves painted? No one can know the answer with certainty, but we are all free to explore our own ideas. This is not just a matter for experts; all our opinions are worthy of respect. When we speculate that these paintings were done for artistic expression, as tributes to the animal spirits, to educate young hunters, as part of ceremonies, as totems, for fertility, or simply for decoration, we are already thinking as art historians. Perhaps the most interesting problem is *how* we should go about trying to answer such questions. What can we know about the art of peoples who lived so long ago, humans who left us no written records? Is such a study hopeless?

It is true that for later ages we have the benefit of written documents of many kinds, but art history always starts with the image itself, and words are secondary. Therefore, no matter what the era, the fundamental problems of art history are the same, and various approaches have been devised that can help us explore our visual heritage. One of the most fundamental of all questions when we see any work of art is, Why does it look like that?

The first answer might be, Because the artist wanted it to look like that. This may seem obvious, but it eliminates the idea that the artist made a mistake or didn't know enough to do anything else or would have wished it differently. Let us credit the artist: all fine art is the result of his or her intentions. These intentions may have been conscious or they may have been so embedded in the culture that the artist was not conscious of them, but in either case let us agree that the artist wanted it "just like that."

We may then ask, *Why* did she or he want it just that way? Now we have reached the starting point for the process of art history. In the attempt to understand works of art, four major approaches have been taken over the years:

1. formal analysis (the artist wanted to relate elements like color and line in a particular way to represent a particular subject matter)
2. biographical (there was something in the artist's background and individual spirit that led to creating the work)
3. patronage and audience (the artist was commissioned to do the work in a certain way or the artist was representing a particular point of view)
4. cultural (the artist was expressing the underlying values of the entire society in his or her time period)

Which of these approaches is best? Perhaps we can ask a better question: Which of them is the most convincing and most helpful to our understanding? The answer may well be that a combination of approaches is most illuminating, but many art historians have emphasized one over the others, as we shall discover.

Formal analysis means studying artistic elements such as color, brushwork, line, and composition. In cave paintings, the colors are natural: black, made from burned animal fat, along with red, yellow, and brown ochres. The colors were applied with brushes or hands, and some pigment even seems to have been blown on, perhaps through a tube of some kind. Most paintings in caves are outlined, but a few are built up of small interior strokes, including groups of dots. In terms of composition, there are many large groups of animals depicted on cave walls, but only rarely is there a grouping (e.g. bisons charging) that makes immediate sense in terms of either pattern or narrative. Other combinations, however, suggest that some cave paintings may represent long-lost stories or myths. In addition, experts studying geometric forms such as groups of dots have speculated that the dots may represent lunar notations; it may be that Paleolithic peoples needed some form of calendar to regularize their nomadic journeys.

Formal analysis is also used in conjunction with the study of subject matter (iconography or iconology). More than half the total of known cave paintings represent large mammals such as bison, oxen, and horses (still wild at this time). These animals are usually painted in profile, but when they have horns, their heads are turned face forward. We may conclude that the animals are in their most recognizable poses, perhaps for the purpose of immediate identification. Occasionally the mammals are shown pierced with spears, and human hunters sometimes appear, suggesting that hunting was at least one of the factors in the creation of the paintings.

Other paintings have subjects such as ibex, boars, fish, masklike human faces, and geometrical forms such as lines, circles, and dots. Moreover, images of hands appear to have been made on cave walls by blowing paint around human hands to define their contours. A few of the hands seem to have been mutilated, since the fingers are not all full size—perhaps marred by diseases such as frostbite or circulatory disorders or possibly by ritual amputation. Handprints, whether whole or mutilated, are very common in cave art. Were they an early way of saying, I was here—a kind of signature?

Although *biographical study* of the cave artists is impossible, we can raise the question of whether the painters were specialists or whether anyone in the group could have become an artist. In *The Social History of Art*, Arnold Hauser wrote: "The elaborate and refined technique of Palaeolithic paintings also argues that these works were done . . . by trained specialists who spent a considerable part of their life learning and practicing their art, and who formed a professional class of their own . . . with schools, masters, local trends, and traditions. The artist-magician, therefore, seems to have been the first representative of specialization and the division of labor."[2]

Hauser's idea is fascinating, but is it true? He came to his conclusion not from any written evidence, but merely from his observation of the paintings and his aesthetic response to their extremely competent execution. Another specialist decided that fourteen different artists participated in painting one group of animals in the Lascaux caves in France. He based his conclusion on what he considered to be different stylistic features in the lines and colors of the paintings. If both scholars are correct, were there fourteen professional art specialists at Lascaux? There is no reason why we cannot study the paintings and come to our own conclusions.

Research into the *patronage* or *audience* of the artwork means studying the small groups of hunter-gatherers who lived and traveled together. It is believed that these seminomadic peoples lived in caves or under sheltering rocks whenever they could. They would return to certain places every year, so the paintings would be available to them only during certain seasons. Would they need certain kinds of paintings at certain times? Did they encourage (or "commission") certain members of their groups to paint? We must remember that paintings were not their only form of art. Early humans also created small stone, calcite, and ivory figurines, some representing women who seem to be pregnant, suggesting that these works may have represented fertility. Other sculptures that these peoples may have carried on their travels included engraved bones and horns, usually with animal designs. Were these possibly used for trade? There are perhaps ten thousand sculpted or engraved objects still extant from this age, attesting to the importance of art for Paleolithic peoples.

Finally, the broader study of *cultural history* would involve relating the paintings to everything that is known about Paleolithic societies. In this case, "everything" is not very much; the art itself forms a major part of our evidence for life in this era. It is known that Paleolithic peoples had tools; for example, they hunted with spears and with bows and arrows, and they fished with hooks. They had the use of fire, for cooking and for light, and made lamps from small hollowed-out rocks filled with animal fat. It is speculated that food, including nuts and berries in season, was abundant for these peoples and that they followed the migration of animals. They must have had a good deal of leisure time during parts of the year, and the paintings may have been done when the pressures of hunting and gathering abated.

The fact that cave paintings are rather similar over large geographic areas suggests that the traveling groups interacted with one another from time to time, sharing their artistic imagery. Our image of these peoples suggests small groups living together but meeting other groups on a regular basis. But we would like to know much more. Today, researchers study the bones of Paleolithic peoples to find out who they were; researchers also inspect their tools to discover how they lived. We need to study their art, however, to know what they believed.

What can we conclude about Paleolithic painting? Although there are no certainties, a few suggestions seem reasonable. First, since large mammals were very frequent subjects, they must have been important to the people. The painted images do not replicate food sources, so we might speculate that large animals represented more than food. What qualities were admired or feared in the large mammals? Energy, power, courage, speed? Or simply their ability to live successfully in traveling and cooperative groups, like the Paleolithic peoples themselves?

Second, paintings were done in large, open caves, where they could be seen by anyone, and hidden in small crawl spaces. This suggests more than one purpose in their creation and use. When we consider that individually or in groups we seldom do anything for only one reason, we should not look for too simple an answer as to why these paintings were created. We may note, however, that today many people still have the feeling that to depict something is to begin to define and control it. We might, for example, say of a good portrait that it "captures the subject." In reverse, people in some parts of the world do not like having their image made or their picture taken by strangers because it might give someone else power over their lives. Since during the Paleolithic period animals were depicted quite realistically but humans were not, we may wonder if the paintings represent some form of power over the animals. If so, the power held by the artists may have made them spiritual or shamanistic leaders in their groups.

Third, most researchers have stressed their belief that cave paintings must have had great importance in the culture, even if we may never know exactly what their meaning (or meanings) might be. The cave walls and ceilings must have been painted in the service of belief and community but perhaps for another reason that relates to a human quality we have difficulty defining. That reason combines tradition with innovation, expectation with surprise, purposefulness with fantasy, and deep seriousness with a sense of play. In a single word: creativity.

It is one of the pleasures of art history that final answers are seldom possible—we all have the chance to inquire freely and then to decide for ourselves. The more we study the more we will know, but unless we use our instincts as well as our intelligence, we will never fully understand art.

Neolithic Art

The first great change in human life came after 9,000 B.C. when humans learned how to control agriculture. Successfully growing grains, fruits, and vegetables meant independence from nomadic hunting and the opportunity to live in one place year-round. With this great change in life-style came a new view of the world, which in turn led to new forms of art.

What might we imagine to be the art of agricultural societies of the Neolithic period? First of all, let us ask what would be most important to people who are farming rather than hunting. The answers must have been the same ten thousand years ago as they are now: good soil, sunshine, rain, and the regular cycle of the seasons. Since these are universal concerns of agricultural peoples, it should not surprise us to find great similarities between the art of Neolithic peoples in Greece, East Asia, eastern Europe, and in the Americas before the arrival of Columbus.

Farming people have a great need for the storage of food, and one of the most important factors in agricultural life was therefore the development of pottery. While the art of the hunters had been of painting and sculpture, the art of the early farmers largely took the form of ceramics. The ability to work the earth was realized not only in planting and harvesting but in forming, baking, and firing clay vessels. These Neolithic ceramics were used for a multitude of purposes, from food storage to cooking, and in some cases even for burying the dead. A great variety of vessel shapes was developed, and incised, impressed, and painted decorations became important features of much early pottery. Although some designs were naturalistic, by far the greater number were abstract, usually with geometric patterns. Why should this be? What could have motivated this enormous variety of decorative motifs?

It is not too difficult to understand why Paleolithic peoples created naturalistic portrayals of animals, for clarity of vision and image is crucial for hunters. This kind of realistic art, however, was of less importance to Neolithic farmers. Their concern was for the regular alternations of sun and rain, warm and cold, spring and autumn. These alternating cycles seem to have inspired much Neolithic art. Again, we have no written documents from this period, so we must rely on a combination of knowledge and imagination to understand the art of early agricultural peoples.

Once more we can apply the four approaches taken by art historians. In Neolithic times there was a great variety of types and styles, but each work can be analyzed formally in terms of style—composition, color, line, and form. In the case of a prehistoric vessel from Gansu, in north-

Fig. 2. China, Middle Yan-shou Period (c. 2000–1500 B.C.), funerary urn, 12³/₄ in. × 18¹/₂ in., from Pan-Shan, Kansu Province. Nelson-Atkins Museum of Art, Kansas City, Missouri.

western China, we can see the swirling spiral designs of the Banshan culture of the third millennium B.C. (fig. 2). This tall jar with a small mouth and wide belly was painted in natural earth colors, and its imposing size is enhanced by the strong and fluid design that takes full advantage of its round form. The "teeth" that notch the spiral designs are typical of Banshan designs, although their meaning is not clear. At one time such jars were thought to have been made only for burial alongside the deceased, but recent excavations have shown they were also in daily household use. Art historians have debated whether an early form of animal-hair paintbrush or some other tool, such as crushed reeds, was used to paint these vessels.

There is not yet much that can be said about Neolithic artists, but again we can speculate: Could anyone be a potter, or were there special-ists who did the work? Some scholars suspect that the quality of the ceramics indicates a professional class of artisans, while others believe that each family may have made its own pottery. It has also been suggested that women were the primary artists in this age while men were more involved in the actual farming, but current agricultural societies do not always display this division of labor. In parts of Africa, for example, women do most of the work in the fields while the men produce the crafts.

The audience for Neolithic ceramics was the family and local community. Although much of the art was clearly utilitarian, such as pottery for everyday use, some pieces were made for ceremonial purposes, including burials. The shapes of the vessels were determined primarily by usage, but the designs that were painted, impressed, and incised on the surfaces must have been created for other reasons. Were they determined by the audience or the artists? Was there a fundamental difference between these two groups, as there often is now? In any case, since the forming, decorating, and firing of clay follows primal rhythms of nature, as does farming, the spirit of this art was surely shared among the Neolithic communities.

Finally, the cultural history of Neolithic peoples reveals much about their art. Despite the lack of written documents, there is considerably more information about early agricultural societies than about Paleolithic peoples, and this evidence is being studied area by area. Generally, when people are dependent upon the regular alternations of the seasons, they are likely to make a religion of nature, and at least some Neolithic art must represent this kind of religious spirit. This is something we can easily understand, for during times of drought, prayers for rain are still prevalent all over the world.

When we raise the subject of religion, more questions immediately come to mind. What had been religion for the hunter-gatherers of the Paleolithic age? How different might religion have been in agricultural periods? Do some works of prehistoric art represent gods? Was nature itself a kind of deity (such as the sun god)? Or, as in some religions today, was the concept of a god too powerful to be directly represented? Such questions are posed to art historians as well as anthropologists, archaeologists, and historians of religion. What is important to realize is that the answers are not settled; this will always be a field to which all of us can contribute.

It may seem that the Paleolithic and Neolithic peoples are very far from our own lives. Yet we have examples of hunting and gathering as well as agricultural peoples near at hand. American Indians as both hunters and farmers have created wondrous paintings and engravings on rock walls (petroglyphs) and magnificent ceramics; Southwest pottery today continues to be an important American art form. Of course, this is not Paleolithic or Neolithic art and shows many differences. Nevertheless, we can both admire and puzzle over the art of such cultures as that of the Anasazi people, who lived at Chaco Canyon and other sites in New Mexico and Arizona nine centuries ago and created fascinating petroglyphs and pottery as well as substantial architecture. What led to such cultural and artistic heights in such an arid land? What are the meanings of their paintings, engravings, and pottery decorations? Why did the Anasazi people disappear in the twelfth century? The latter question seems to be related to a decline in the total amount of moisture that parts of the Southwest received, but the questions about the Anasazi have never been thoroughly answered. Their imaginative (rather than the naturalistic) representations of animals and humans on the cliff walls and the dramatic geometric patterns on the ceramics are often hauntingly beautiful. Do they relate to the art of earlier eras in human history?

Urban Civilizations and Naturalism

The third major period in human culture, which began at different times in different parts of the world, is labeled *historical,* because it is when systems of writing were first devised. This period has featured the use of metals and the development of urban civilization—when people are no longer concerned primarily with animals or with the cycles of nature but with each other. If we buy our food from a grocer rather than hunting it or growing it ourselves, we tend to become human centered. Thus, life in towns and cities, in contrast to nomadic or agricultural life, has focused upon the interaction of human beings. Urban cultures appeared at different times in different parts of the world, but when they developed, people began performing a variety of specialized roles in a more complex social fabric. Since this historical and mostly urban civilization has lasted to the present, it covers a great many different cultures and generalizations are risky. Nevertheless, we can ask once more: What is most important to people who have complex urban life-styles? The answer, clearly, is other people, and the historical period is one in which the primary artistic subject matter has often been the human figure.

We may take depictions of humans for granted, but we should remember that they were not very important in the art of Paleolithic or Neolithic peoples, and therefore they represent something new in the history of art. Furthermore, in most cultures, over a period of time, humans are gradually represented less in stylized fashion—that is, more "realistically." Another indication of a human-centered focus during this urban period is the emergence of signed works of art—Greek paintings of the sixth century B.C. This means that human beings had become important not only as a subject for art but also as individual artists. Why this new need for people to be recognized as individuals? This topic will be explored in the following chapter. For now we may note that many urban societies throughout history have produced "realistic" representations of individual humans.

Perhaps we should take a moment to consider the question of "realism." We take that word now to mean an accurate visual representation of what we see, as though from a photograph. However, what is considered "real" varies from society to society and from time to time. Some people believe that what we see with our eyes is not as real as the unseen forces of nature or of the spirit. The Bible tells us: "Now we see as through a glass darkly, but then we shall see face to face." People who do not believe that our eyes can see the deeper reality of life do not create art that is "realistic" in the current sense. Is it possible to say that *all* art is realistic and that only the conceptions of what is real change?

Some art historians believe that a more useful word than "realistic" is "naturalistic," meaning images that faithfully represent how forms appear in nature. Only in urban civilizations have humans been depicted naturalistically; before that it was obviously not considered necessary or desirable. One may see the process historically. In many religions there has been a gradual change from not representing gods semiabstractly to depicting them as very idealized human images to portraying them naturalistically. We can, for example, follow this progression very clearly over the centuries in both Christian and Buddhist art.

While many art historians in the past have seen the trend toward naturalism as a sign of progress, others now suggest that naturalism actually represents a lessening of the power of belief and therefore a loss of spirituality in the images. For example, an eighteenth-century painting of the Madonna and child is more humanistic than a medieval image, but is it more expressive as a work of art? The answer obviously depends upon the vision of the beholder. Those differences of vision from one person to another is one of the reasons art history can be so fascinating.

The historical period has produced the largest number of works of art, or at least the majority of those that are extant. It is also the period that has been most researched by specialists. The following three chapters investigate how art historians have studied the artworks, artists, audiences, and cultural histories of differing eras, as well as the methods by which we study our own cultural heritage.

NOTES

1. Quoted in John E. Pfeiffer, *The Creative Explosion* (Ithaca, N.Y.: Cornell University Press, 1982), p. 23.

2. Arnold Hauser, *The Social History of Art* (New York: Vintage Books, 1957), p. 16.

2

Traditional Views of Art

Greek Art and Theory

The art of Greece has been vital to the formation of the Western artistic tradition. Through the ages, the combination of humanity and nobility in Greek sculpture and painting has represented many of our highest human values. Therefore, it is not surprising that Greek art has long been a major field of research. Art historians have especially sought to understand the stylistic evolution of Greek sculpture and painting in relation to Greek history and culture.

Greek art-historical inquiry must incorporate something that the study of Paleolithic and Neolithic art lacked—the written word. The ancient Greeks wrote the earliest theoretical and historical documents of art, providing concepts of art that have been studied and reformulated by art historians ever since and have influenced our own views of the meaning and value of art. The ideals of Greek sculpture and painting were the fundamental basis of European and American aesthetics over many centuries (the uniting of the teaching of art history and aesthetics is discussed in chapter 9). Clearly, a study of the relationship between Greek art and art theory helps us understand our own visual heritage.

Greek art theory is especially fascinating when studied in conjunction with the historical evolution of Greek art. However, the ancient Greeks had no single view of the meaning of art. Plato disagreed with Aristotle's aesthetic theories, just as later Greek writers would disagree with theories of "golden age" (fifth century B.C.) philosophers.

It should be no surprise that art theory changes as art changes. But which transformation comes first? Artists like to believe that they are in the vanguard of change, but it might be that life changes, and with it both art and art theory. Though scholars lack a single complete theoretical text about art before the first century A.D. (only fragments of writing survive from before this time), we nevertheless can trace the art theories of major Greek philosophers and artists.

Plato set down the most important tenet of early theory: that art was fundamentally "imitation" (mimesis). In Greek legend, drawing was invented when a man traced the outline of a horse in sunlight; painting, when someone filled in the shadows of a man and woman on a white tablet. But what did Plato mean by imitation in a philosophical sense? In book 10 of *The Republic*, he uses the example of the couch to illustrate his idea. To him, fundamental reality is conceptual, the *idea* of something (in this case the couch), which includes all of its various forms and possibilities. The carpenter makes a couch in some particular form, but because he limits the total concept of couch to his specific example, his couch is one step removed from the reality of the idea. A painting of the couch would be reality twice removed, only an appearance from a specific angle in a particular light. Thus the broad concept of the couch becomes more and more limited, the artist always far removed from the ultimate reality of the idea. Plato therefore distrusted art as several dangerous steps away from truth. He wrote, "Shall we not say that we make an actual house with the art of building, and with the art of painting we make another house, which is a kind of man-made dream. . . . [The problem is] the weakness of the human mind on which the art of painting in light and shadow, the art of conjuring, and many other ingenious devices impose, having an effect upon us like magic."[1]

Perhaps we should call Plato's conception of art's magic his second basic notion of art, because although art is removed from reality, it still has the power to affect our beliefs. There is an early Greek legend about a painting contest. An artist paints a picture of grapes so realistic that birds come down to peck at them. A second artist then secretly paints a curtain over the grapes. When the first painter returns, he demands that the curtain be removed. When he discovers that it, too, is a painting, he knows that his imitation of reality has been less effective, and he loses the contest.

The relationship between image and reality has remained a fundamental question up to the present day. When we look at a photo of a movie star, we may imagine that we are actually seeing his or her face. Watching a live broadcast of a sports event, we frequently act as though the game were really in front of us. If we have the good fortune to view Leonardo's *Mona Lisa* in person, we may consider the eternal question of why she is smiling, when actually all we see is paint. No one is there to smile but ourselves.

Of course, we all realize that a photograph is only a piece of paper, a television program merely an electronic image, and a painting nothing more than a two-dimensional depiction. Nevertheless, we suspend our disbelief while we look at the photograph, program, or painting. If they do not convince us, we may revoke this suspension at any time and simply disbelieve.

Plato asks: "Do you perceive that the images are very far from having qualities which are the exact counterpart of the realities they represent?"[2] We are supposed to answer yes. Plato believed that an image could never express full reality, and therefore the illusion was one only of appearance. The mimetic effect creates a likeness that is ultimately far from the truth, and its potentially magical effect can be dangerous to rational thought.

Plato's concept of mimesis greatly affected later ages. Many drew the conclusion that if art was imitation, it should imitate nature. Yet previous to the Greeks, the idea that reality was what we can see with our eyes was not common. Many cultures have believed, and still believe, that reality lies *beyond* rather than *on* the surface of things and must be represented in symbolic ways. In contrast, Plato's conceptions were particularly important for the naturalistic Western tradition in the fine arts.

Aristotle was more sympathetic than Plato to the idea of art, created through a combination of inner knowledge and technique. Aristotle, commenting as did Plato on the carpenter, observed that the artisan's hands shape the wood but the soul or spirit of the artist moves the hands. This soul or spirit combines tradition and imagination to create form, in which order produces beauty.[3] Aristotle praised idealistic over naturalistic art. He compared three painters: Polygnotus, who depicted humans as better than they are; Pauson, who showed them as worse than they are; and Dionysius, who portrayed them exactly as they are. Aristotle preferred Polygnotus because he believed that artistic images should be ideal models for their viewers.

From the two great "classical" Greek philosophers, two of the most important theories of art emerged: that art imitates nature and that it should serve a moral purpose. These theories still are current. Even abstract artists sometimes claim that their art follows (imitates) their own inner nature; they, too, celebrate a form of mimesis. The theory that art should serve a moral purpose is more controversial, adopted by groups spanning the religious and political spectrum, from communist regimes in the former Soviet Union and China to the religious right in the United States. As we shall see in chapter 5, moral education was one of the first goals of art education in schools. The opposite point of view, that art should exist only for itself ("art for art's sake"), also has its current adherents, many of them creative people. However, most artists probably hope their works will lead the viewer to a higher state of awareness, which may be a kind of moral purpose in itself.

The 1990 debate about the exhibition of Robert Mapplethorpe photographs was primarily about censorship. However, it can be seen also as an argument in terms of Greek theory. On one side were neo-Aristotelians, demanding that art have an elevating moral purpose, or at least display no immorality. On the other side were neo-Platonists, believing that art is an imitation of life, in which homoerotic activities certainly do exist. Most of us, even the most fervent civil libertarians, would probably agree that art can and does affect its viewers; if it did not, why would we bother with it? The important question is whether we want to *regulate* art in order to control its effect. If so, there are problems: Who decides what effect the art will have? Might it not have different effects upon different people? Who, therefore, could or should regulate it? One solution has been adopted by the film industry. It does not censor itself but labels its creations, presumably to keep children from seeing certain movies. Will we eventually have PG-, R-, and X-rated art exhibitions? What would Plato and Aristotle have thought?

Having examined some aspects of Greek art theory, we may ask how well it represents Greek art. Before the days of Plato and Aristotle, the art of Greece had been symbolic rather than naturalistic. It was only gradually, over time, that naturalism became dominant, and there are interesting historical connections that suggest how vision and belief matched each other. From circa 1100 to 700 B.C., much art was created with abstract or semiabstract designs; thus the period is called "protogeometric" and "geometric." Greece then was primarily an agricultural society, and the cycles of nature were represented in the patterned designs on much early Greek pottery.

Around 700 B.C., Greek urban centers began to supplant agricultural life, and the geometric basis of design moved toward the figurative. At first, an aristocratic societal structure dominated, a system of rule by class and inheritance. People were born into their positions, rather than earning them through individual talent, and their images were of the eternal gods that reinforced the myths of a stable culture. However, in the "archaic" statues of the time, we can already see the special Greek vision of the human form as beautiful in itself. The temple maidens called *kore*, immortalized in stone, combine innate spirituality with a sympathetic expression of natural feminine beauty.

Even before the classical era, Greek sculpture and painting had a human quality that gave it a special flavor. Although Greek culture received some influence from Egypt, its art was clearly different in spirit. Consider the inscription on an Egyptian temple of the sixth or seventh century B.C.:

> I am all that exists,
> And all that did exist,
> And all that shall exist;
> No human has lifted my veil.[4]

This is the kind of powerful religious vision that produces the sphinx, with all its mysterious beauty and grandeur, but does not produce fully naturalistic images of humans. The "archaic" period in Greek art was one in which naturalistic and iconic forms merged and blended into fascinating combinations of mythic and human, otherworldly and mundane.

In contrast to Egypt and Mesopotamia, in the early fifth century B.C., aristocratic society in Greece began to break down. A new economy developed in which merchants took a more important role, and individuals who were not necessarily from the highest classes rose up to take control of the government. The Greeks' defeat of the Persians in 480 B.C. was an event of great magnitude, giving the Greeks new confidence in their abilities. During this period, a form of democracy developed, based upon the belief that human beings could and should choose the most talented among themselves as leaders instead of following aristocratic birthrights. It was in this era that the Greeks came to believe that "all norms and standards, whether in science, law, morality, mythology, or art, are creations of human minds and hands."[5]

Belief in the power of human minds and hands was crucial to Greek thought and to Greek art. When there is confidence in humanity, there are also opportunities for each human being. It is not surprising that artists began to sign their works during this period, for individual genius was already being recognized in other aspects of Greek life. The Olympic games, for example, honored personal achievement in athletics, and winners of the games were immortalized in sculpture and poetry. The spirit of competition and personal success was also recognized in politics and business. It was no longer necessary to be born into an aristocratic family; each individual above the level of slave had the chance to excel and to define his or her own destiny.

What of religion, the basis of so much artistic achievement? When there is confidence in humanity and in individual genius, there is less emphasis upon the supernatural, and so it was in Greece. Empedocles wrote a poem in the fifth century B.C. celebrating the artist as a kind of deity. He described the painter as someone who blends colors to produce a lifelike world and suggested that the entire universe around us was created in the same way, by the mixing of elements. As a view of creation, this is surely more scientific than religious and helps to explain the Greek emphasis upon naturalism.

The beliefs of Plato and Aristotle were appropriate to the art of their time. In the fifth and fourth centuries B.C., Greek sculptors blended naturalism with a reverence for the ideal. Their sculptures are still admired as the epitome of Greek artistic expression. The Parthenon, the most famous Greek temple, was constructed from 438 to 432 B.C. under the influence of the great sculptor Phidias (c. 490–432 B.C.). It is significant that he and Pericles (c. 495–429 B.C.), the greatest leader in the history of Athens, were contemporaries.

Pericles declared, "We are lovers of beauty with simplicity, and we cultivate our minds without loss of manliness." He set out to glorify Athens as a cultural as well as a political center and patronized artists in his effort to celebrate Athenian triumphs. He insisted, "Now that the city [is] sufficiently supplied with the necessities of war, [the people] ought to devote the surplus of the treasury to the construction of these monuments, from which, in the future, would come everlasting fame . . . shining with grandeur and possessing an inimitable grace of form . . . as if some ever-flowing life and unaging spirit had been infused into the creation of them."[6]

The Parthenon was constructed when Athens was at the height of its power, and unlike many religious buildings, it was built to human rather than divine scale. To many admirers, it still represents the most harmonious blend of idealism and humanism in all of Greek art. Its proportions, slightly off mathematical balance to adjust to the human eye, have seemed particularly satisfying to generation after generation of viewers. Reflecting the grandeur of classical Greek culture, the Parthenon remains one of the great architectural sights of Europe. It celebrates a human, rather than a supernatural, ideal that has retained its appeal through the ages. However, in Greece this sense of human confidence and glory was not to last for long.

Athens went into decline after the death of Pericles, beginning with a terrible plague and continuing with long and often disastrous warfare. Greek confidence in self-rule was severely shaken, as Thucydides wrote in his study of the Peloponnesian War: "All parties dwelling rather in their calculation upon the hopelessness of a permanent state of things, were more intent upon self-defense than capable of confidence."[7]

The death of Alexander the Great in 323 B.C. ended the most glorious era in Greek history. Not surprisingly, changes in art mirrored the changes of the time. What might one expect from the art of a culture that was experiencing its own decline? Gods in human form and idealized naturalism no longer expressed the vision of life experienced by the Greeks. Instead, more stress was placed upon emotional expression and sensual gratification. Female nudes became a popular subject for sculpture, as did portraits of males in intense emotional states. Instead of expressing the cultural values of the group, art came to depict the experiences of humans as individuals. These changes in art parallel those in the writings of Greek (and Roman) theorists.

In the fifth century B.C., the artist Polyclitus wrote a *Canon* that became the most celebrated text on art during the classical period. He stressed symmetry in modeling the human form, instructed sculptors about the ideal proportions to achieve beauty, and emphasized tradition over imagination. His theories embodied the confidence of Greeks living in a period when democratic ideals blended with belief in a glorious military and artistic heritage.

In the third century B.C., Xenocrates still defined the doctrine of beauty as a combination of symmetry, rhythm, and precision. He added, however, that the imagination of the artist was also an important element. His art theory therefore moved beyond imitation into a world of individual creativity, still bound by traditional laws of proportion and symmetry but also responsive to inspiration. Earlier philosophers had written that inspiration was the province of poets and musicians but not of "artisans." Now it became an important element in the theory of all the fine arts.

In the first century A.D., a teacher of rhetoric named Dio wrote an oration completely devoted to sculpture and painting. Noting that artists want to avoid seeming "untrustworthy and to be disliked for making innovations," he adds that they are capable of "contributing their own ideas, becoming in a sense the rivals as well as the fellow-craftsmen of the poets."[8] This was an important step for artists, since poets had previously reigned supreme in freedom of expression. Horace's famous dictum *Ut pictura poesis* (painting is the same as poetry) is even more succinct. However, Dio believes that the fine arts could have an even greater power. Recalling the work of the sculptor Phidias, Dio argues that the artist can give physical form to the divine: "But you, by the power of your art, first conquered and united Hellas and then all the others by means of this wondrous presentiment, showing forth so marvelous and dazzling a conception that none of those who have beheld it could any longer form a different one."[9]

Dio praises just what Plato had distrusted—the magical power of art to shape our sense of reality. He suggests that if an artist's creation is powerful enough, that creation will shape our perception from that time forward.

Is this true? Do we have any pictorial images that define our ideas? Think of the classic photograph of the marines planting the flag at Iwo Jima during World War II. Does it define our vision of war? Does Grant Wood's painting *American Gothic* help to establish our conception of farmers? An especially interesting example is Leonardo's *Last Supper*, an image that will be discussed later; for now we should note that Leonardo's vision was so compelling that many people have come to imagine Christ and his disciples according to Leonardo's conception.

In Greece in the third century A.D., Plotinus took issue with the idea of mimesis in his *Enneads*, writing that "artists do not simply reproduce the visible, but they go back to principles in which nature itself had found its origin; and further, they on their own part achieve and add much."[10] Following this principle, Philostratus wrote in *The Life of Apollonius of Tyana:* "Imagination wrought these, an artificer much wiser than imitation. For imitation will represent that which can be seen with the eyes, but imagination will represent that which cannot."[11]

According to these philosophers, the direct imitation of nature was no longer vital. Why did this change take place? Perhaps it was because there was no longer much confidence that humans could control their world through idealistic actions. Thus, artists turned the focus inward.

The movement toward imagination over mimesis in art theory is reflected in late Greek and early Roman sculpture. Artists began to create dramatic gestural figures, such as the famous *Laocoon*, depicting a father and two sons trying to break free from the grip of a giant serpent. Many viewers prefer these later sculptures over the calmer classical works because they powerfully express human feelings. They maintain a fundamental naturalism and humanism but not a classical balance and restraint. Would we say Greek art gradually became more realistic? Only if we find drama more real than serenity, movement more real than calm, and imagination more real than tradition.

One idea remained the same throughout the mature periods of Greek art, namely, that the human figure represented the highest form of beauty. Figurative art became the perfect visualization of "humanism," the fundamental idea passed down to us from classical civilization. Sophocles wrote in *Antigone*, "Wonders are many, but none is more wonderful than man." Aeschylus had one of his characters say, "I am human, celebrate me as a man and not a god." The religious ideal had given way to humanism; and the belief that people should manage their own fate, no matter how severely shaken at times, has been crucial in the development of Western civilization.

The artistic consequences of humanism have been great. Not only are classical Greek statues still copied in some art schools, but, more important, the human figure has remained for more than two thousand years the most dominant theme in Western art. We may take this for granted, but it has not been true in other cultures. In Chinese painting, for example, landscape has been the major subject of the past millennium, while in Islamic art, abstract geometric designs have dominated. Why was the human figure the focus in ancient Greece?

One possible answer was suggested in the previous chapter: people in urban societies deal less with animals, plants, or the cycles of nature than they do with each other. Yet Chinese and Islamic artists also worked primarily in urban centers. Here we enter into religious, social, and cultural history, which many art historians believe crucial to their studies. These studies begin by asking good questions: How did the Greeks think about their lives? How did they differ from Chinese and Islamic peoples in that conception? In each of these societies, how did people live? How did they relate to one another? And, finally, in what traditions did they express their beliefs?

These broad questions provide major themes for art-historical study. We can take this same approach to examine the art in our own lives. How do we decorate our homes and our rooms? What do we put on the walls of our schools? Do we use posters, sculptural objects, ceramics, prints, drawings, photographs, or paintings? What subjects do we prefer? What does all this tell us about our ideals and our beliefs? Is the art just decoration? If so, why have we chosen particular works? Are they merely pleasing combinations of color, line, and form, or do they hold symbolic meanings for us? Most Americans may be content to allow the art historian to be the "expert," but that is not enough. It is also our job to learn how art affects us and, more generally, how it relates to the values that people of every culture and every historical period have held. This is a major task that can never be completed but is a delight to explore and will be discussed in later chapters.

Chinese Theories of Art

One of the oldest and richest artistic cultures in the world is that of China. As a major influence on neighboring cultures, China has much in common with Greece, but its art and artistic theories developed in different directions (a sample lesson plan is given in appendix 2). The forms of art most often discussed in China have been painting and calligraphy, although artists also worked in jades, bronzes, textiles, ceramics, and architecture.

Painting actually was one of the later arts to develop in China, not reaching prominence until the fourth century A.D. It has maintained its traditions for more than fifteen hundred years. One of the great names among early artists was Ku K'ai-chih (c. 345–406 A.D.), famous for his mastery of thin brushstrokes that looked like "iron wires." He commented that human figures were the most difficult to paint, followed by land-scapes and animals, but his fame came from his extremely elegant depictions of men and women in narrative scenes. For the next five hundred years, human figures were an important theme for Chinese artists. Unlike the Greeks, however, they were not interested in the body as an object of beauty in itself. Instead, humans were shown as models for good actions. "People are interested in paintings because noble scholars are represented," wrote one early theorist. Another added: "Of those who look at pictures, there is not one who, beholding the Three Majesties and the Five Emperors, would not look up in reverence; nor any that before a painting of the degenerate rulers of the Three Decadences would not be moved to sadness."[12]

Thus according to one early Chinese theory, the value of painting came from its capacity to convey noble qualities to emulate or degenerate qualities to avoid. Aristotle would have agreed. This theory was also important for religious art, and many of the Chinese paintings that survive from early periods were inspired by Buddhism.

Even earlier, however, there was the suggestion that painting was an activity that could go beyond the representational to become something creative in itself. The philosopher-mystic Chuang-tzu wrote in perhaps the third century B.C. about a king who invited all the painters in his domain to his court to demonstrate their talents. While the others were politely lined up waiting to pay their respects, one artist sauntered into an inner chamber, removed all his clothes, and began to paint. The courtiers were horrified, but when the king heard about him, he exclaimed that because this man was totally devoted to his art, he must be a true master.

A related anecdote concerns an emperor who invited two artists to his court to paint the scenery of the Yangtse River. One artist carefully made sketches for weeks, then painted the scenery slowly, with great precision. The other wandered for months alongside the banks of the river, finally arriving at court just in time to dash off a bold ink sketch of the scenery. The emperor declared them both masters, praising one artist for capturing the details of the landscape and the other for capturing its essence.

Perhaps the most important theoretical writing in the history of Chinese art involves the concept of "Six Rules" formulated by Hsieh Ho around 500 A.D. Five of these rules describe how to build structure through brushwork, capture the forms of the objects depicted, employ appropriate colors, and create a unified composition based on the techniques of past masters. The first rule, however, has been the most important: *rhythmic vitality and life-movement.* This phrase has been discussed and argued about for more than a millenium. The consensus is that it means a painting must have an inner sense of life. Whether an artist has a bold or a detailed style and whatever the subject matter, if there is no spiritual force within the painting, it will lack vitality.

One major theory of Chinese art stresses its value as memory. The artist Tsung Ping (375–443 A.D.) wrote how he treasured the sight of great mountains and river gorges, but because of his age he could no longer travel to scenic locations. "Therefore I have taken to painting forms, arranging colors and constructing clouds over mountains. We see a truth perceived by someone long, long ago can be understood by those coming a thousand years after. . . . Without leaving the crowded human habitations, I roam and wander in the solitary wilds of nature."[13]

This kind of substitutional theory became especially important after the tenth century, when landscape became the most important theme of Chinese painting. The major eleventh-century artist Kuo Hsi wrote that the sage cultivates his spirit in seclusion among the mountains and streams and then is able to convey the purity and grandeur of nature through painting. "Without leaving your room you may sit to your heart's content among streams and valleys. . . . Look with a heart in tune with forest and stream."[14]

Kuo Hsi divided landscape paintings into those through which the viewer can travel, those in which the viewer can wander, and those in which the viewer can live, preferring the latter. The artist was able in his own works to express the magnificence of Chinese mountain scenery while still painting in a representational manner. His grand landscapes combine great power of conception with full control of brushwork.

Once artists had mastered representational skills in landscape paintings, an appreciation for the individual spirit of the painter emerged. One of the great poets and calligraphers in Chinese history, Su Shih (Su Tung-p'o, 1037–1101), became a spokesman for the new viewpoint. He claimed that those who looked only for mimesis in painting lacked maturity. Su believed a painting should be a visual poem that expresses the nature of the artist as well as the nature of what he or she is depicting—that indeed the two are one and the same. Su wrote a poem about his good friend Wen T'ung, a painter of bamboo, in which he describes how the artist unifies himself with his subject:

> When Wen T'ung paints bamboo
> He sees bamboo and does not see people.
> Why does he not see people?
> Trance-like, leaving his body behind,
> He becomes a bamboo
> Endlessly putting forth new growth.[15]

Su also wrote two prose poems on "The Red Cliff" that became among the most famous of all Chinese texts. In one, Su and a friend are drifting in a boat at night and the friend laments the impermanence of life: "We are nothing more than the flies of summer between heaven and earth, grains of millet on the waste of the sea! It grieves me that life is so brief, and I envy the long river that never stops." Su sympathizes with his friend but replies that "if we view life through the vision of change, there's not a moment of stillness in all creation. However, if we understand the changelessness of things, then all beings including ourselves have no end. Why should we be envious? The breeze whispering on the river, the bright moon over the mountains, which our ears hear as music and our eyes see as beauty, we may enjoy freely and they will never be exhausted."[16]

The sense that beauty should be appreciated from within became even more apparent in the work and thought of scholar-artists in later generations and eventually came to dominate much of Chinese painting. Theorists insisted that "if meaning is there, don't see for outward likeness," or "an excellent painter is skilled at meaning, not at superficials."[17] One of the most admired of scholar-artists was Ni Tsan (1301–74). His own mocking self-appraisal shows how far the idea had developed that painting is the expression of an inward state of mind:

> By the eastern sea there is a sick man,
> Who calls himself "mistaken" and "extreme."
> When he paints walls and sketches on silk and paper,
> Isn't it an overflow of his madness?

Ni Tsan also wrote that he painted bamboo "merely to sketch the exceptional exhilaration in my breast, that's all. Then, how can I judge whether it is like something or not?"[18]

If art springs from the inner life of the painter, it becomes vitally important that to make art one cultivates oneself in poetry, music, and philosophy as well as nature. To put it in more modern terms, if art is self-expression, it is vital to have a cultured and noble self to express. Thus Chinese painters were advised to read books and ramble through mountains as well as practice their brushwork. As early as the late eleventh century, Kuo Jo-hsu wrote that "the great masterpieces of the past were created mostly by great scholars of high position, or by hermits living close to nature. Because they lived the lives of true men and sought relaxation in the arts, steeped themselves in them, this high thinking and elevation of spirit found expression in their paintings."[19]

The flexibility of the Chinese brush, held in the fingertips, makes it an extraordinary instrument for artistic expression. Every movement of the fingers, hand, wrist, shoulder, and body is instantly transmitted into line and form. For this reason, the Chinese idea that brushwork reveals the full personality of the artist can easily be understood. The Chinese felt that there was no need to strive for originality—it would come on its own since each person is different. Hence, there was no struggle to find "one's own style." Painters were content to learn by copying, for their own spirit would certainly shine through their brushwork. Furthermore, the more one studied, rambled through nature, and experienced life, the deeper and richer one's paintings would become. It was expected that painters' work would improve as they got older, and artists proudly signed their works with their ages when they passed sixty and seventy years old. Whether or not this was a self-fulfilling prophecy, most experts today agree that many Chinese artists did their best work in their final years.

The question of methods was important to Chinese painters and theorists. As time went by, model books were printed that showed how to depict trees, mountains, buildings, boats, figures, and plants. A kind of orthodoxy developed, even among many free-spirited literati (scholar-poet) painters, which led to several interesting theoretical discussions. Wang Kai warned painters using his method book that:

> neither dexterity nor conscientiousness is enough. Some set great value on method; others pride themselves on dispensing with method. To be without method is deplorable, but to depend entirely on method is worse. You must first learn to observe the rules faithfully; afterwards, modify them according to your intelligence and capacity. The end of all method is to seem to have no method. . . . Study ten thousand volumes and walk ten thousand miles. . . . If you aim to dispense with method, learn method. If you aim at facility, work hard. If you aim for simplicity, master complexity. . . . He who is learning to paint must first learn to still his heart, thus to clarify his understanding and increase his wisdom.[20]

In a culture where the writers about art were almost always the artists themselves, theory was always tied to the creative production of painters, and thus the issues were not just theoretical but practical. Therefore, the important question of methodology was taken up by later artists in different ways. Some felt that by copying the ancients one could not only achieve a sense of universal values but also develop one's own style within the parameters of accepted practice. Others felt that this was too restrictive and argued for greater personal freedom.

The seventeenth century was one of the most artistically fertile ages in Chinese history. However, it was a very difficult period politically. Following a great deal of unrest within the Ming government, foreign Manchu forces (considered "barbarian" by many Chinese) invaded the country. After a protracted struggle, they were able to establish the new Ch'ing dynasty, which was to last until 1912. As might be expected, such serious governmental changes affected people's views about their country and themselves, leading to a variety of artistic expression.

While some painters continued to follow conservative literati traditions, others explored new paths in the new age. One of these was Shih-t'ao (1642–c. 1707). A descendant of the Ming royal family, Shih-t'ao was lucky to escape with his life when his family was massacred after the Ming dynasty fell. He was taken to a Zen Buddhist temple where he studied old books, practiced calligraphy, and began to paint. Even in his youth he was determined to follow his instincts. He inscribed on a painting at the age of fifteen that he disdained the usual traditions of painting and instead used his own method.[21]

As an artist who was outside normal society, because of both his family background and his life as a monk, Shih-t'ao was able to ignore the pressure to conform. His art expressed an individual spirit that has made him one of the most admired masters in later Chinese history. In fact, painting seems to have been more important to him than his religious practice, and after much travel through China, he eventually settled in the city of Yangchou as a professional artist. Although he was to some extent responsive to the wishes of patrons, he was still able to paint from the dictates of his own spirit, and he constantly emphasized in his inscriptions the need to go beyond the imitation of the past. He noted that the early painters had no models to imitate, and they were nonetheless able to create works of great artistic power. "Yet, ever since these ancients established methods, latter-day painters are not permitted to go beyond them," he lamented.[22]

Around the age of sixty, Shih-t'ao wrote a text called *Enlightened Remarks on Painting* that expressed his philosophical views and theories about art. These were not entirely different from the views of the past, but he strongly emphasized the importance of individual creativity: "All things have both a constant aspect and one which responds to circumstances; similarly, any method must be capable of transformation. . . . Painting is the greatest method for representing the world in the process of transformation and interaction, for capturing the essential beauty of landscape's dynamic forms, the eternal activity of creation. . . . The important thing is whether one is capable of fully valuing one's perceptions. . . . Our function lies not in brushwork itself, but in what it can transmit; it lies not in ink quality alone, but what it can convey."[23]

Shih-t'ao is considered the epitome of the individualist painter in China, and his theories as well as his art have been very influential ever since the seventeenth century. By providing an alternative to conservatism, he enabled the world of brush painting to increase its scope, thus providing for its longevity. In this century, when Western styles of art have become known to Chinese painters, it is fascinating that even those artists trained in Europe have tended to return to Chinese brushwork traditions whenever they were allowed to do so by the changing political tides that governed their careers. The strength of Chinese artistic tradition, enlivened by individualists like Shih-t'ao when it was in danger of stultification, has persisted to the present day. It could not have lasted for so long had it not been amenable to inspiration as well as transformation.

Art and Art Theory in India

Greek art can be characterized broadly as humanistic, and Chinese literati theories emphasize the expression of the cultivated self, but the art of India is more directly religious. This is because almost all Indian art seems to have a sacred function, even when it appears most secular to Western viewers. Paintings of beautiful women, for example, symbolize the human soul longing for union with the divine. Sculptures of embracing couples, which may seem to verge on pornography, are also expressions of Indian religious ideals.

To appreciate any art, one must have some understanding of the culture. India is a vast land, primarily agricultural and heavily populated. Over the centuries a caste system developed, in part to provide hereditary occupations within the strongly structured society. Although everyone is born into a caste that will dictate much of his or her life, there is great religious freedom. First, different religions coexist. Although India is the birthplace of Buddhism, for the last millennium the primary religion has been Hinduism. This is not a monotheistic religion like Buddhism or Christianity. Instead, there are many gods to worship, some of whom take on various powers that can be represented in art by multiple heads and arms. One may worship any deity in the pantheon, and even in the same household it is not unusual for one family member to accept Shiva as a personal deity and another to pray to Krishna.

Life in India is a unique mixture of structure and freedom. Birth into a family and caste determines much of one's future, and in most ways there is little opportunity for individualism. A personal and private response to religion, however, is common, and this may be more possible when other forms of individuality and particularity are not insisted upon. Art has the same combination of structure and freedom. Aesthetic response in India comes within a structure of traditional values; the spiritual function of the art provides the opportunity for both artist and viewer to partake in a shared vision.

Throughout the ages, the human form has been the primary source and subject of Indian art. Yet Indian art is not necessarily similar to the art of Greece. In contrast to Greek classical art, which relies upon symmetry and balance, Indian art expresses vibrant sensuality. A sense of physicality and movement enlivens it and gives it a unique combination of idealism and sexuality.

One of the leading writers on Indian art was Ananda K. Coomaraswamy, a native of Ceylon who served for many years as curator at the Museum of Fine Arts in Boston. He believed that the art of India is an exemplar of traditional, as opposed to individualistic, values, and he often compared it to the medieval art of Europe. He felt, for example, that naturalism is "antipathetic to religious art of all kinds" and that Christian and Indian icons both express ideas rather than serving as likenesses. According to Coomaraswamy, "True art, pure art, never enters into competition with the unattainable perfection of the world, but relies exclusively on its own logic and criteria. . . . only our response to its qualities of energy and characteristic order will enable us to judge it as a work of art."[24]

Communicating an idea is not the same as idealism, however. The Indian work of art, according to Coomaraswamy, is neither a memory image nor an ideal in the humanistic sense; rather, it is a symbol that could be ideal only in the abstract sense. Indian art tends to ignore the transient and the momentary in favor of the eternal and absolute. What makes it fascinating is that these eternal values are expressed in human terms. Although there have been stylistic variations in Indian art over the ages, many of the themes, even the poses, have remained constant. The distinctions between one work and another are those of intensity and energy rather than originality. "When the themes are felt and the art *lives*, it is of no moment whether the themes are old or new."[25]

In his essay "The Theory of Art in Asia," Coomaraswamy describes how a traditional Indian artist goes about preparing to create an image. First, the artist eliminates all emotions and distractions through meditation. Next, he visualizes in his mind the image he is about to create. He then concentrates to achieve total self-identification with the image (much like Wen T'ung "becomes a bamboo"). If the image is a god or goddess, the artist must transcend himself into unification with the deity. Only now is the artist able to begin work. Coomaraswamy supports his description with a quotation from the Hindu classic *Brhadaranyaka Upanisad:* "Whoever worships a divinity as other than the self, thinking 'He is one, and I another,' knows not."[26]

The Indian artist, having identified with his subject, is able to depict the form in which the deity is manifest. Since the formal idea was cultivated, rules were established as to the ideal proportions for such spiritual images. This may seem strange to us, since we disdain rules for artists, but it worked well in India. According to one fifth-century text, the unit of measurement was the face, from the chin to the top of the forehead. For example, a standing Buddha image would be nine faces tall.

Today we might find such instructions to be confining, but Coomaraswamy believed that "such convention is a far greater help than hindrance to real art. It does not prevent a man of genius from producing the most beautiful work possible, although ensuring that it shall so far conform to an accepted standard as to be immediate and universal in its appeal."[27]

If the artist is to some degree controlled by a canon of forms that represent an ideal of superhuman grace and beauty, art can represent a supernatural order beyond the limitations of the individual artist. This view of art presupposes that people believe that what we see here and now in our daily lives is illusion and that ultimate truth lies beyond our limited vision. Naturalism alone is not enough, for it lacks spirituality. For this reason the Indian artist identifies with the divine and is content to follow formulas in his or her work to produce an ideal image.

One of the most surprising aspects of Indian art for Westerners is the union of sexuality and spirituality. To see sculptures of couples in passionate embraces upon the walls of Hindu temples is puzzling to those who have been taught to separate sensuality and religion. Coomaraswamy explains that "in India, the conditions of human love, from the first meeting of the eyes to ultimate self-oblivion, have seemed spiritually significant, and there has always been a free and direct use of sexual imagery in religious symbolism."[28]

Some scholars feel that in India, which is an agricultural society, fertility has always informed art. Would this necessarily lead to sensuous deities, to whom prayers are offered for abundant crops as well as for abundant families? It is not true of all agricultural societies, yet in India the sexual union that is considered the highest bliss to achieve on earth is an intimation of union with the divine. There are no cultures that have shown the beauty of love more rapturously than India. Because sex is not shameful or sinful, it can be celebrated in spiritual as well as physical terms. It is true that mystic Christian poets in Europe have also presented sexual unity as a metaphor for the rapture of union with Christ, but Indian artists have represented this rapture in the most direct way possible.

In Indian religion, the earthly world is not denied, but it is not celebrated for its own sake. The purposes of art and life are the same—enlightenment and release from the bondage of earthly concerns. Art therefore follows a cosmic rhythm rather than an earthly one, and the artist must achieve spiritual harmony beyond any sense of selfhood. The artist, in this view, becomes an instrument through which the divine may operate. Just as the Greeks had muses who inspired poets and artists, many cultures have postulated some force beyond artists who could guide their inspiration.

Those of us who consider ourselves completely secular might find it difficult to accept this view of creativity; yet hasn't everyone experienced at one time or another a sense of "feeling the flow" without conscious effort, whether during painting, playing music, writing, or some physical activity? When this feeling is gone, every activity seems to take great effort and we wonder where the natural flow has gone.

The sense of natural flow is one of the most striking features of Indian art. Within the seeming restrictions of traditional proportions and stylistic features, artists have been able to create images in which the life force of their beliefs is given vigorous form. Unlike later Greek art, there is little emphasis upon individuality in Indian art. Images are not particular representations of individual people; and artists traditionally did not sign their works. Instead, Indian art through the ages celebrates the eternal truths of the sacred world through sensual, and often sexual, images of beautiful women and heroic men, with a sense of movement that suggests the influence of dance. Paintings are small in format but rich in color; carvings are ornate and full of life; textiles are lushly designed. The earthly and spiritual splendor of the Indian vision of life emerges in all of its arts.

The Middle Ages in Europe

Unlike the art of Greece, China, and India, medieval European art did not celebrate naturalism, nature, or spiritual sensuality. In fact, the biblical injunction against "graven images" confronted the Christian world of the early Middle Ages with a serious problem. Was it immoral for artistic images to be created? Or was the injunction merely against the *worship* of images? Many works from antiquity remained, and images of emperors could be found on coins. Even if these were not sinful, many questioned whether images could ever approach the sense of the divine they meant to convey. Clement of Alexandria wrote, in "Exhortation to the Greeks": "A statue is really lifeless matter shaped by a craftman's hand; but in our view the image of god is not an object of sense made from matter perceived by the senses, but a mental image. God, that is, the only true God, is not perceived by the senses but by the mind."[29]

Some churchmen argued that prayers offered to images actually pass through the images to God. They believed that the image thus helped bridge the gap between the believer and the deity. After much dispute, during which some images (known as icons) were destroyed (by "iconoclasts"), this second view prevailed, and in the fifth century artists began to create the images that led to the great artistic triumphs of the Romanesque and Gothic eras.

Considering the popularity of medieval art today, it is strange to think how it was once regarded as part of the "dark ages," during which the light of Greek humanism was almost extinguished. This was, of course, a Renaissance perspective, frowning upon the lack of naturalism and overwhelming religious content of most medieval art. However, the noble sculptures, handsome tapestries, splendid metal work, evocative mural paintings, exquisite illuminated manuscripts, and above all magnificent architecture of the Romanesque and Gothic cathedrals are surely among the wonders of world art.

One of the most influential books on medieval art is Henry Adams's *Mont-Saint-Michel and Chartres*, first published in 1904 and frequently republished thereafter. The author was a novelist and historian who turned away from the materialism of his day to write about an era of faith and artistic creation. Though not trained in art history, he made a great contribution to the field. By focusing his attention upon two great monuments, one of the Romanesque period and one of the Gothic period, he gave voice to the spirit of the Middle Ages.

How can we explain the success of Adams's account? First, his style immediately involves the reader. Discussing the Romanesque, he writes: "Serious and simple to excess! is it not? Young people rarely enjoy it. They prefer the Gothic. . . . No doubt they are right, because they are young: but men and women who have lived long and are tired—who want rest—who have done with aspirations and ambition—whose life has been a broken arch—this repose and self-restraint as they feel nothing else. The quiet strength of these curved lines, the solid support of these heavy columns, the moderate proportions, even the modified lights, the absence of display, of effort, or self-consciousness, satisfy them as no other art does." In contrast, describing the Gothic style of Chartres Cathedral, Adams comments, "No two men think alike about it, and no woman agrees with either man. . . . To most minds it casts too many shadows; it wraps itself in mystery. . . . Our amusement is to play with it, and to catch its meaning in its smile; and whatever Chartres may be now, when young it was a smile."[30]

To help us understand the religious fervor that animated the builders of great cathedrals, Adams offers us legends, stories, history, poetry, biographies, and music as well as plans of the monuments and descriptions of the art. In short, he takes us into the lives of those who created the magnificent cathedrals. Churchmen of the times wrote how everyone in the community, high and low, pitched in to help, even if they could offer nothing more than their labor:

> The inhabitants of Chartres have combined to aid in the construction of their church by transporting the materials. . . . men brought up in honour

and wealth, nobles, men and women, have bent their proud and haughty necks to the harness of carts, and like beasts of burden, they have dragged to the abode of Christ these waggons. . . . often when a thousand persons or more are attached to the chariots—so great is the difficulty—yet they march in such silence that not a murmur is heard. . . . when they have reached the church they arrange their waggons about it like a spiritual camp, and during the whole night they celebrate the watch by hymns and canticles. On each waggon they light tapers and lamps; they place there the infirm and sick, and bring them the precious relics of the saints for their relief.[31]

Understanding the transportation of huge stones as a religious act helps us to realize how such a magnificent cathedral could have been built. Further, it explains the glory of Chartres as the visual expression of the profound beliefs of an entire community—indeed, of an entire continent.

In today's world we gain a great deal from the diversity of our backgrounds and beliefs. Furthermore, through the arts of the past we can learn about the ideals of many cultures throughout the ages. But, perhaps inevitably, we have lost something in the process: the overwhelming force of a unifying religion that can give hope and solace to every member of society. It is this religious force that is expressed in most medieval art, and today we can only look upon the cathedrals and art objects with admiration and wonder.

The Renaissance

The Renaissance brought forth a different view of the world and therefore led to different artistic values. Classical learning was revived; the cult of the individual rose against the more communitarian spirit of the past, and the basic struggle of philosophers and artists was to harmonize Christianity with a view of humankind as "the measure of all things." While religious subjects continued to be depicted in painting and sculpture, the focus was different. Instead of iconic representations of a divine reality, images were humanized to the point where a Venetian artist painted himself as Christ and his twelve best friends as disciples, while another artist painted his mistress as the Virgin Mary. In many ways, the artistic progression was similar to that of the ancient Greeks. Beginning with somewhat abstract images, a change occurred to idealized humanism, and finally to more emotional and expressive naturalism as the Renaissance moved into the baroque.

The most influential writer in English on Renaissance painting has been Bernard Berenson. Although his major study, *Italian Painters of the Renaissance*, is based on four essays published between 1894 and 1907, the clarity and humanity of his writing are still luminous today. Late in his life, adding a preface to yet another edition of his book, Berenson comments on art education:

> Many see pictures without knowing what to look at. They are asked to admire the works of pretended art and they do not know enough to say, like the child in Andersen's tale, "Look, the Emperor has nothing on." . . . children are not taught what to look at . . . and unless they are brought up in families of taste as well as means, they are not likely to develop unconsciously a feeling for visual art. . . . Happily visual language is easier to acquire than spoken language. . . . [My book] does not attempt to give an account of the painters' domestic lives or even of their specific techniques, but of what their pictures mean to us today as works of art, of what they can do for us as ever contemporary life-enhancing actualities. . . . We must look and look till we live the painting and for a fleeting moment become identified with it. . . . No artifact is a work of art if it does not help to humanize us.[32]

It is with this humanistic spirit that Berenson discusses the various schools of Italian painting and helps them come alive for the reader. He divides his book into sections on Venetian, Florentine, central Italian, and northern Italian painters, ending with an essay on "The Decline of Art." While critics today might not always agree with Berenson's evaluations, anyone who has studied Italian painting owes him a great debt.

To take one example of how Berenson uses wider cultural contexts to explain schools of painting, we can compare what he has written about Venetian and Florentine artists. He begins with the understanding that he is seeking to discover what aspects of the human spirit the art embodies. Berenson believes that the Venetian painters are similar to poets in their harmonious unity of intention and execution. He also admires the Venetians for their musicality, writing: "Their coloring not only gives direct pleasure to the eye, but acts like music to the moods, stimulating thought and memory in much the same way as a work by a great composer."[33]

Berenson discusses a number of Venetian painters before moving on to the Florentines. Here he notes that "the history of art in Florence can never be, as that of Venice, the study of a placid development. Each man of genius brought to bear upon his art a great intellect. . . . Forget that they were painters, they remain great sculptors . . . architects, poets, and even men of science. They left no form of expression untried." Admiring the range and greatness of the Florentine masters, Berenson concluded that they were primarily concerned with form. By their prowess in stimulating the tactile imagination of the viewers, Florentine artists could increase the sense of reality and offer a heightened sense of intensity and beauty in their works. From the time of Giotto, "every line is functional;

that is to say, charged with purpose. . . . no matter what his theme, Giotto feels its real significance."[34]

Berenson believed that Italian painting declined after the High Renaissance, lacking what he considered the crucial balance of form, movement, and space in composition. Perhaps the change, which Berenson saw as a decline, was inevitable. Trying to blend the values of the Greeks and the Christians was a difficult task, yet it may be that this tension created the nobility of the art of the Renaissance. For many great masters of the fourteenth through the sixteenth centuries, creativity demanded a balance between opposing forces. By the end of this period, humanistic values triumphed. Michelangelo, for example, sought out religious force in the figurative subject matter, vital to the Greeks but subordinated in the Middle Ages. He wrote, "Nowhere does God, in his grace, reveal himself to me more clearly than in some lovely human form, which I love solely because it is a mirrored image of himself."[35]

Michelangelo believed that God was the source of all beauty and that the artist received a gift from heaven. However, he also felt that to create images of God, the artist must be more than a skillful painter or sculptor—he must live a blameless life. For this reason, even in his final years, Michelangelo was haunted by a sense of sin and felt that his great accomplishments were of no use. He wrote a sonnet about his fear in facing not only physical but also spiritual death:

> My course of life has already reached
> Through stormy seas on a flimsy vessel
> The common port, at which we land to tell
> All conduct's cause, good or bad,
> So that the passionate fantasy, which made
> Of art a monarch for me and an idol,
> Was laden down with sin, now I know well,
> Like what all men desired against their will.
> What will become now of my amorous thoughts
> Once gay and vain, as toward two deaths I move,
> One known for sure, the other ominous?
> There's no painting or sculpture now that quiets
> The soul that is pointed towards that holy love
> That on the cross opened its arms to take us.[36]

When we consider it was Michelangelo who painted the harrowing scene of the *Last Judgement* on the wall of the Sistine Chapel, we can understand him as both exemplar and victim of the Renaissance attempt to integrate religious and humanistic views of the world.

Later European Art and the Rise of Individualism

Once secular values had triumphed over religious ones, humans could consider themselves the central force in the universe. This allowed for a great sense of freedom but also demanded responsibility and confidence in the human intellect. The Age of Reason brought forth great achievements in philosophy and literature, but reason and fine art have never sustained a totally comfortable relationship. Perhaps the sensuality of form, line, and color seems dangerous to the rational spirit; or it may be that the visual image is inherently more emotional or spiritual than pure logic would allow. In any event, there was an inevitable rejection of the overly optimistic belief in human reason, and this led to more powerful changes in the world of the arts.

Without the boundaries of common and fervent religious belief, there was nothing to stem the emotional reaction against the rationalists, who predicted that humans could control and improve their lives through reason and logic. The French Revolution, in particular, led to great hopes—all the more disillusioning when smashed. Beethoven dedicated his Third Symphony to Napoleon, then tore up the dedication when Napoleon proclaimed himself emperor.

Through these historical changes, the move toward individualism in art persisted. By the Romantic period of the nineteenth century, the humanistic vision had clearly triumphed over that purely religious in spirit. Early nineteenth-century painters had new demons to contend with: the rise of the industrial state, modern conceptions of full-scale warfare, and the horrors of the human mind that had previously been attributed to personal devils. Goya, serving as a court painter in Spain, spent much of his time depicting the disasters of war and acts of human folly in etchings that spared no sensibilities. Subjects that previously would have been considered too depressing or horrific now blossomed forth. Goya believed that "the sleep of reason creates monsters." This encapsulates how optimism about control over human destiny through rationalism gave way to a more pessimistic worldview.

William Blake, a remarkable English poet and artist, began his career with illustrated poems called *Songs of Innocence and Experience* that contrast the natural beauty of existence with its fierce and turbulent nature. He believed that these two contraries produce all energy and life; yet he also decried the human destruction needlessly caused by the industrial revolution, with its child labor and separation of people from the land. Through his middle years, disillusioned with the spirit of his age, he composed mystic and prophetic texts which he printed with his own visionary illustrations. Blake stated: "The Nature of my Work is

Visionary or Imaginative; it is an Endeavor to Restore what the Ancients call'd the Golden Age. . . . I will not Reason & Compare: my business is to Create. . . . If the doors of perception were cleansed every thing would appear to man as it is, infinite. . . . In your own Bosom you bear your Heaven and Earth & all you behold; tho'it appears Without, it is Within, in your imagination, of which this world of Mortality is but a Shadow."[37]

Toward the end of his life, Blake designed and printed a set of illustrations to the biblical story of Job following the traditional storyline: Satan taunts God that even the virtuous Job would lose his faith if he were denied all his earthly happiness. Thus Job is subjected to severe trials, at the end of which he has retained his faith and is again graced with God's blessings. Blake, however, adds some commentary that demonstrates his own conviction that "without contraries there is no progression." One example is his etching *Hell is naked before him & Destruction has no covering*, the sixteenth in the Job series (fig. 3). The artist depicts a powerful image of God sitting in judgment, with souls descending into Hell, while Job, with his wife, looks on in wonder. Blake adds his own words on the etching to those from the Bible, such as: "It is higher than Heaven what canst thou do, It is deeper than Hell what canst thou know." For Blake, Job has invited his own downfall because of his materialism, and it is not until he finds his own spiritual and creative powers that he is redeemed. The powerful imagery of these etchings shows how the religious vision of the past was not totally lost but was transformed through personal vision.

The concept of the artist as rebel against society came into being in the nineteenth century. It is an idea that we often assume today although it is comparatively recent. In previous ages, artists expressed the values of their entire culture, or at least its important segments; but in the 1800s, the image of the lonely individual protesting the evils of society became paramount, at least in the popular imagination. The Impressionists being reviled by the art critics of their day, Vincent Van Gogh's mental instability, and Marcel Duchamp painting a mustache on the Mona Lisa all have helped redefine the role of the artist. One has merely to visit the art department of any university to see how, at least outwardly, young artists express this persona in their clothes and attitudes. It is not a trivial matter, for how we see ourselves contributes to how we create.

How we see ourselves also affects our value systems, including philosophy. Two of the major German philosophers, Kant and Hegel, wrote about art as an expression of human and spiritual values, and both stressed Greek and Renaissance ideals. To Kant, who lived in a revolutionary period, Greek figures represented a form of freedom. Although he sought natural beauty without human intervention, Kant believed that

Fig. 3. William Blake (1757–1827), *Thou Hast Fulfilled*, from the "Job" series (1823–25), etching, ink on paper, 8⅜ in. × 6½ in. Private collection.

ultimately the only true ideal is human, because only humans can be conscious of beauty. To the properly attuned person, art is an aesthetic experience of the highest order.

For Hegel, historical and cultural meanings of art were important in addition to aesthetics. He too admired the Greeks because they could portray the harmony of body and spirit. He felt that the art of the Middle

Ages emphasized spirit over the body, while the spirit was not fully expressed in Egyptian or Oriental art. We would probably adopt a different view today, finding the art of many other cultures extremely spiritual. Nevertheless, Hegel's interest in the balance of human and ideal elements still informs much of our attitude toward art history.

Other Important Traditions

There is neither time nor space to discuss here all the differing and fascinating artistic traditions that are available for art-historical inquiry. We might point out, however, that during this century the arts of Africa have been increasingly collected, studied, and appreciated all over the world, after being largely ignored or derided. African sculptures in particular have inspired artists such as Picasso and Braque and have also allowed us to share a unique and powerful artistic vision. In Africa, however, art has traditionally held specific meanings and uses. One of the questions that we must face is whether we, who often appreciate African works for their form, are missing the crucial cultural meanings that animate the art.

We shall see in the next chapter that some art historians of recent decades have argued against formal analysis of the object, stating instead that art should be seen as part of the ideology of a culture, illuminating each stratum of society. In tribal societies, most masks and sculptures carry well-understood meanings in rites and festivals and were never meant for ordinary circumstances. When we put them on display in museums, is it enough to appreciate them as art objects, or are we losing sight of their intrinsic value? Can we learn, or do we intuit, some of the force that they hold in their own cultures?

These are some of the questions raised by the study of African art, and these questions can help us to reflect on other art we usually take for granted. Should art only be seen in its original context? What does this mean for museums and for the methods of display? How might this idea affect the way we teach? There are many questions and few answers, but perhaps the fact that we are asking ourselves such questions means we are on the right track.

Some of these issues also concern the study of the art of early South America. Certainly the Incas and Mayans, for example, produced some amazingly powerful images, but the original meanings are bound up in the beliefs of the cultures, which historians and art historians are working together to uncover. Similarly, the art of Himalayan countries like Tibet and Nepal is strikingly bold, even frightening, but it begins to make sense when one studies how Buddhism combined with more fearsome native religions to foster such conceptions of wrath and the divine.

Other issues are raised by the study of folk arts, which exist even in the most "advanced" urban cultures and sometimes seem to contradict the assumptions we have made about the role of art in complex societies. American folk art, for example, often seems diametrically opposed in spirit to the "high art" being produced at the same time. What are its values? And what are the values of art historians who study it?

First, we must understand that folk art has its own traditions, which may not be as naïve as is often supposed. Patterns of style can be seen over the course of many generations, as well as favorite subject matter, techniques, and media. Nevertheless, folk art can usually be characterized as less technically polished than much high art and less centered upon individual expression. Instead, it expresses the values of at least one segment of society, usually a segment that is not at the forefront of "high" culture.

Recent studies have shown that folk art (and especially its variant "outsider art") is now often created by the disfranchised: women, the elderly, and eccentrics. It is generally studied by those art historians who seem to have some strong points of view in common. First, they see a purity of expression in original folk art that is being corrupted and destroyed by the influx of high culture. This seems to reflect a worldview that harkens back to a golden age before the advent of modernism. Belief in a golden age is common to many traditional cultures, but our own belief in "progress" has made a golden age obsolete. Second, those who admire folk art tend to believe in the essential goodness of humanity and to distrust industrial society as a distorter of human values. Third, they celebrate nature and bemoan urban society for making us lose our roots. In short, they cling to a view of life that espouses what might be called old-fashioned virtues. Ironically, it is the loss of these virtues that has placed new value on the pastoral and led to the celebration of folk art.

Perhaps it is not until something is about to be lost, or at least is perceived as threatened, that it is recognized as important. The study of folk art has certainly broadened our perception of artistic values. In addition, it has provided a much-needed counterpoint to the study of "masterpieces," which are a tiny percentage of all works of art and often only embody the values of one small element of society. Studying masterpieces such as the *Mona Lisa* leads to an understanding of art as the history of individual geniuses, while the study of folk art allows us to see a history of the natural expression of people's traditional beliefs. Similarly, the study of crafts as art can widen our appreciation of artwork whose function and beauty interrelate, rather than limiting our conceptions to "art for art's sake." All too often in the past, high art has been admired by those with a disdain for utility that reinforces the distinctions between upper and lower classes.

One final form of art should be mentioned: the art of popular culture. Even those art historians who appreciate folk art often have trouble with mass-produced consumer goods. Yet there is no question that everything, from cars to soft-drink bottles, is designed with visual impact in mind. These designs can not only be enjoyed but also studied as cultural artifacts that tell us a great deal about ourselves. Most people, even those who appreciate them, would not call such objects art. But when a recent exhibition at the Brooklyn Museum of Art featured the "modernistic" designs of cars, radios, and toasters from the 1930s, it proved surprisingly popular with the art-going public. Is this an example of the theory that when something is exhibited in a museum it automatically becomes art? Or, more generously, does it show that at least some mass-produced items can be seen to have aesthetic as well as historical values? Chapter 7 offers some practical projects for studying popular culture that show how the process of inquiry can enrich our understanding of many different artistic and human values.

Art has been such a difficult word to define that many have given up the quest, but it is certainly true that what we consider art helps to define our values. Should art be for the few or for the masses? Should "cultural leaders" define what art—or even "good art"—is? If so, who are these cultural leaders? Art teachers, critics, museum curators, collectors, professors? If we would like some guidance, to whom should we turn? Reflecting on some of these questions may lead us to an understanding of whether we would consider the artifacts of popular culture art or why we would consider one car or advertising poster as art and not another. This may not be a negative process; in fact, it may be one of the most useful ways of examining our own perceptions.

In the so-called fine arts we must ask the same questions, because we are again touching on our own value systems. Whatever the style or medium, from whatever age or country, do we prefer art because it appeals to us through its visual and formal qualities? its spiritual dimension? its decorative delights? its intellectual components? its emotional connotations? its cultural function? Each of us must discover our own answers and then, just as important, realize that different answers may be just as meaningful to other people.

One thing we can learn from the study of folk and popular arts is that art history need not be exclusive. Complex urban cultures such as those of Greece, China, India, and Europe have certainly produced magnificent works. However, there is no reason to neglect the art of other cultures, including our own at all levels. We may undertake formal analysis of the designs of contemporary ceramics as well as of Renaissance paintings and study the biography of a fine craftswoman as well as Leonardo. Furthermore, when we understand the patronage of quilt makers who produce works for their families and friends, we can learn as much as we do from studying the patronage of Italian princes. We will be drawn to the works that hold the deepest meaning for us (and they may be the enduring monuments), but we should never disdain any artistic expression of the human spirit.

The study of culture cannot rest with the history of the governmental and societal leaders. It was not from the White House or jet-set society that some of the most significant events of past decades have sprung. The civil rights, women's, and ecology movements came from everyday people,[38] and without an understanding of American culture as a whole, we could never understand the success of any of these movements. Similarly, the entire range of art can be appreciated for the many different values it encompasses, including, ultimately, the understanding of all humanity.

NOTES

1. Plato, *Sophist* 266c, and *Republic* X 602d.

2. Plato, *Cratylus*, 432d.

3. See Moshe Barasch, *Theories of Art* (New York: New York University Press, 1985), pp. 9–14.

4. Inscription on an Egyptian temple to Neith at Sais. Immanuel Kant believed that "more sublime words were never uttered, nor a thought ever expressed more magnificently" (*Kritik der Urtheilskraft*, 1790).

5. Arnold Hauser, *The Social History of Art* (New York: Vintage Books, 1951), p. 92.

6. Quoted from Plutarch's *Life of Pericles* in J. J. Pollitt, *Art and Experience in Classical Greece* (London: Cambridge University Press, 1972), p. 66.

7. Thucydides III, 83, quoted in Pollitt, *Art and Experience*, p. 112

8. Dio, *Oration XII*, quoted in Barasch, *Theories of Art*, p. 27.

9. Ibid.

10. Quoted in Erwin Panofsky, *Idea: A Concept in Art Theory* (New York: Harper and Row, 1968), p. 26.

11. Translation from Pollitt, *Art and Experience*, p. 53.

12. Wang Ch'ung (27–c. 100) and Ts'ao Chih (192–232) quoted in Susan Bush and Hsio-yen Shih, *Early Chinese Texts on Painting* (Cambridge, Mass.: Harvard University Press, 1985), pp. 25–26.

13. Quoted in Lin Yutang, *The Chinese Theory of Art* (New York: G. P. Putnam's Sons, 1967), p. 31.

14. Quoted in Bush and Shih, *Early Chinese Texts*, p. 151.

15. Unpublished translation by Stephen Addiss.

16. Unpublished translations by Stephen Addiss.

17. Quoted in Susan Bush, *The Chinese Literati on Painting* (Cambridge, Mass.: Harvard University Press, 1971), p. 110.

18. Ibid., p. 134.

19. Lin Yutang, *The Chinese Theory of Art*, p. 82.

20. Wang Kai, quoted in Mai-mai Sze, *The Way of Chinese Painting* (New York: Random House, 1959), pp. 130, 131, 133.

21. See Richard E. Strassberg, *Enlightened Remarks on Painting by Shih-T'ao* (Pasadena, Calif.: Pacific Asia Museum Monographs, 1989), p. 15.

22. Ibid., p. 31.

23. Ibid., pp. 64, 66, 90.

24. Ananda K. Coomaraswamy, "The Theory of Art in Asia," *The Transformation of Nature in Art* (New York: Dover, 1956), pp. 4–5, 25–26.

25. Ibid., p. 35.

26. Ibid., p. 7. In fifteenth-century Italy, Dante echoed this idea when he wrote: "Who paints a figure, if he cannot be it, cannot draw it."

27. Ananda K. Coomaraswamy, *Medieval Sinhalese Art* (New York: Pantheon, 1956), p. 48.

28. Ibid., p. 44.

29. Quoted in Barasch, *Theories of Art*, p. 52.

30. Henry Adams, *Mont-Saint-Michel and Chartres* (New York: Mentor Books, 1961), pp. 20–21, 93–94.

31. Ibid., pp. 106–7.

32. Bernard Berenson, *Italian Painters of the Renaissance* (London: Phaidon Press, 1956), pp. ix, xii.

33. Ibid., p. 3.

34. Ibid., pp. 39, 45.

35. Quoted in Anthony Blunt, "Michelangelo's Views on Art," *Readings in Art History*, vol. 2 (New York: Charles Scribner's Sons, 1976), p. 76.

36. Translation by Stephen Addiss.

37. William Blake, from *A Vision of the Last Judgement, Jerusalem, The Marriage of Heaven and Hell*, and again *Jerusalem*.

38. This idea was well expressed by Charles Kuralt in a talk given in 1989 at the University of Kansas.

3

Twentieth-Century Methodologies in Art History

This century has been by far the most active in terms of art-historical development, largely due to its great variety of artistic movements and theories. Even more important, museums across the country now exhibit the arts of almost all cultures and historical periods. We may take this for granted, but it was not always the case. Public museums are only two hundred years old, the products of democratic systems of government. The much more recent exhibition of non-Western art has been spurred on by greater communication among peoples around the world.

During the twentieth century, the field of art history has been altered by developments in photography, which led to accessible reproductions of artworks in print/poster, slide, and book form. Art exhibitions, classes, reproductions, books, journals, films, and videos have stimulated a wide variety of approaches to art-historical study that may seem confusing if not understood in context. Differing approaches and methodologies in art history can be as delightful as the variety of artistic traditions available to us, and can increase the richness of the field. We have the unprecedented opportunity to see and appreciate the arts of all times and places. As a consequence, the history of art has the potential to become an important part of all our lives. Chapter 6 offers suggestions for how to utilize art history as a process of inquiry rather than a process of information acquisition, while chapter 8 offers suggestions for the scope and sequence of art studies at the elementary and secondary levels. In this chapter we will investigate what art history has become in this century and how the many approaches that are being explored can enliven our own understanding of the opportunities art history offers.

Style and Iconography

Two of the great names in twentieth-century art history are Heinrich Woelfflin and Erwin Panofsky. Both scholars tend to focus more on the artwork than the artist, the audience, or the culture, although Panofsky also stresses context as a major factor in understanding art. Their work on style and iconography has inspired much of the best art-historical research and writing of our century. Although they have recently been depreciated by those who prefer other methodologies, their work remains seminal to the field of art history.

Woelfflin's great contribution is his analysis of principles of style.[1] Two main features distinguish his work, the first being his understanding that style can be divided into personal, national, and period aspects. He writes that just as each of us sees an artwork differently, so each artist sees the same subject differently, even if his or her wish is nothing more than mimesis. Each human being has a different temperament; thus, each painter will make brushstrokes that are quick or slow, confident or delicate, energized or serene. Woelfflin argues that even in the smallest detail, the creator's individuality is apparent. It is this belief in individual style that led an art historian to decide that there were fourteen different painters at work in the cave at Lascaux.

Woelfflin also writes that artists, despite their individuality, cannot help but be part of their own respective national traditions: "The course of development of art, however, cannot simply be reduced to a series of separate points. Individuals fall into larger groups. Botticelli and Lorenzo di Credi, for all their differences, have still, as Florentines, a certain resemblance when compared with any Venetian. . . . That is to say: to the personal style must be added *the style of the school, the country, the race.*"[2] For an example, Woelfflin contrasts Rubens's Flemish sense of activity and massiveness with the subtlety and restfulness of Dutch landscape painting. However, he feels that beyond personal and national styles a third division is necessary, that of period. As the human vision of the world changes through time, it produces a new ideal of life and a new relationship between individuals and their surroundings. In the late twentieth century, we simply do not see the world in the same way our grandparents—nor persons of any other period—did.

These ideas of personal, national, and period styles are so common among art historians today that we cannot believe they were not familiar from ancient times. In fact, to some extent they were. Aristotle had divided the work of artists by whether they painted humans idealistically, realistically, or disparagingly. Many early Greek writers praised one painter over another by comparing use of color, attention to detail, and other stylistic features. In terms of national style, the Greek artist Theodorus compared the naturalistic sculptures of Greece with the preordained styles of Egypt. Period style was also observed by the early Greeks, often with aesthetic preferences for one period over another. Xenocrates postulated that Greek sculpture reached its stylistic peak in the fifth and fourth centuries B.C., a notion that is still current among those who prefer classical Greek sculpture. Cicero agreed, writing that the same development occurred in painting.

Although Woelfflin's ideas on personal, national, and period styles are not entirely new, they do create a clear structure for analysis, supported in his writings by lucid examples from European art of the Renaissance and baroque eras. Woelfflin's second major contribution to stylistic analysis is more controversial: he divides two-dimensional art into pairs of categories, based on what he considers a progression from the linear to the painterly. An emphasis on outline, he feels, led to a vision of subjects as individual, tangible, limited, and volumetric, as can be seen in the clearly outlined paintings of the High Renaissance. In the baroque era, on the other hand, a new way of seeing and painting evolved that is less tangible. Artists presented objects as limitless, no longer dependent upon outline but seeming to shift and merge into one another. Woelfflin writes: "Linear vision is permanently bound up with a certain idea of beauty and so is painterly vision. If an advanced type of art dissolves the line and replaces it by the restless mass, that happens not only in the interest of a new verisimilitude, but in the interests of a new beauty too."[3]

Woelfflin is trying to avoid the classical preferences of many art lovers and critics in the early part of this century. These preferences had led to seeing certain periods of Greek art as superior to the others and to the belief that High Renaissance art was superior to that of the baroque. To Woelfflin, stylistic changes through time are not a matter of quality but merely reflect "a different attitude to the world." What was this new attitude? The emergence of baroque art suggests that the Renaissance tension between religion and humanism gave way to a new interest in human subjectivity and emotion.

To support his major distinction between the linear and the painterly, Woelfflin creates four more categories. First, he believes that spatial treatment evolved from a series of planes to more gradual recession. Renaissance space was therefore specific and orderly, more logical than the fluid space in baroque paintings. Second, he believes that forms developed from closed and finite to open and relaxed. Instead of clearly articulated and outlined forms, objects gradually became less defined and more integrated with each other. Third, composition changed from multiplicity and individuality to unity. This did not imply simplicity but meant that the emphasis upon individual forms gave way to a more unified sense of totality. Finally, Woelfflin argues that the artistic presentation changed from absolute to relative clarity of expression: while painting was once seen as depiction of a subject or group of subjects (humans, objects, buildings, trees, etc.), people's conception of it changed and it was seen as emotional expression. An art based upon line became an art based upon paint and color.

How effective are Woelfflin's principles? They have been studied in art history classes for more than fifty years, and many scholars have found them to be extremely useful for understanding the differences in artistic vision that led to certain major historical developments in art. Woelfflin stresses that painters of the baroque era had their own sense of vision and were not merely "decadent" or unable to maintain the clarity and balance of Rennaissance painting traditions. He taught that artists should be understood in the context of their own traditions rather than criticized for not following the ideals of another period.

Although these principles have been influential in twentieth-century art history, they are not uncriticized. Some scholars feel that Woelfflin's linear and painterly distinction is accurate for certain periods of art but becomes artificial and misleading when applied to others. It does not work well, for example, with much twentieth-century art. A more complex criticism comes from the well-known art historian E. H. Gombrich, who feels that Woelfflin's principles constitute a "norm" of art that polarized periods into "classical" and "nonclassical." Even though Woelfflin himself gives equal merit to baroque art, which is nonclassical, his norm is still based upon a polarization that might inhibit fresh views of art and artists. Criticism also comes from practitioners of the new art history who argue that the primary emphasis upon style is misguided. Nevertheless, Woelfflin's conceptions of style remain important to the field and form a background for much twentieth-century art-historical research and writing.

The second major art historian to provide a new impetus to the field is Erwin Panofsky, one of many important European intellectuals who came to the United States prior to World War II. In this context, his article "The History of Art as a Humanistic Discipline" takes on additional force, particularly his suggestion that "even he who merely transmits knowledge or learning participates, in his modest way, in the process of shaping reality—a fact the enemies of humanism are perhaps more keenly aware than its friends."[4]

Panofsky defines the art historian as a humanist whose primary material consists of works of art. He agrees with Woelfflin that the content of an artwork depends on the basic attitude of a nation, period, and individual. However, he adds that the social class of the artist and his or her religious or philosophical persuasion can also be important. Panofsky stresses that the humanist must "re-create" the work of art by searching for the intention of the artist. Of course, intention can never be fully understood, but Panofsky believes one should aspire to that goal by balancing artistic sensitivity (aesthetic response), visual training (historical research), and cultural conditioning. Realizing that cultural backgrounds are different in various countries and historical periods, Panofsky believes that it is essential for the art historian to "make adjustments by learning as much as he possibly can of the circumstances under which the objects of his studies were created."[5]

This kind of broad humanistic approach to art history is enriched by Panofsky's research in iconography, the study of subject matter. He began his major work on this theme with a definition: "Iconography is that branch of the history of art which concerns itself with the subject matter or meaning of works of art, as opposed to their form."[6] This was the first great challenge to purely formal analysis, and it has been especially influential in the study of historical (rather than contemporary) art.

To focus attention on the deeper levels of this research, Panofsky utilizes the term *iconology*, which he divides into three parts. The first part seeks the factual meaning of the subject. Panofsky uses the image of a man lifting his hat. We see the man and his action the same way someone who came from an entirely different culture would. At this level, Leonardo's *Last Supper* is a painting of thirteen men who are gathered around a long table exhibiting various gestures and facial expressions.

The second part deals with specific cultural conditioning which helps us further understand meaning. In Western culture, lifting one's hat is an act of greeting rooted in the knight's custom of lifting his helmet to show he has no warlike intentions. Most people in our culture know that the *Last Supper* represents an important event in the life of Christ. Someone from a different culture might not be aware of this specific meaning.

Panofsky's third level of iconographic meaning is more difficult to define. He calls it "intrinsic meaning or content" and characterizes it as "those underlying principles which reveal the basic attitude of a nation, a period, a class, a religious or philosophical persuasion—unconsciously qualified by one personality and condensed into one work." This does not mean the *expressive* quality, such as a man tipping his hat happily or sadly; for Panofsky, that is part of the first or factual layer of meaning. What then does "intrinsic meaning" imply? In the case of Leonardo's *Last Supper*, we might consider what the artist added that was national, personal, or specific to his period. At this time the iconic importance of religious images was declining in favor of individualization and specific emotions, just as it had done in late Greek art. In earlier paintings of the Last Supper, artists usually depicted the moment when Christ declared that the bread and wine were his body and blood. In church history, this was the crucial beginning of the sacrament of communion. Leonardo, however, chose to depict the moment when Christ revealed that one of the disciples would betray him. This is the psychological, rather than the theological, high point of the scene. It shows a new emotional attitude toward symbolic values, which was specific to Leonardo in Italy during the High Renaissance. This is an example of what Panofsky calls "iconography in the deeper sense . . . [showing] essential tendencies of the human mind."[7]

In summing up the three levels of analysis, Panofsky writes that the first requires practical experience from the viewer; the second demands knowledge of cultural sources, themes, and concepts; and the last calls for synthetic intuition, an understanding of the human spirit. He believes that ultimately we do not divide our reactions consciously into three sections but rather apprehend an artwork's iconography in an organic process that at its best makes use of all three levels simultaneously.

An Example from The Far East

When we examine the art of a culture that we have not studied, we omit one level of understanding, and our reactions are certainly changed as a consequence. For example, when Westerners see Chinese calligraphy, they examine the lines and shapes and perhaps can intuit some of the spirit of the work, but they cannot read the words, and thus they lose the level of specific verbal meanings. A more subtle example might be that of a Japanese Zen painting. It is an interesting exercise to take such a work, which has a very obvious meaning to people in one culture, and to see how it is understood by those in a different culture. Without being told its referents, how do you view and react to the *Daruma* by Shunso (fig. 4)? Before reading the following paragraph, examine the reproduction closely while imagining that its actual size is more than four feet tall.

We will offer some explanation and then ask you to look at the photograph again (this exercise would be much better, of course, with an original artwork). What does this work mean to someone with the appropriate cultural background? First, Japanese would know that Daruma was a Buddhist monk who in the sixth century traveled from India to China, where he became the founder of East Asian Zen. He is said to have meditated in front of a wall for nine years with an intensity of spirit that brought him to enlightenment. According to one of many legends about him, when his eyelids grew heavy, he plucked them off and threw them on the ground so he could continue his meditation.[8] The face and eyes of Daruma therefore reflect both his foreign origin and his determination not to sleep. The intensity of his look, however, is primarily an attribute of his total commitment to meditation. To a Japanese, Daruma is both the patriarch of Zen Buddhism and a model for complete dedication to a task.

Fig. 4. Shunso Shoshu (1750–1835), *Daruma* (1828), ink on paper, 49³/₄ in. × 20¹/₄ in. Private collection.

Looking at the work again, do you have the same reaction as before? The factual subject matter remains the same; what you see is still the bust of a figure painted with ink upon paper. Furthermore, the formal line, composition, and tone also remain the same and have the same expressive potential. Adding the second level of specific cultural meaning, however, gives us the opportunity to see the human values of the work in a new light. When we learn that the painter was not a professional artist but rather a Zen master who had spent a great deal of time in meditation, perhaps our reaction changes again.

Or perhaps not. The most challenging element in the study of art is that we each have our own personal reactions. These are often based on our immediate visceral response when first seeing an artwork. We may have so loved, hated, or been indifferent to the *Daruma* from the start that we have no interest in changing our opinions. In most cases, the immediate response to a work of art does not change as much as it develops and deepens with further study. Like most things in life, the more we give of ourselves to understanding and appreciating art, the more we gain in the depth of our response. This is one reason why the study of art history can enrich us as human beings, and it should guide us in how we teach the understanding of artworks of both past and present.

Nontraditional Methodologies in Art History

A number of new approaches to art history have emerged in this century. Some are rooted in the past but have new areas of emphasis, while others are quite different from anything that has come before. The appearance of new methodologies was not an accident; a few scholars have been convinced for some time that art history is a discipline so conservative as to be labeled reactionary. For example, in 1983 Norman Bryson wrote: "It is a sad fact: art history lags behind the study of the other arts. . . . while the last three decades or so have witnessed extraordinary and fertile change in the study of literature, of history, of anthropology, in the discipline of art history there has reigned a stagnant peace . . . at an increasingly remote margin of the humanities. . . . little can change without a radical re-examination of the methods art history uses—the tacit assumptions that guide the normal activity of the art historian."[9]

One of the most pervasive of the new methodologies is sometimes called Marxist, as it stresses social and economic elements that led to the production and dissemination of the art. Marxist art history has now been practiced through several generations and has evolved just like other methodologies. In general, it has deemphasized the study of the individual work of art or artist to stress the importance of the audience, particularly the patrons who commissioned or purchased the artworks. Marxist and post-Marxist art historians do not ask who made the art as much as what effect it had on society.

Vytautas Kavolis, in *Artistic Expression: A Sociological Analysis*, proposes that we must focus on the economic and political determinants of artistic style. These affect how art reinforces community structure through stratification systems, such as those of social class in both pre-urban and urban societies. He writes that both naturalism and abstraction (geometricism) are to some degree functions of the level of economic development of the society in which the art was created. Thus, nomadic peoples have tended toward naturalism, while agricultural peoples have preferred geometric regularity. Furthermore, a static economy with little trade leads to formal art styles, while more dynamic economies stimulate more spontaneous and informal styles. Kavolis insists, however that other factors, such as political absolutism or religious orthodoxy, can "predispose artists towards stylistic rigidity."[10]

From this point of view, artistic change can respond to economic and political factors. For example, Germany's move to industrialization was more rapid than that of England. Kavolis suggests that the resultant emotional stress may have been a factor leading to expressionism as an important artistic style in Germany, although it made few inroads in England. Further, autocratic political systems tend toward favoring formal styles of art that glorify their regimes, often in monumental proportions. Conversely, diffusion of political power results in more spontaneity in art and more "equalitarian treatment of the parts of a work, without the establishment of a central focus of attention to which other parts are subordinated."[11]

Within urban society, class structure has had an important effect on art styles. Kavolis believes that class influences our lives in ways we may not realize. For example, how we function within our social class may help to determine our artistic responses. To illustrate this point, Kavolis constructed a graph: earlier societies are divided into aristocrats, who preferred dignity and refinement in arts of elegant lyricism, and peasants, who stressed their mastery over nature in arts of geometric simplicity and heaviness. For urban societies, the chart is more complex. The upper middle class prefers refined sensuousness or "spiritualized" emotionality. The lower middle class tends toward simplified rigidity, distortion, or sentimental realism. The working class favors bold simplification or photographic realism.[12]

These kinds of generalities are, of course, simplistic and potentially dangerous. It would not be difficult to find examples that show opposite tendencies, but the effort to identify class tastes, as well as other social or economic factors, leads to interesting new ways to view art. Kavolis has many challenging hypotheses in his book, and if not all of them bear up under intense scrutiny, they do at least stir us to examine art in terms of societal values.

A classic example of Marxist analysis is *Art History and Class Struggle* by Nicos Hadjinicolaou. The author believes that it is a mistake to view art history as the history of artists or of masterpieces. These are constructs, he argues, of art historians who themselves represent middle-class points of view. Furthermore, discussing individual, national, or period styles is missing the most important point: that works of art represent the point of view of a particular social class. Therefore, every painting or sculpture reveals the world of a particular ideology. Hadjinicolaou states at the outset that "the fundamental function of ideology is determined by class relations. . . . The dominant ideology, while it ensures that people keep their place within the social structure, at the same time aims at the preservation and cohesion of this structure."[13]

From this point of view, much of the art of the world can be considered "the history of ruling class visual ideologies. Pictures are often the product in which the ruling classes mirror themselves."[14] Indeed, portraits of kings and princes are no different from statues of presidents and politicians; they all reinforce the dominant class. Perhaps the most controversial aspect of Hadjinicolaou's book is his denial that artists have personal styles. For most art historians, personal style is a fundamental belief, and to have it denied is shocking. Hadjinicolaou recognizes that just as every leaf on a tree is different, so is each human being, and in that sense he does not deny some personal elements in art. However, he believes that studying individual artists neglects the most important questions of how an artwork reflects one or more of the visual ideologies of the time.

Hadjinicolaou, in his argument against personal style, proposes that some artists, due to their success in representing a dominant ideology, never change their manner of painting and thus seem to maintain a personal style. Others, due to shifting patronage, appear to change styles, either chronologically or simultaneously. As an example of chronological change, Hadjinicolaou cites the painter David, who lived before, during, and after the French revolution. David first produced flattering portraits of would-be aristocrats, then a stark rendition of the assassinated revolutionary Marat, and finally elegant depictions of the newly dominant French bourgeoisie. Because David was commissioned by people with different ideologies, in each case he represented their class interests in a visually convincing fashion. Trying to define a consistent personal style for David in these works is difficult; understanding them in terms of their patronage is more convincing.

Hadjinicolaou chooses Rembrandt as an example of a painter working simultaneously in different styles. The author points out that art historians are likely to accept only one of Rembrandt's styles, featuring the emotive use of light and shadow, and they tend to ignore his other works. Nevertheless, throughout his career Rembrandt painted mythological scenes and portraits of wealthy businessmen in what seem to be rather different styles. How can we account for this if we regard Rembrandt as an example of a genius with a personal style that shines through all his work? Hadjinicolaou has an explanation: Rembrandt painted some works in the ideology of the court, for which dramatic versions of mythological scenes were appropriate. His portraits were done for members of the Dutch upper middle class and represent their ideology. The paintings we most identify with Rembrandt, including those on religious themes, were for a special segment of middle-class people described by Max Weber as having "an extraordinary capitalist business sense ... combined in the same persons and groups with the most intensive forms of a piety which penetrates and dominates their whole lives. Such cases are not isolated, but these traits are characteristic of many of the most important churches and sects in the history of Protestantism."[15] Rembrandt's deep sense of shadow in these works reflects the visual ideology of this religious-capitalist class, which because of its puritan spirit did not admire the more colorful and ornate sacred paintings in the Italian style.

According to this approach to art history, not only the subject matter but also the formal qualities of art depend less upon individual genius than on the class beliefs and ideologies of patrons. As Frederick Antal writes, "we can understand the origins and nature of coexistent styles only if we study the various sections of society, reconstruct their philosophies and thence penetrate to their art."[16]

There is no doubt that the Marxist approach has helped illuminate art history in many ways, but it has also been attacked. One objection is that it tends to ignore our aesthetic response, the sense of beauty that artworks can convey. Hadjinicolaou has a straightforward response: "Aesthetic effect is none other than the pleasure felt by the observer when he recognises himself in a picture's ideology. It is incumbent on the art historian to tackle the tasks arising out of the existence of this recognition. ... this means that from now on the idealist questions 'What is beauty?' or 'Why is this work beautiful?' must be replaced by the materialist question, 'By whom, when and for what reasons was this work thought beautiful?' "[17] This is fascinating, but is it enough? Certainly we will gain a great deal by analyzing why people have thought a work of art beautiful, but can responses to art, historical as well as contemporary, be only ideological? Don't we respond to works of different classes and beliefs than our own?

Like many new points of view, Marxist art history burst upon the scene with some important insights but also something of a chip on its shoulder. To present its case, it often tried to discredit other approaches. In this it was unsuccessful; most members of the current generation of socioeconomic art historians also take an interest in formal analysis, iconography, and the lives of artists.

One of the most interesting scholars currently taking what we might call a post-Marxist approach is Albert Boime. In 1987 he published the first in a projected five-volume series on the social history of modern art, *Art in an Age of Revolution, 1750–1800.* Believing that the French revolution and the English industrial revolution together constituted a "great divide in human history," Boime sets out to capture their consequences through a study of the art of the period. He comments in his preface:

> While traditional art history had generally isolated its subject, treating it as an almost autonomous phenomenon, the social history of art seeks to set the artist and the work of art into a broad historical and economic context ... [and] presents the familiar artist and works as inseparable from the historical context. The imagery of the period visually records the way in which people of a certain status perceived, accepted, or rejected the social, political, and cultural changes of their time. ... Art continued to serve as the emblem of good taste, as the means of aggrandizing the patron, and as an active agent for advancing official ideology.[18]

Boime then discusses the art of the first half of the nineteenth century from the point of view of a social historian. In studying the art of William Blake, for example, he contrasts Blake's political liberalism and hatred for slavery and oppression with his relationships with conservative patrons. Boime especially focuses upon Blake's complex attitude toward the industrial revolution, that is, his crying out against its excesses while perceiving its potential for social progress.

Boime does not neglect the personal and original contributions of individual artists, but he wants above all to "make sense of artistic achievement in a total human context."[19] He represents the current, more sophisticated approach of socioeconomic art historians. That kind of methodological sophistication is also seen in the recent work of many scholars who follow the older traditions of biographical and stylistic analysis. It is clear that although the original Marxist approach may have been one-sided, its trenchant analysis of how patronage and politics have affected works of art has been very influential. The new social approach to art history has added a great deal to the field, and few current scholars have not widened their range of study as a result.

Feminist Art History

The study of art history from a social and cultural point of view has been further enriched by those who examine the role of women, both as subjects for art and as artists. There has been interest in this topic for more than a hundred years, with books on women artists appearing as early as the mid-nineteenth century. However, the recent surge in feminist art history was given great impetus by a special 1971 issue of *Art News* devoted to women in art. This issue included a controversial article by Linda Nochlin entitled "Why Have There Been No Great Women Artists?" Her answer is primarily that restrictive institutions and educational systems so hindered women that they could not achieve their rightful place in the world of art.[20]

During the succeeding two decades, interest in women artists grew considerably. One of the first tasks was to focus attention on neglected women artists of the past, many of whom had been famous in their own day. A number of books gave us a much clearer idea of how many women artists of note worked, despite considerable disadvantages, during the Renaissance, baroque, and Romantic periods. Surprisingly enough, it has only been in the last century that they were virtually forgotten. The recent revival of interest has led to some thorough biographical and stylistic studies that considerably change our viewpoint on the importance of women in the art worlds of Europe and America.

The attention upon women artists has spread from Western culture to that of the Orient. Research for Patricia Fister's exhibition and book *Japanese Women Artists, 1600–1900*[21] led her to the conclusion that in traditional Japan, women were even more constrained than in Europe. Nevertheless, some outstanding female artists were able to make their way in an almost completely male-dominated field, utilizing a combination of talent and determination. Since women had been historically important in fiction and poetry in Japan, many artists were able to enter the visual arts through literature, such as the haiku poet and artist Chiyo (1703–75), the *waka* poet and literati painter Gyokuran (1728–84), and the poet, potter, calligrapher, and painter Rengetsu (1791–1875). Significantly, two of these women (Chiyo and Rengetsu) attained some artistic freedom by becoming nuns after the deaths of their husbands.

In her book, Fister demonstrates that women artists in Japan did not always paint in an overtly "feminine" style. Nevertheless, there is an overwhelming conviction in Japan today that women's work must be somehow charming and graceful but lacking in boldness or strength. Indeed, since Japanese scholars have never written on women artists, Fister was interviewed in Japan frequently at the conclusion of her research. In one newspaper article she was quoted as saying that Japanese women artists were "very feminine," although she had never uttered any such words. Did the reporter simply invent this "quote"? Or was his cultural conditioning so strong that he imagined that she *must* have said it? Some of the examples of painting and calligraphy in Fister's book surely disprove this cliché, demonstrating the kind of artistic power and force that are visually startling.

Later in 1988 an exhibition and book-catalog on Chinese women artists appeared, entitled *Views from the Jade Terrace: Chinese Women Artists 1300–1912*. In her opening essay, "Women in the History of Chinese Painting," Marsha Weidner points out that the women artists were usually either members of the scholar-official class or courtesans serving this class. Generally denied the opportunity to function as professional artists, some women were able to take advantage of the literati spirit in which painting became a private expression of one's cultivated self. As Weidner comments, "Since the home was the sole completely sanctioned arena for female activity, gentry women were able to discover their talent for painting only after scholars had made this a domestic pursuit."[22]

Even in the Chinese literati world, women were restricted by a strong Confucian society and were expected to maintain the male "equation of fragility with femininity."[23] As a result, women artists were discouraged from being innovative, and their art was less varied than that of their Japanese counterparts. Women were usually expected to adhere to bird and flower themes, although some became adept at the primary subject of landscapes or at painting figures, most often beautiful women. Fan paintings were plentiful, although women also painted hanging scrolls and hand scrolls. In general, delicate styles predominated over more forceful brushwork.[24]

In traditional China, the pressure on women to conform to male expectations had the effect of confirming those expectations. Cultivated women could demonstrate their talents in art only when they did not challenge the dominant cultural view of proper feminine behavior. Many fine women artists emerged, such as Guan Dao-sheng (1262–1319), an extraordinary painter of the "gentlemanly" subject of bamboo.[25] The fact that women made a significant contribution to the history of Chinese painting under the restrictions of a patriarchal society is a tribute to their perseverance as well as their skill.

The initial task of reviving attention upon European, American, and East Asian women artists has met with some success. For example, general histories of art, which at one time did not discuss or illustrate women artists, now usually include at least at few. H. W. Janson's *History of Art* did not mention women artists in the first edition of 1962, but in the most recent edition (1986) there are 21 women painters, sculptors, and photographers among a total of 430 artists discussed.[26] This is less than 5 percent, but it is certainly an improvement.

Who are the women from the past who have now been accepted as

Fig. 5. Guerrilla Girls (Contemporary), *Do Women Have to Be Naked?*, poster, ink and color on paper, 11 in. × 28 in. Private collection.

major artists? Among the Western female masters most often recognized are Artemisia Gentileschi, Angelica Kauffmann, Rosa Bonheur, Mary Cassatt, Berthe Morisot, Kathe Kollwitz, Georgia O'Keeffe, Louise Nevelson, and Helen Frankenthaler. In *Introduction to Asian Art*, Patricia Fister discusses and includes illustrations of works by Guan Dao-sheng, Gyokuran, and Rengetsu. Marilyn Stokstad, now concluding a major new survey of world art, will have a more responsible overall representation of women artists than ever before in her two-volume text.[27]

Nevertheless, problems still exist. In the past decade, women artists in New York City have discovered that their representation in museums and galleries was far below what their numbers warranted. They formed an organization, the Guerrilla Girls, and began appearing in public wearing gorilla masks, papering the streets with their unique posters. One poster proclaimed, "Bus Companies are more enlightened than NYC art galleries," and offered the following statistics: 49.2 percent of New York City bus drivers are women compared to only 16 percent of the artists represented in New York galleries. Other posters chided critics, art magazines, and museums for not representing a reasonable share of women artists. Perhaps their most fascinating poster asks, "Do women have to be naked to get into the Met. Museum?" (fig. 5). The gorilla mask on the nude is graphically effective in making us pause and absorb the message that the women in the Metropolitan Museum of Art collection are almost always bodies, not artists. The Guerrilla Girls' posters, with their no-frills approach, were originally created for use on the streets, but to the surprise of the artists, they are now avidly collected by major museums.

Beyond focusing attention on women artists, in the past few years feminist art historians have taken on a more difficult problem: rethinking the history of art without automatically following the traditional male point of view. They argue that it is not enough to accept the subsidiary position of women in European, American, Chinese, or Japanese society and evaluate women artists in comparison with the male artists of their day. Instead, they declare that a realization of the class and sexual structures of the societies is vital to understanding the work of women artists. Artistic production is not just the result of individual creativity but is influenced by every aspect of life and culture. Until we know how women artists received their training, how their works were (all too rarely) shown and purchased, what encouragement or discouragement they received in terms of subject matter, and how their position as women gave them their sense of artistic vision, we can never truly understand their art.

One book that takes this new approach is *Old Mistresses: Women, Art, and Ideology* by Rozsika Parker and Griselda Pollock. Borrowing some Marxist concepts, the authors stress that "the way the history of art has been studied and evaluated . . . is a particular way of seeing and interpreting in which the beliefs and assumptions of art historians, unconsciously reproducing the ideologies of our society, shape and limit the very picture of the history of art. . . . a radical reform, if not a total deconstruction of the present structure of the discipline is needed in order to arrive at a real understanding of the history of women and art." Part of the new understanding must come from studies of a woman's place in the artistic world of her time. Often, however, only women's names are known, such as those of most Greek and Roman women artists. Boccaccio, writing in the fourteenth century, gives brief biographies of three classical women artists, borrowing from Pliny. Yet Boccaccio reflects a biased point of view even while praising these women's art, stating: "I thought these achievements worthy of some praise, for art is much alien to the mind of women, and these things cannot be accomplished without a great deal of talent, which in women is very scarce."[28]

Understanding women artists only as exceptions and considering creativity a primarily male virtue was common until this century and is still the norm in certain circles. In terms of worldly success, women artists were severely handicapped by inadequate educational opportunities and relegation to second-class status. Artistic education for women was drastically limited in Europe before and, even more so, after the French revolution. Drawing from the nude, the single most important educational practice in Europe, was generally forbidden to women, although as time went on women became the subjects of nude studies more and more often. Furthermore, women painters were often restricted to subject matter considered less important by most male artists (such as portraiture and genre paintings), only to find these same subjects commandeered by men when they became fashionable.

More serious in many ways was the relegation of certain art forms to a lesser status because they were traditionally practiced by women. This has been difficult to combat, since we are imbued with the idea that painting and sculpture are "high art" and other media, such as textiles and ceramics, have lesser value. It is a curious fact that in Japan, where every form of art is considered capable of the highest aesthetic quality, American quilts have been highly honored, while in our own country they are often considered a form of folk art that is of marginal interest.

Most restrictive of all, women became the subjects of circular reasoning. If females are considered less creative than males, then what they make must perforce be less artistic. If their work is judged inferior, male superiority is reaffirmed. In a male-dominated society, this conveniently reinforces the status quo. As Parker and Pollock state: "Art is not a mirror. It mediates and re-presents social relations. . . . Women's practice in art has never been absolutely forbidden, discouraged or refused, but rather contained and limited to its function as the means by which masculinity gains and sustains its supremacy in the important sphere of cultural production."[29]

Today, most art historians are willing to acknowledge the earlier biases of the field. But if women are to be allowed their just place in art history, how must it be accomplished? Some authors have accepted the traditional values of our discipline and only asked that women's work be judged equally with that of men. Others have gone further, arguing that traditional art-historical values are so male-oriented that they need to be reexamined before merely adding a few women artists to the list of accepted masters. As Karen Peterson and J. J. Wilson wrote in their book on women artists, "The danger of having a fixed, or unexamined, art history perspective is that it all too frequently predisposes us to look only at certain kinds of art, to see only superstars, chosen by biased criteria."[30]

One way to rethink our approach to artistic value judgments is to see the value of feminine points of view within various geographical and historical contexts. For example, Weidner states: "To date, our approaches to Chinese painting have been based almost exclusively on the roles of men, usually scholars, in the Confucian social order. . . . [Women] did not have the personal connections that resulted from [travel] experiences and from holding office. . . . Most spent their days serving their families at home. It is with the family and home, then, that the study of women painters must begin. As men have led us through the upper political and intellectual reaches of Confucian society, women can lead us into the heart of its fundamental institutions." Parker and Pollock reinforce this idea in their discussion of the work of Mary Cassatt, commenting that she "manipulated space and compositional structure to endow what women did in the home with respect and seriousness, while at the same time being able to make us recognise the limitations resulting from the confinement of bourgeois women in the domestic sphere alone."[31]

One example of a woman artist working from her own experience is Margo Kren (b. 1939) in her 1982 series of lithographs entitled *Dreams and Memories*, printed by Mike Sims at the Lawrence Lithography Workshop. One of the prints recalls a time in Kren's childhood after she had all her hair cut off because of ringworm, common in Texas at the time. When her hair had finally grown back, Kren's memory is of the sheer sensuality of having it combed by her grandmother (fig. 6). She and her grandmother didn't talk much, so the combing of hair became an important expression of kinship. In the background is another moment in time. Her grandmother, in her eighties, had lost her memory and was living in a retirement home. Kren depicts her mother and aunt combing their own mother's hair. The style is expressionistic, and Kren conveys how memory combines the events of the past with the emotions of the present. Thus, she portrays at once the vividness of a child's feeling and the bittersweet quality of the adult's recollection.

To avoid tokenism or assumptions that any artist can sum up every woman's experience, we should explore many different possibilities inherent in the field of art history. For example, it can be an enlightening experience to examine the work of women in arts other than painting, graphics, or sculpture. Have such outstanding photographers as Julia Margaret Cameron, Margaret Bourke-White, and Diane Arbus conveyed artistic visions of which male photographers might not have been capable? Have we missed much of the beauty of other arts, such as textiles, by relegating them to inferior status despite their worldwide historical importance? Most of all, have we tended to consider the word *feminine* in narrow contexts, despite the fact that women are at least as diverse as men in emotion and experience? In short, have we deprived ourselves of the understanding and appreciation of much art of great value? If so, we are all the losers, for the study of women artists offers not merely insights into the life of women in their time but a greater sense of the entire artistic world that is our inheritance.

Other Recent Methodologies

One of the most interesting explorations in art has been Rudolf Arnheim's study of visual perception. Although he is not generally regarded as an art historian, his work is of interest to anyone concerned with teaching art. Arnheim's research demonstrates how we do not really "see" in complete ways but rather find visual structures that enable our minds to

Fig. 6. Margo Kren (b. 1939), *Hair,* from the "Dreams and Memories" portfolio (1982), lithograph, 7³/₁₆ in. × 9¹/₂ in., gift of the artist. Spencer Museum of Art, University of Kansas.

determine what we have seen. For example, a circle with a few dots and lines becomes a face. The implications of this study are far-reaching. In particular, we must realize that our knowledge intrudes upon our visual perception at almost every point. We see what we *think* we see, based upon visual clues rather than total organic perception. Art teachers, facing this problem, often try to persuade their students to "draw what you see, not what you know." It is a difficult task.

How can we train ourselves really to look and see what is before us and not just absorb a few clues? We must first ask ourselves how much new experience we really wish to have. We may imagine that we want to see things forever new, but do we not value the "old friend" quality of an artwork that is well loved? If so, what is the balance between fresh perception and memory? Most of us are willing to experience some novelty if it does not take us too far from the familiar and the comfortable. For example, a new work by an artist we know may be more appealing than one by a total unknown. We often go to concerts of well-known performers and familiar music, and exhibitions of French Impressionism draw many more people than do those of art from unfamiliar cultures or time periods. Yet isn't our visual perception more likely to be heightened by what is new to us?

The viewing of art is changed by time and repetition. When we hang a new painting, photograph, or poster in our home, it is a fresh and enlivening experience. But for how long? Do we not begin to take it for granted after a time and no longer truly perceive it? The Japanese solve this problem by having only one place in the traditional home for hanging a painting. They place a hanging scroll in a special alcove called *tokonoma* and then after a week or two roll it up, put it away in a box, and unroll another scroll. This way their experience of the paintings remains fresh, even if the scrolls are not entirely new.

If we change and rotate our art, in the home or in the museum, a painting may be remembered, but because it is not constantly on view, the memory fades enough for the new viewing to take on additional excitement when the work reappears. It may even seem new; between viewings the painting will not have changed, but *we* may have. Similarly, you can't step into the same river twice, not only because the river changes constantly but because you are different. Therefore, when we see a painting again after a respite, our changed selves may perceive things we had not noticed before.

Whether a work is totally new or has been seen before, what matters is our perception and especially our readiness for fresh perception. In an age when we are bombarded by images in the media, it is all too easy to allow our eyes to get lazy and pay attention only to the most dramatic of images. Advertisers know this, and further dull our perceptions with visual overstatement. Visiting a museum may help, but unless we participate in the artistic and art-historical process, we are severely limiting our perceptive potential.

Arnheim suggests that we "have neglected the gift of comprehending things through our senses. . . . Too many persons visit museums and collect picture books without gaining access to art." He divides his major book, *Art and Visual Perception: A Psychology of the Creative Eye*, into chapters on balance, shape, form, growth, space, light, color, movement, dynamics, and expression. He concludes by commenting that "the human mind receives, shapes, and interprets its image of the outer world with all its conscious and unconscious powers."[32] While Arnheim's studies may not open us up to pure perception, which is probably impossible, he offers fascinating glimpses into our patterns of vision.

Several other approaches to art history have been investigated in recent decades. One of these involves psychoanalysis, in which works of art are investigated for their unconscious symbolism. Freud himself wrote about artistic creation, believing that unconscious impulses resulting from unresolved childhood experiences can trigger the artist. For example, Leonardo was raised by two "mothers," a peasant mother and the wife of his father, and he later made a large-scale painting of the Virgin Mary and St. Anne with the Christ child in which the three figures, through gesture and composition, seem to merge into one. According to Freud, this unique painting stems from Leonardo's childhood wish to unite with two mothers. Leonardo's scientific interests and his obsessive work habits also resulted from childhood trauma, according to psychoanalytic theory.

Many art critics' psychoanalytic interpretations are sexual, often surprisingly so. David Lubin, in *Act of Portrayal*, analyzes *The Agnew Clinic* by Thomas Eakins. Lubin sees this painting of a famous doctor demonstrating a new surgical technique as "a live sex show with an all male audience, a male superstud, and a dainty damsel, helpless, supine." While we may feel that this commentary is extreme, we might also agree that an atmosphere of inchoate sexuality can be sensed in many nineteenth-century American paintings. In defense of his analysis, Lubin writes that "the best way to read a portrait is to coax from it as many viable interpretations as it will yield."[33] Others would not agree, believing that a painting may admit multiple interpretations, some surely more valid than others. How, then, to determine which are the most "viable" or "valid" interpretations? Most art historians would answer that one must study the work thoroughly and learn everything one can about the artist, the patron, and the culture, after which more meaningful understanding will emerge.

A more subtle writer on art from a psychoanalytic point of view is the English critic Adrian Stokes. Many of his essays have been gathered and republished in *The Critical Writings of Adrian Stokes*, including studies of painting, sculpture, architecture, and Greek culture. In his writings about the nude, Stokes discusses how from infancy we sometimes treat objects outside ourselves as though they were part of us. The baby eventually learns that the breast of its mother belongs to a separate person, and the relationship that develops between infant and mother sets the pattern for future relationships with all other people, either by unity or by contrast. Until we can deal successfully with otherness, we cannot function effectively in life.

According to Stokes, the nude is the "promise of sanity," of great potential power as the ultimate other. The act of painting the nude therefore becomes a matter of representing the other as "an entire presence, engaging the allegiance produced in the act of drawing." The artist maintains a temperate separation from the subject of the work so that he or she can re-create this otherness; ultimately, the experience of the painting can be understood as "the invitation to merge with the object."[34] Stokes believes that in our increasingly fragmented society there will be ever greater need for art to provide us with life-giving symbols of things outside ourselves to which we can relate harmoniously.

Psychoanalytic approaches to art offer a range of possibilities. They can center upon studies of how childhood experiences may give birth to certain kinds of subjects or forms; how subconscious (often sexual) symbolism is hidden in works of art; or, more broadly, how basic human drives and needs are fulfilled through the artistic process. While this methodology offers new and often surprising approaches to interpretation, it has encountered a good deal of resistance from those who believe that it leads to distortions of the art's original meanings. Focusing upon hidden or subconscious meanings, psychoanalytic interpretation neglects the more overt personal and cultural interpretations that many art historians find most enlightening.

A second new approach is deconstruction, in which established systems of interpretation are broken down to find new meanings in works of art. Some followers of this approach believe that it is impossible (and therefore useless) to seek the original meanings of a work or to plumb the artist's original intention. Therefore, all meanings we find today can be considered valid, as seen earlier in the case of David Lubin's interpretation. This methodology has been criticized, as has the psychoanalytic approach, for distorting meaning. For those who do not believe that it is impossible to reach at least a good approximation of the original meanings of artworks, there remains the responsibility to discover and adhere to them.

Deconstruction does not always entail finding personal meanings in works of art from the past. An early study that we might consider deconstructionist but that stays within historical boundaries is Morse Peckham's *Man's Rage for Chaos*. Peckham begins by stating that the branch of philosophy called aesthetics has tried in the past two hundred years primarily to answer the age-old question, What is art? His view is that "few intellectual enterprises have so utterly failed." This is in part because theoreticians have assumed that we create art to make order of a chaotic world. Not so, claims Peckham. First, he disputes the notion that experience comes to us in a chaotic blizzard of phenomena. Instead, he believes that all data reach the human brain through patterns of perception. Art does not need to create order because it is already established in the mind. Instead, art offers us the experience of (controlled) disorder.[35]

Peckham writes that it is only when we go beyond the previously accepted order that we can be creative, whether we are scholars, poets, or painters. Creative activity occurs after disorienting experiences and acts as a construction of perceptual fields that express the innovation of the creator. The art is then perceived by the viewer, listener, or other audience, and this perception is also a creative act. Both artists and viewers must have some tolerance for discontinuity, some sympathy for expression different from that experienced in the past.

Art, according to Peckham, is "a biological adaption which serves to keep man alive, aware, capable of perceiving that he is . . . capable of innovation."[36] Because we cannot live entirely within order, we must learn how to deal with disorder. In this sense we cannot only accept but can actually welcome a certain limited amount of artistic chaos in our lives—chaos that is usually confined within the carefully nurtured boundaries of protected environments. We go into a museum or a gallery of modern art expecting new visual experiences we might not tolerate elsewhere. We have special formats for new artistic experiences: books or magazines for poems; exhibitions for art; concert halls for music; theaters for dance, drama, or film. In contrast, street theater can appear dangerous because it brings a touch of chaos into our lives at a time when we may not be prepared for it. Art that uses chance operations, such as the music, words, and graphic art of John Cage, enrages many people because it suggests that someone is not sufficiently ordering the experience of chaos for us. Of course, Cage is actually controlling the parameters of his art while allowing chance operations to function within prepared boundaries. Nevertheless, he makes many otherwise "art-loving" people very nervous.

Peckham not only uses a form of deconstruction but also a third new approach to art history called semiotics, or the study of images as signs for the transferral of meaning. These signs or signals are not always obvious to the uninformed viewer but within each culture they are generally accepted by means of education and tradition. As a rule, we stay within well-defined limits in our use of signs, though occasionally we go so far as to render our communication unintelligible, a situation that confronted the first viewers of cubism. Peckham comments: "The artist constructs fields of signs: in producing stylistic dynamism, he changes the signs the perceiver has been using. . . . Generally the new signs are so few, so similar to the old, and so controlled by rules, that the power of the situation continues to identify the field as an occasion for playing the perceiver's role. But at times, as in the case of Picasso and Braque, the new signs are so different, and so many, and violate the rules so strongly, that the perceiver is unable to play his role."[37]

The study of visual signification is not new, but this method offers fresh possibilities. One methodology is to divide images into those that function as icons, directly resembling their referents, and those that are symbols, relying upon interpretation. For example, an image of the crucified Christ is an icon, while a simple cross may carry the same meaning as a symbol to those who know its cultural import.

One problem with the semiotic approach to art has been that, while words are almost always abstract referents (there is nothing directly connecting the sound or spelling of most words to their meaning), images are often direct referents, being a picture of their primary subject. Therefore, the methodology originally developed for the study of words needs some adjustment before it will work well for images. Furthermore, don't we usually experience images in conjunction with words? At a gallery or museum, when we may think we are occupied purely with painting, prints, photographs, or sculpture, we spend a large part of our time looking at labels. We may even talk with a friend about the art as we view it, or take a guided or taped tour. In other contexts we may listen to an art history lecture that is accompanied by slides or (as you are doing right now) read a book and look at reproductions. How do the verbal and visual elements mix in our experience?

This question is taken up by Norman Bryson in *Word and Image: French Painting of the Ancien Régime.* He concludes that "we have not yet found ourselves able to dispense altogether, in our dealings with the image, with some form of contact with language." Not only can the caption on a photograph or the inscription on a painting affect us, but the implied verbal message of many works can influence our thinking while we are absorbing the visual impression of the art. Bryson notes that an image may be less important as we look at it "than it is as anticipated memory: the moment of its impact may be intense, but only so that the visual impression can go on resonating within the mind after it has ceased to contemplate the actual image. Present qualities—as in advertising— are subordinated to future ones, and the qualities likeliest to endure are those that cluster around verbal components."[38]

Do we agree? Are the works of art that we can call to mind memorable because they attach themselves to words and concepts? Or are there images that resonate in us just for their visual qualities? We are so habituated to using words within our minds to frame our experiences that it may be difficult for us to make the distinction. With instrumental music, we know we are not in a world of words and can allow the form of a nonverbal experience full sway. But in painting, can we (or should we) eliminate words as part of the experience of viewing?

This discussion touches upon a more traditional distinction between content (subject) and form (artistic qualities). A painting of the Crucifixion has specific meanings that may arouse certain responses in the viewer. The formal qualities of the painting itself, such as line, form, and color, may also arouse responses. Some viewers are more intent upon the former, some the latter, but most would agree that it is the combination of content and form that creates a fine work of art. When abstract art began as a protest against content, painters wanted to fix our attention purely upon form, and many comparisons were made to music. But most art signifies in two different ways, as subject (more verbal) and as form (more visual). Some art historians believe that we can explore these significations by borrowing from new methodologies in linguistics and anthropology. In this way semiotics, if properly utilized for visual materials, may prove very useful in art history.

Psychoanalysis, deconstruction, and semiotics are three of the newer and still controversial approaches being employed to illuminate the history of art. There is no doubt that each offers different ways of seeing and interpreting, but will they supplant the older methods of biographical, stylistic, and iconographic study? Probably not. But as long as no methodology is taken as the only valid system, art history will surely continue to grow more rich and fascinating.

NOTES

1. The following discussion is based on several writings of Heinrich Woelfflin, especially *Principles of Art History: The Problem of the Development of Style in Later Art* (New York: Dover, 1932).

2. Ibid., p. 6.

3. Ibid., p. 16.

4. Erwin Panofsky, "The History of Art as Humanistic Discipline," originally published in *The Meaning of the Humanities* (Princeton, N.J.: Princeton University Press, 1940), reprinted in *Meaning in the Visual Arts* (Garden City, N.J.: Doubleday Anchor Books, 1955), p. 23.

5. Ibid., pp. 10, 17.

6. Erwin Panofsky, *Studies in Iconology: Humanistic Themes in the Renaissance* (New York: Harper and Row, 1962), p. 3.

7. Ibid., pp. 7, 8, 15.

8. According to legend, where his eyelids had fallen tea plants grew up. This story shows how truths can be hidden in legendary forms, since tea was indeed cultivated by monks who sometimes used it as a slight stimulant before periods of meditation.

9. Norman Bryson, *Vision and Painting* (New Haven, Conn.: Yale University Press, 1983), p. xi.

10. Vytautas Kavolis, *Artistic Expression: A Sociological Analysis* (Ithaca, N.Y.: Cornell University Press, 1968), p. 20.

11. Ibid., p. 27.

12. Ibid., p. 88.

13. Nicos Hadjinicolaou, *Art History and Class Struggle*, trans. Louise Asmal (London: Pluto Press, 1973), p. 11.

14. Ibid., p. 102.

15. Max Weber, *The Protestant Ethic and the Spirit of Capitalism* (London: London University Books, 1971), p. 43.

16. Frederick Antal, *Florentine Painting and Its Social Background* (London: Routledge and Kegan Paul, 1948), p. 4.

17. Hadjinicalaou, *Art History and Class Struggle*, pp. 182–83.

18. Albert Boime, *Art in an Age of Revolution, 1750–1800* (Chicago: University of Chicago Press, 1987), pp. xix–xx.

19. Ibid., p. xxv.

20. Early books on women artists include: Ernst Guhl, *Die Frauen in die Kunstgeschichte* (Berlin: Gutentag, 1858); Elizabeth Ellet, *Women Artists in All Ages and Countries* (New York: Harper and Brothers, 1859); Clara Erskine-Waters, *Women in the Fine Arts* (Boston: Houghton-Mifflin, 1905); and Walter Shaw Sparrow, *Women Artists of the World* (London: Hodder & Stafford, 1905; republished New York: Hacker Books, 1976). Nochlin's article is one of many in *Art News* 69, no. 9 (January 1971).

21. Patricia Fister, *Japanese Women Artists, 1600–1900* (Lawrence, Kans.: Spencer Museum of Art; and New York: Harper and Row, 1988).

22. Marsha Weidner et al., *Views from the Jade Terrace* (Indianapolis Museum of Art; and New York: Rizzoli, 1988), p. 13.

23. Ibid.

24. The hand scroll *Pine Trees* by Cai Han (1647–86) is a notable exception, being rendered in forceful and dramatic brushwork. See Weidner, *Views from the Jade Terrace*, pp. 112–13.

25. Bamboo is considered to be like the scholar-gentleman because it bends but does not break in the wind.

26. H. W. Janson, *History of Art*, 3d ed. (New York: Harry N. Abrams, 1986).

27. Patricia Fister, *Introduction to Asian Art* (New York: Harper and Row, 1993).

28. Rozsika Parker and Griselda Pollock, *Old Mistresses: Women, Art, and Ideology* (London: Routledge and Kegan Paul, 1981), pp. xvii–xviii, 47–48. Boccaccio is quoted in ibid., p. 14.

29. Ibid., pp. 119, 170.

30. Karen Peterson and J. J. Wilson, *Women Artists: Recognition and Re-Appraisal from the Early Middle Ages to the Twentieth Century* (New York: Harper Colophon Books, 1976), pp. 6–7.

31. Weidner, *Views from the Jade Terrace*, pp. 27–28; Parker and Pollock, *Old Mistresses*, p. 41.

32. Rudolf Arnheim, *Art and Visual Perception: A Psychology of the Creative Eye* (Berkeley: University of California Press, 1974), pp. 1, 461.

33. David Lubin, *Act of Portrayal* (New Haven, Conn.: Yale University

Press, 1985), pp. 72, 74–75. I am indebted to Thomas Dedonker for bringing this book to my attention.

34. Adrian Stokes, *The Critical Writings of Adrian Stokes*, ed. Lawrence Gowing (London: Thames and Hudson, 1978), pp. 304, 305.

35. Morse Peckham, *Man's Rage for Chaos* (Philadelphia: Chilton Books, 1965), p. 3.

36. Ibid., p. 314.

37. Ibid., p. 79.

38. Norman Bryson, *Word and Image: French Painting of the Ancien Régime* (London and New York: Cambridge University Press, 1981), pp. 5, 30.

4

How Art Historians Work

We have investigated various periods of art, both prehistorical and historical, and discovered many ways of seeing, perceiving, and theorizing. In the process we have found how different approaches to art history can offer new illumination, from direct study of artworks to broader research into society and culture. However, the question remains: What exactly do art historians do, and how do they go about doing it?

Study of a Single Project

It might be helpful first to examine one particular art-historical project to see the specific methodologies involved and the results obtained. I will choose one of my own projects so that I can relate all the steps involved. The project was a study of the artistic world of a Japanese painter, poet, and calligrapher named Kameda Bosai (1752–1826). I was interested in Bosai's art but also in how he lived in, reacted to, and influenced the world around him, and especially his connections with other intellectuals and artists. My goal was an exhibition, accompanied by a full catalog that could stand alone as a book (this is now known as an "accompanying book").

The beginning of the process occurred when I chose the theme of Bosai and his world. I had seen a few of his works from time to time, although he was not often published in books or catalogs about Japanese art. The informality and freedom of Bosai's landscape paintings and the wild dance of his calligraphy very much appealed to me. I then noticed that his works were beginning to be collected in America, mostly by private collectors such as noted New Orleans eye surgeon Kurt Gitter. Since I was serving as adjunct curator of the New Orleans Museum of Art, I discussed with the director, E. John Bullard, the possibility of an exhibition. He was enthusiastic, so I next talked with the staff of the Spencer Museum of Art at the University of Kansas. After again receiving a positive response, I determined to go ahead with the project.

Like most art-historical research, the study of Bosai and his world had two parts. The first consisted of background reading and study. Much of this I was able to do in the United States, because books and articles on Japanese history, culture, and art of the Edo period (1600–1868) were plentiful in the University of Kansas library or available through interlibrary loan. Since the Edo period had been the focus of most of my previous research, I was already acquainted with much of the literature involved. Furthermore, I had studied a good many paintings, either in person or in reproduction, by Bosai's contemporaries. However, I made a systematic effort to review the material I knew, examined many photographs and slides, and tried to find any new or obscure literature I might have missed. I searched for this material partly by talking with friends in the field or related fields and partly by checking bibliographies and notes in the books and articles I was reading or rereading. All of this background study took a good deal of time, but since I could work at my own pace, it was not onerous.

The more difficult part of my project was more specific to Bosai and his world, and most of this research I could accomplish only in Japan. The research divided into three parts: finding written materials; seeing artworks; and discussing Bosai with scholars, collectors, and interested others. I was able to visit Japan one summer early in the research period, and I made preliminary efforts toward all three avenues of study. It seemed that few academicians knew of Bosai more than slightly, and no scholar in art history had done any serious study of his life and work. I did, however, meet a few collectors and dealers who showed me examples of Bosai's work, with calligraphy being more common than paintings.

During that summer in Japan I determined to locate whatever research materials were available. I went to the National Diet Library in Tokyo, the equivalent of the Library of Congress, and found there were as yet no books on Bosai. By checking indexes of Japanese periodicals, I was able to find some articles, most of which were published in journals of some age. Since most were held in the library, I then filled out special forms, waited on line, and eventually received bound volumes of the journals. I was able to make photocopies within the library system, and I eventually took these copies home to the United States to read more carefully than I could in Japan.

Finally, near the end of the summer, I was told that a librarian named Sugimura at Tokyo University had been studying Bosai's life and poetry for some years, and therefore I tried to meet him. Unfortunately, in the short time I had left it proved to be impossible, but after returning to the United States I wrote Sugimura a letter expressing my interest in his work on Bosai. He responded favorably, and after several letters back and forth he invited me to join him on a trip to northwestern Japan to retrace the route of Bosai's longest journey, a leisurely tour that took him almost three years. Although we would move at a faster pace, I realized that I would need more time for research in Japan than my academic schedule permitted; so I started to apply for grants that would enable me to take one term off from teaching.

While I was back in the United States, Sugimura published and sent to me his book, appropriately titled *Kameda Bosai.* This volume turned out to be a detailed study of Bosai's life, with a large number of poems included in the text. There was some mention of Bosai's art and small illustrations, but no serious art-historical study was included. Sugimura's book proved to be the most valuable single source I had for my study of Bosai, and I took the time to translate it in full for my own use. The poems were the most difficult parts to translate, since they were almost exclusively in Chinese rather than Japanese, but I did my best, aided by some annotations provided by Sugimura in his book. When I was finished, I still had a large number of questions, too many to try to resolve by letter. I wrote them down and saved them for the time I might meet Sugimura and ask him in person.

Filling out grant applications was a long and burdensome task, but it did have the advantage of focusing my attention on exactly what I wanted to do. I was lucky; I received a grant from the Metropolitan Center for the Study of Far Eastern Art that enabled me to spend five months in Japan. It was clear to me that by studying an artist who was currently little known, I had cut myself off from discussions with many art historians who did not know his work. On the other hand, those few scholars and collectors interested in Bosai were most pleased to aid my research. In fact, they were delighted that a foreigner was interested in this once famous but now obscure Japanese artist. I wrote to Sugimura and he arranged a trip to the northwest region to search for works by Bosai and to view the countryside that the artist had seen and painted.

I went to Japan late in the summer and did not return home until shortly before Christmas. The journey with Sugimura came early in my stay. We traveled mostly on trains, which operate very efficiently in Japan, and often were welcomed at the homes of well-to-do farmers and merchants where Bosai himself had stayed almost two centuries earlier. I discovered that a traveling artist in those days could simply move from one patron's house to another, receiving hospitality in return for good conversation and perhaps a painting or calligraphy. One large calligraphy that had by now made its way into an American collection had originally been created when Bosai visited the house of a man with a garden featuring two beautiful pine trees. Bosai's poem about the two pines (fig. 7) formed the text of his calligraphy; undoubtedly it originally had been a present in return for hospitality:

> Your ancestors planted pine trees a few inches high:
> Did they realize that they would become a pair of dragons?
> Frosty trunks and snowy branches are firmly rooted below;
> Green whiskers and black colors stand proud throughout the winter.
> In auspicious mist they engage the miles-high moon,
> Their pure music wafts on high to harmonize with heaven's wind.
> Twisting branches look like dragons fighting for the magic jewel;
> The dense greenery of their leaves is like the shaking of long manes.
> One might take them for arching whales slapping the vast sea,
> Or watch, amazed, as they clutch at clouds rising to the azure sky.
> Mulberry fields and oceans, how many times have they alternated?
> But your house, Sir, will surely endure as long as the trees themselves,
> Generation after generation carrying on your ancestor's enterprise,
> Forever together with this pair of pines, lasting without end.[1]

One wonders if the pines, the house, and the family still exist.

Calligraphy is a medium that many Chinese and Japanese over the centuries have regarded at the pinnacle of all art forms. This may seem strange to us; we may consider an example of handwriting attractive but hardly a work of art. Yet we collect autographs of famous people, and we believe that we can see something of a person's character in his or her penmanship. East Asians believe calligraphy is the true expression of a person's individual personality. In addition, calligraphy, which utilizes the same flexible brush that is used in painting, is a visual feast of lines, shapes, and forms stemming from the fifty thousand possible character forms in Chinese and Japanese. In some ways calligraphy resembles abstract art (although the graphs all have meanings) or action painting, in which gesture, like dance, produces expressive form.

Bosai's calligraphy is written seven columns wide in regular script (which is most like printing and is easier to read than running and cursive scripts). He clearly wanted his host to understand and enjoy the flattering references to the garden, but he also gave the scroll a sense of rhythmic life by his alternations of heavier and lighter strokes, thicker and thinner lines, and straight and curved shapes. Reading from top to bottom, right to left, we can follow the strokes as they flow down the paper. In this way calligraphy is an art like music, moving through time, as well as like painting, to be seen in its entirety, instantly.

I discovered that Bosai's tour gave him the chance to see much of northwestern Japan, and the mountains and rivers along his journey surely encouraged his painting of landscapes. Like all scholar-artists, he

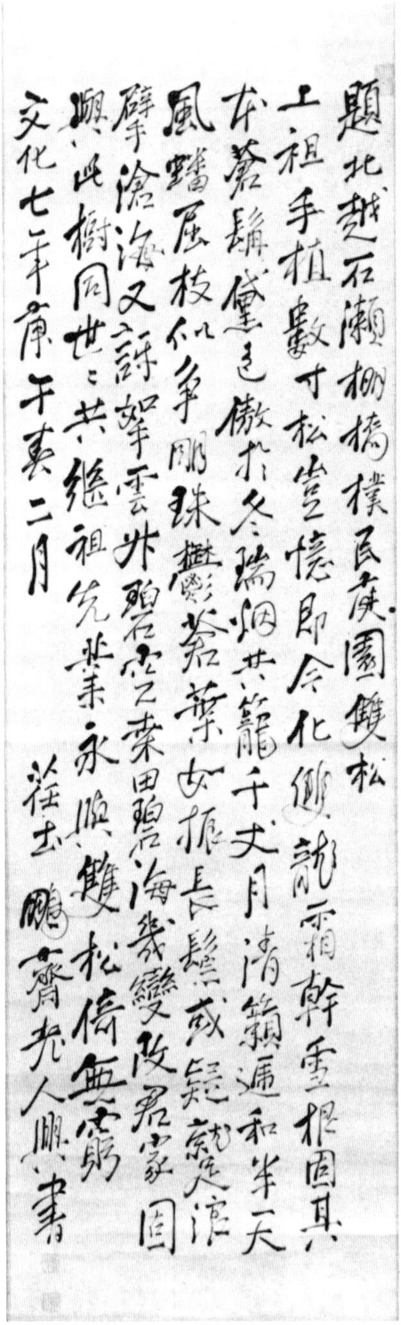

Fig. 7. Kameda Bosai (1752–1826), *The Pair of Pines* (1810), ink on paper, 44¼ in. × 13⅜ in. Private collection.

presented his own individual vision with allusions to the past. He also loved to combine the "three treasures" of the scholar: painting, poetry, and calligraphy. One of his landscapes, dated 1807, refers with admiration to the Chinese poet Su Shih, author of the "Red Cliff" prose poems discussed earlier. In it Bosai portrays a scholar-poet crossing a bridge beneath high mountains, with a lonely pavilion near the peak (fig. 8). The same brushwork brings forth and unites painting and calligraphy with Bosai's poem:

> The Red Cliff is eight thousand feet high,
> A rainbow bridge connects two peaks over the river.
> Where is the old immortal Su Shih now?
> I know he has entered the heavens
> And is no longer within the confines of the world.
> How can anyone lengthen life by only celebrating himself?[2]

Bosai's art shows us that he was able to commune with nature while visiting old and new friends. By following in his footsteps, I tried to emulate his experiences. Among the interesting people I met on my trip were a monk who lived on the side of a mountain and collected rubbings of calligraphy by Bosai and his friends; a farmer who had inherited a collection of Bosai's works, some probably painted or written in his house; and the curator of a local historical center who had several works by Bosai but had not yet found time to study them. I was also able to view the sites Bosai had seen and celebrated in his poetry, many of which were little changed by modernization. Best of all, I had the chance to get to know Sugimura and to benefit greatly from his knowledge and kindness. I spent hours on trains with him asking questions drawn from his book and discussing the many aspects of Bosai's life. In return, I showed him how I had been taking photographs of Bosai's paintings and calligraphy and also of his signatures and seals. From these I was able to begin to sort out genuine Bosai works from imitations, which were copious. In this way I felt I was able to contribute something to our scholarly exchange, although I certainly received much more than I gave, other than my enthusiasm and appreciation.

At the end of the trip, perhaps from sleeping on too many Japanese floors, I had some annoying back trouble, and Sugimura took me into his home near Tokyo for several days until I could walk again. He also showed me various research materials he had gathered over the years, and we discussed Bosai's paintings and calligraphy at some length. Sugimura was able to expound on the biographical and poetic sides of Bosai's art, while I contributed my comments on his brushwork, use of color, and compositional schemes. I think it is fair to say we both enjoyed the conversations a great deal. My good fortune in finding a helpful scholar

Fig. 8. Kameda Bosai (1752–1826), *Rainbow Bridge* (1807), ink and light colors on paper, 38¼ in. × 13¼ in. Manyo-an Collection.

was very important to the success of the project, all the more fruitful because my research complemented rather than copied his.

I had taken a great many slides and photographs of Bosai works, and I spent a good deal of time making comparisons with two slide projectors.

Having seen the works in person was a great help, as I could recall my original impressions, aided by the notes I had taken. In addition, my notebooks of seal and signature reproductions had grown, and I was able to put dates on the use of certain seals and to chart the evolution of Bosai's signatures. Only a minority of Bosai's works were specifically dated by him, but I could now create a chronology for both dated and undated works. I also had a number of slides and photographs of works by Bosai's teachers, friends, acquaintances, and pupils. I discovered that Bosai, particularly in his later years, was fond of getting together with friends and doing collaborative works, scrolls on which each artist would contribute a small painting or poem. These works very effectively demonstrate Bosai's artistic world and I determined to include some of them in the exhibition.

Translating Bosai's calligraphy and inscriptions was very difficult. First, the words had to be read, not an easy task with cursive script calligraphy. Since there are so many possible Chinese characters, deciphering them can be an endless task. I was able to obtain some help in this regard from a few experts (older Japanese are now worried that the younger generation will totally lose this skill). Once the characters were identified, it was still not easy to translate the works, since Chinese-style poetry is often deliberately ambiguous. Again, I sometimes had to turn to friends for help in establishing the meanings, and only then was I able to try to re-create the poems in English. A few of the more difficult longer prose and poetry texts I sent to an American friend, Jonathan Chaves, who is one of the leading translators of our time. He was kind enough to provide elegant readings for these texts.

What did I discover about Bosai while doing all this work? Primarily, that biographical, poetic, and artistic elements all blended together to shed light upon the artist and his milieu. It soon became clear how Bosai's life affected his art. Born in Edo (Tokyo), Bosai was so precocious as a child that he was given a full Confucian education. His teacher had helped develop a new kind of eclectic Confucianism in which each person could freely select his or her own moral and philosophical stance. When Bosai's education was complete, he opened his own Confucian academy, and soon his brilliant lectures and kindly personality drew hundreds of students. During this period, Bosai followed his teacher's lead in developing his poetry, calligraphy, and informal landscape painting, but only as a sideline to his Confucian studies. He published several books on scholarly topics and seemed destined for a brilliant career.

Then came disaster. The Japanese government, fearful of new ways of thought that stressed individual freedom, issued a decree against "alien teachings." Enrollment declined precipitously and soon Bosai was forced to close his school. It was at this time that he took his long journey to the northwest, staying at the homes of friends and acquaintances and turning his attention more to the arts. By the time he returned to Edo, he was a much more accomplished painter, poet, and calligrapher than before. His final decades were spent as a kind of free-lance literatus, contributing prefaces to books, giving away his paintings and poems to friends and followers, and surviving on a very small income.

This kind of biographical study led me to specific projects that made my research come alive. For example, I discovered that Bosai had admired a group of the most famous heroes in Japanese history, the Forty-seven Ronin. He composed a long text eulogizing these men, and his words were carved into a stone memorial tablet and erected at the temple where the Forty-seven Ronin were buried. He wrote, in part: "Moral heroism derives from inner sincerity, and moves Heaven and earth. . . . if a man has a human heart, how can he not admire their spirit and empathize with their determination?"[3]

Sugimura and I visited the temple with the stone memorial, and I made a rubbing of Bosai's inscription that was later included in the exhibition. We also visited other sites where Bosai's calligraphy had been carved into stone at temples and private gardens. This helped give me a picture of how art was made public during that period of Japanese history, as well as more understanding of Bosai's patronage and his calligraphy itself. Finally, I visited the descendants of the Kameda family and discovered that they owned a marvelous portrait of Bosai that they were willing to lend to the exhibition.

All these activities used up my time in Japan more quickly than I would have imagined, and I returned to the United States with much work still to be done. The main tasks at this point were choosing the remaining works to be included in the exhibition and writing the accompanying book. Due to the difficulty of arranging loans from Japan, where possible I chose works by Bosai and his artistic circle from American and English collections. But when only a Japanese work would demonstrate some important aspect of Bosai's art, I included it. After some thought, I decided to add one painting forgery and one calligraphy forgery, to be displayed and discussed next to Bosai's genuine works as examples for connoisseurship study. I believe that one way we can learn the true essence of an artist is by comparing a genuine work with a copy. In the case of Bosai, the forgers could imitate his general sense of composition, but the actual linework of the copies lacked the rhythm, tension, and dynamism of the originals.

Writing the catalog was not as difficult as I had feared. By this time, I was so immersed in Bosai and his world that I found the writing flowed fairly easily in most sections, although there were some paragraphs that needed to be rewritten again and again. My first question, and one that confronts anyone preparing an exhibition catalog, was whether to write individual entries for each artwork or a through-composed text. I chose the latter for two reasons. First, the paintings and calligraphy seemed to mesh beautifully into an account of Bosai's life and times. Second, by putting them in chronological order and discussing artistic issues as they came up in relation to his life, I found that I could write a relatively seamless account of Bosai's life and work.

Sugimura kindly consented to write an introduction, which I translated. My chapters consisted of "The Early Years," "The Years of Travel," "The Final Years in Edo," "Bosai's Followers," and a conclusion. Illustrations fit in comfortably along the way, and I relegated long translations to an appendix to avoid burdening the text. For a second appendix, I prepared life-size photographic reproductions of the forty-seven seals of Bosai that I considered genuine. The New Orleans Museum published my text as a large-scale softcover catalog, and the University Press of Kansas published a hardcover edition. In this way my text served both as book and catalog.

The exhibition itself seems to have been a success. Although Bosai's work is deeply embedded in the values of traditional Japanese literati culture, the freedom of his brushwork communicated well to an American audience. Labels that included information about Bosai and translations of the poems were an important feature of the exhibition, and I hope that my text was useful for those who wanted to pursue a deeper interest in Bosai's art. I received a number of compliments from Japanese colleagues, probably because no one in Japan had done an exhibition or book on Bosai's art, but also because of my stress on Bosai's "world" as well as on Bosai himself, an approach not often used in Japan.

Through this experience I learned first how much time a project like this can take; if I had not been involved in exhibitions before, I would never have guessed the many complications they involve. Second, I realized how fortunate I had been to receive help from Sugimura and others; if we want to go beyond a narrow interpretation of art history, the advice and cooperation of those in allied fields can be vital to the success of a project. Third, I was thrilled when the works were all gathered together and displayed; even at this late moment, one finds there is much more to be learned. A former teacher of mine once commented that the best time to write a catalog is when the exhibition is over; alas, that is not possible.

The World of Kameda Bosai was just one of the many kinds of projects that an art historian can undertake. This one involved travel to a foreign country and delving into old documents in another language, but a project might just as easily be the study of a contemporary artist in one's own vicinity, the architecture of selected buildings and homes in one's city or town, or the popular art of one's childhood. In most cases, the work will involve intellectual study and aesthetic response; projects go best when the two are balanced. Both can be developed through such activities as planning an exhibition, giving a talk, or writing a book or article. We hope that this volume is helpful in encouraging everyone to consider trying the art-historical process. There are many books that can help, including discussions of art historians and other kinds of art-historical resources.

Art Historians at Work and Writing about Art

A volume published by the Getty Art History Information Program entitled *Object, Image, Inquiry: The Art Historian at Work* is the most recent study to date of how art historians work. It begins with interviews of a representative sampling of art historians and concludes with studies of the projects they undertook. A certain amount of difference is revealed between what art historians say they do and how they actually spend their time, but many insights emerge to illuminate the richness and variety of the field.

A number of themes covered in this book give us a glimpse into the visions of art historians; these visions determine the course of their work. First, doing research in the field usually means not only dealing with masterpieces but being inundated by works of every quality and style. It is important to see as many works in person as possible, but one scholar wrote: "When you . . . see this vast number of copies and replicas and questionable works and unassignable works, damaged things, fragments, you really come face-to-face with another kind of reality in the realm of art."[4]

Art historians deal with this mass of raw visual information in a number of ways. Many make notes (index cards are still very useful, although more and more work is being done with computers), photograph anything that might be of interest, organize categories, and write outlines. It is important to try to find new ways to ask questions about material. Many art historians read books in anthropology, history, literature, and other fields as well as in art history and allow intuition to function in addition to reason.

A second problem is finding resources. One solution is to question colleagues, not only in art history but also in other fields. Librarians are often excellent sources of information, especially when one is stepping beyond one's field of specialization. Archives are helpful, although not always easy to use. Searching for information can range from "detective work" to "browsing." One writer commented: "you go on certain trails, on the scent. There is an openness to chance all the time."[5]

Third, having seen the artworks, taken or obtained photos, and located and studied the reference sources, the art historian must still write and publish. This is sometimes the most difficult part of all. As a contributor to *Object, Image, Inquiry* noted: "Writing for me is painful; it's excruciating. I am a very constipated writer, so I dread the thought of having to write anything. I approach it dutifully as a requirement, but I'd much rather talk about [my ideas]; talking is a much more natural mode of communicating . . . for me."[6]

A problem art historians mention is their desire to communicate the visual excitement of the art rather than writing in a dull or dry academic manner. One explained: "The hardest thing going is to write vividly when you are writing thoroughly, and I don't know how to do that except not to be afraid of the affective power of works of art."[7] For many art historians, the objects offer sheer pleasure and joy, but they question how that can be conveyed. When writing about art goes badly, there is nothing more frustrating. When it goes well, it can be exhilarating, a creative act that can give intense satisfaction in those rare moments when the writing seems to flow of itself.

Publishing is another question. Young professors at colleges and universities *must* publish to get tenure, so the pressure can be intense. Much writing must be approved by "readers" who can be devastatingly critical. Even when accepted, articles may take several years to appear because journals are so slow in publishing. Popular art magazines move more quickly and even pay authors, but they may have less prestige in the academic community.

Books can be even more problematic unless the writer is famous in his or her field. Art books tend to be expensive to publish because of the cost of reproductions, and, of course, most art historians want to include as many (often color) reproductions as possible. Fortunately, there are a number of university presses that supplement commercial firms as potential publishers, although they are less likely to print as many elaborate color plates.

For many art historians, both within and without museums, a major publishing opportunity is an exhibition catalog. At one time these were basically no more than checklists of works in the exhibition, perhaps with a short essay or brief notes. This has entirely changed. Nowadays, many catalogs are large in scale and serious in purpose, and they often contain some of the most important and lively writing in the field. The only drawback is that exhibitions cannot be delayed. Often, the catalog must be written in a hurry, without time for extensive scholarship or, even more important, extended thought about the art. Furthermore, one must write about the works that are available for the exhibition, rather than choosing any example in the world. Nevertheless, the chance to write about the art people see in an exhibition is exciting, and more and more scholars are taking up the challenge.

In reading *Object, Image, Inquiry*, it is clear that current art historians have mixed attitudes toward two recent developments in the field—new methodologies and computers. Some art historians dismiss new methodologies, but many more take an interest and read some of the writers (mostly from other fields) who have influenced new art history. These include Ferdinand de Saussure, Roland Barthes, Jacques Derrida, Michel Foucault, Claude Lévi-Strauss, Noam Chomsky, and Walter Benjamin. How useful have the new ideas been? One art historian writes: "We need to sew the study of the arts back into the study of history and society and culture. The methodologies . . . to do that are coming from parallel disciplines." Two other views are less positive: "I find much of my own discipline now engaged in what I call, disparagingly, intellectual ambulance chasing. . . . it tends to breed . . . a kind of slavish imitation"; and "One could say you're creating a theoretical structure which has no necessary reflex in the art itself . . . which is utterly divorced from the actual artistic object."[8]

The basic difference lies between those who want to expand art history as a field into many cultural levels and those who argue that both the artist and the work of art are being lost in the process. However, most agree that the new cultural emphasis has been invigorating. Furthermore, there is a new understanding that the study of art is not merely a method of illustrating historical issues of the past: "Art is not simply another visual document, is not simply a passive reflection of history, but rather an active shaper of it."[9] According to this understanding, artists not only respond to but also help to define the world around them. Therefore, the art historian, presenting us with the artistic vision from many cultures and time periods, can help to shape our own sense of reality.

While few art historians dispute their use of computers in assembling information, some find that it does not help in the fundamental, creative side of the art-historical process: "In the end I'm really deeply skeptical about a lot of the enthusiasm about the computer from my fellow academics. . . . You can have all the data you like, beautifully arranged before you, but if it doesn't come together in some intuitive order, if you've asked dull questions, you will have a massively dull book."[10] The use of word processing for revising manuscripts, however, is widely hailed as a great benefit to the field. The opportunity to make changes again and again without having to retype an entire manuscript allows art historians to reconsider, revise, and polish their manuscripts more than ever before.

For those who wish to explore this theme further, a useful book is *Computers in the History of Art.* The volume is divided into four sections: "Overview," "Electronic Imaging," "Databases and Data Modeling," and "Applications." The overview begins with the caveat that the probability of a breakdown in a military computer annihilating humanity is "100 times more likely than the likelihood that computers—used by art historians—can contribute anything substantial to the enrichment of culture."[11] The overview continues on a more positive note with an examination of six ways the computer can be helpful: collecting data; retrieving data; examining issues; reconstructing, producing, and simulating objects; administrating and organizing people and objects; and communicating things of beauty. The later sections of the book are more technical but are written clearly enough to encourage those art historians who wish to take advantage of the computer's potential.

Another book that demonstrates how computers are being used for art history is *Census: Computerization in the History of Art,* a volume inspired by a conference in Pisa that lists no fewer than 162 computer projects ranging from catalogs, lexicons, and sources to iconographies, bibliographies, and photo archives. There are short abstracts about each project, including some that specifically address art-historical uses of the computer.[12] It is encouraging to see that by 1984 there was such a great variety of projects from all over the world; undoubtedly, many more were not described.

Four other books shed light on the work of art historians and on the skills needed to write about art. The first is *Art History: Its Use and Abuse,* by W. McAllister Johnson, a professor at the University of Toronto. Johnson has thorough chapters on research, bibliography, writing, university and public life, and cataloging theory and practice, mostly directed to the art historian in academia. Fortunately, a sense of humor (that blessing) enlivens his text. For example, his preface lists typical art historical phrases with translations:

It has long been known that . . . *I haven't bothered to look up the reference*
It is obvious that . . . *I can't explain it*
It is generally believed that . . . *A couple of others think so too*

> While it has not been possible to provide definitive answers ... *Nothing worked out*

The author also notes why he writes as he does: "the essay form is likely to be most effective because it is inevitably irritating."[13]

Johnson has useful things to say about research, particularly that "the only sane way to approach research is to know that you will do more work, and a rather different type of work, than you anticipated. . . . Both method and knowledge are specific manifestations of curiosity, which is essentially an altruistic selfishness."[14] He stresses that we must be practical, realizing how much there is to do even on the simplest project. He urges us to consider what we can accomplish in the time that is available; we may have false starts, false leads, and setbacks, yet we must be willing to continue to a conclusion, always with the realization that more could have been done. On the one hand, we must be thorough; on the other, the urge to learn more and write more must at times be resisted, or nothing will be completed.

Johnson has helpful suggestions regarding the process of using a library. He tells us that each collection or library is its own world and has conventions and procedures that must be understood if one is to find what one needs. Art librarians can be of enormous help, but the definition of one's subject must come first. We are dependent upon resources, but libraries, archives, and museums must be approached with sufficient insight so that information does not crowd out knowledge. Research ideally will lead us toward meaning rather than mere facts, so we should always leave ourselves time to think about what we are learning. If we are studying the art of a previous time period, what was its importance to the people of that culture in that era? And what kind of meaning can it have for us today?

A second useful book for those involved in art history is Sylvan Barnet's *Short Guide to Writing about Art.* The author, whose personal expertise ranges from Shakespeare to Japanese Zen calligraphy, divides his guide into the following chapters: "Writing about Art"; "Analysis"; "Writing a Composition"; "How to Write an Effective Essay"; "Style in Writing"; "Manuscript Form"; "The Research Paper"; and "Essay Examinations." The book can be helpful to scholars at every level but is especially useful to those who are writing about art for the first time. Barnet believes that "we write about art in order to clarify and to account for our responses to works that interest or excite or frustrate us. In putting words to paper, we have to take a second and a third look at what is in front of us and what is within us. And so writing is a way of learning."[15]

Barnet suggests that we begin by considering our audience, which consists of ourselves and those who may share our interests, so that we explain enough and not too much. He makes clear the difference between sociological, biographical, iconographic, and analytic studies, and asks us questions that may help us define just how a work of art makes its effect. Giving examples of successful essays along the way, he takes us through the use of comparison, the ways to achieve a clear style, and the preparation of a manuscript, including footnotes, endnotes, and bibliographies. Most helpful of all, Barnet is always humane in his suggestions, never letting us forget that our goal is the communication, through our own study and understanding, of what artists have created.

Writing about Art, by Henry M. Sayre, also contains many insights into the seeing and writing process. The author begins by explaining that writing about art is the best way to understand one's own feelings about the visual world. He notes that "in order to see aesthetically, most of us . . . need to be prodded" and that this prodding can come from visiting a museum or a gallery but also by making the effort to express in words what we see and feel:

> We all carry all manner of baggage with us when we see works of art . . . and what we carry affects what we see, let alone how well we see it. Seeing art, then, is as much a self-critical as it is a critical operation. It involves, absolutely, our own prejudices and preconceptions. . . . But a work of art needs also to rise above whatever ignorance or misunderstanding we might initially bring to it. . . . In my own writing I have usually found that the best pieces I have done have resulted not from my attempt to explain what I already know . . . but from my attempts to engage a work that I find in some way powerful even as I am unable at first to articulate just what the sources of that power may be. Writing then becomes a kind of exploration. This leads in turn to better writing, because the sense of mystery, excitement, and discovery involved in the process of exploration is never lost.[16]

There are a number of important admonitions in Sayre's book. For example, he discourages the overuse of quotes, suggesting that "when you quote, always move on from the quotation and continue to develop the paragraph by developing the idea the quotation initiates."[17] This advice is surely useful to those who feel they cannot say something better than did the source they have found. No matter how fine the quotation, it can and should be integrated into the text through further comments and explanation.

Although most of Sayre's book is narrative in style, each chapter concludes with a summary that lists specific suggestions for the aspiring writer. Toward the end, the book includes several fine examples of short essays composed by Sayre's students rather than by professional art historians. Sayre comments that they are not beyond the skills of any one of us, surely an encouragement to us all. It will depend upon each reader whether Sayre or Barnet is the most useful, but both can be recommended to those either beginning or further along in their writing about art.

Finally, in *Art History in Education: An Annotated Bibliography and History*, Paul Brazier attempts to combine two aims.[18] One is historical: he analyzes both English and North American art education (primarily at the university level) over the past century. The second is bibliographical: Brazier includes annotated listings of books and major journal articles dealing with art history and art education. For example, he describes the *Journal of Aesthetic Education*, the *College Art Journal*, and the *Art Bulletin*, among others, citing articles he finds of particular interest. In total, 356 books and articles are cited in the text. While there are no doubt many omissions, for those with an interest in seeing how art education has progressed in English-speaking countries, this book should prove useful.

Art History Resources

Although the greatest resource for an art historian may well be another art historian, librarian, or archivist, we do not find everything through personal contacts. There are a number of useful reference volumes and sets that can make research immeasurably easier if we know how to use them. The following owes much to the advice of Susan Craig, art librarian at the University of Kansas, who suggested some resources that are available at many libraries across the United States and Canada. It should be emphasized that these are only a few of the hundreds of reference volumes that have been published.

Largest in scale is the *Encyclopedia of World Art* (London: McGraw-Hill, 1965), which has many extended essays within its seventeen volumes and also includes many high-quality illustrations. Since it was originally written in Italian, it is most helpful for Italian and other European art. Next comes the *McGraw-Hill Dictionary of Art* (London: McGraw-Hill, 1969), which has a large number of shorter entries in its five volumes. Among one-volume references, *The Oxford Companion to Art* (London: Oxford University Press, 1970), has been widely utilized, although it has been somewhat supplanted by the more concise *Oxford Dictionary of Art* (London: Oxford University Press, 1988).

There are also a host of specialized reference books divided into categories of different kinds. Some represent the art of a particular country, such as Matthew Baigell's *Dictionary of American Art* (New

York: Harper and Row, 1979). Others cover a certain historical period such as the Renaissance, the nineteenth century, or the contemporary era. Furthermore, some art dictionaries are organized by topic or medium; two examples of the latter are *The Dictionary of World Pottery and Porcelain* (New York: Charles Scribner's Sons, 1971) and Frances Phipps's *Collector's Complete Dictionary of American Antiques* (Garden City, N.Y.: Doubleday & Company, 1974). Finally, if you are having trouble writing, you will find that you are not alone if you consult Kenneth Hudson's *Dictionary of Diseased English* (New York: Harper and Row, 1977).

For finding the right book, the first and foremost source is *Art Information: Research Methods and Resources* (Dubuque, Iowa: Kendall Hunt Publishing, 1990; previous editions lacked the second word of the title), by Lois Swan Jones. This large paperback volume is eminently practical. You will learn how to compile a bibliography; consult museum catalogs; locate reproductions; solve research problems of many kinds; and use encyclopedias, biographical dictionaries, library catalogs, indexes, abstracts, reference books, directories, iconographical references, and much more.

The first third of Jones's book consists of a narrative description of the research process, including how to plan a research project, utilize a library, and compile a bibliography. The larger section of the book consists of listings of reference books. Two examples of Jones's bibliographic entries follow; the first is from the section "Documents, Sources, and Criticism" and the second is from "For Art/Museum Educators":

Friedenthal, Richard. *Letters of the Great Artists.* Trans. by Daphne Woodward et al. London: Thames & Hudson, 1963.
Vol. I: From Ghiberti to Gainsborough.
Vol. II: From Blake to Pollock.

Bunch, Clarence, ed. *Art Education: A Guide to Information Sources.* Art and Architecture Information Guide Series. Detroit: Gale Research Company, 1978. Includes all types of topics of interest to art educators, such as research, creativity, exceptional and disadvantaged children, teaching processes and materials, teacher resource materials, financing art education, and children's art books.[19]

These two examples help make it clear how this volume opens up the world of art research by means of useful, often annotated, bibliographies. *Art Information* concludes with appendixes of foreign language and English special terminology, a listing of databases, and an index to publications, subjects, and professions. There is no single book as helpful to an art researcher; and, fortunately, it is updated frequently.

Another fine general book on art history resources is Etta Arntzen and Robert Rainwater, *Guide to the Literature of Art History* (Chicago: American Library Association, 1980). It is divided into sections on general reference sources (e.g., bibliographies, dictionaries), general primary and secondary sources (e.g., methodologies, documents), the particular arts, and serials. This book has over four thousand entries and a useful index, but it is now more than a decade old and will not contain many important recent references. Even older but still useful is Mary W. Chamberlin's *Guide to Art Reference Books*, also published by the American Library Association but dating to 1959. Included are 2,565 entries including many foreign-language books. Finally, Donald Ehresmann's *Fine Arts: A Bibliographic Guide* (Littleton, Colo.: Libraries Unlimited, 1979) is somewhat more up-to-date and includes 1,127 listings of books and handbooks, with helpful commentaries.

Much of the best art-historical writing is contained in articles rather than books. Fortunately, there are excellent resources for locating these articles through periodical indexes. *Art Index* (New York: H. W. Wilson Co., 1929–   ) covers about two hundred journals. More than three hundred journals are covered in the *RILA: International Repertory of the Literature of Art* (Santa Monica, Calif.: J. Paul Getty Trust, 1975–   ). The most complete reference is in French, the *Repertoire d'Art et d'Archeologie* (Paris: Centre de Documentation Sciences Humaines (1910–   ), and indexes more than 1,175 periodicals (almost 40 percent in English), covering art history from 200 A.D. to World War II.

For twentieth-century art, including photography, *Art Bibliographies: Modern* (Santa Barbara, Calif.: ABC–Clio Press, 1969–   ) is a helpful resource. More complex, since it lists references to subjects, authors, citations, and institutions in four separate volumes, is the *Arts and Humanities Citation Index* (Philadelphia: Institute for Scientific Information, 1979-   ). Although this work is not the easiest to use, it can be especially valuable since it covers all the humanities, giving a wider focus to art-historical inquiries. For exhibition catalogs, which are often ephemeral, the best source is *Catalogs of the Art Exhibition Catalog Collection of the Arts Library, University of California at Santa Barbara* (New York: Chadwyck-Healey, 1977-   ). This computerized system has listings for more than sixty-seven thousand catalogs. Finally, one may find newspaper articles on art through the *Newsbank Review of the Arts: Fine Arts and Architecture* (New Canaan, Conn.: Newsbank, 1975-   ), for which there are full-text microfilms available if one does not have access to the original newspapers.

References to Museums and Institutions

There are a number of reference volumes that can help art historians locate museums and other institutions; in some cases, they offer information about the holdings or other activities of the museums. The most complete reference may be *Museums of the World* (Munich: K. G. Saur, 1981), which briefly lists museums of all kinds by country and city, with an annotation on the speciality (e.g., local history, decorative arts, botanical). For fine arts, Virginia Jackson's two-volume *Art Museums of the World* (New York: Greenwood Press, 1987) may be more useful since it contains essays on museums with commentary on their collections. For America and Canada, *The Official Museum Directory* (Washington, D.C.: American Association of Museums) is published every two years. It contains listings by state and city, giving addresses and telephone numbers, personnel, collections, activities, hours, and other information. The *American Art Directory* (New York: R. R. Bowker), published every year or two, is similar but adds listings of art organizations, libraries, and art schools. The *International Directory of Arts* (Munich: Muller Verlag) is published every two years in two volumes with the addresses of museums, galleries, and dealers.

References for Artworks

Following our four main approaches to art history in order: first, where can we find information if we wish to study a particular artwork? If we need a reproduction or permission and we know a work's whereabouts, *The Picture Researcher's Handbook: An International Guide to Picture Sources and How to Use Them* (New York: Charles Scribner's Sons, 1979) is useful but unfortunately does not include most museums. We can also consult the appropriate museum catalog, journal, register, or bulletin. What if we do not know the exact work or its whereabouts but merely have a subject or an artist's name? Yala H. Korwin's *Index to Two-Dimensional Artworks* (Metuchen, N.J.: Scarecrow Press, 1981) indexes the reproductions in two hundred primary books by artist, subject, and title. Patricia Pate Harlice's *World Painting Index* (Metuchen, N.J.: Scarecrow Press, 1977) is also useful. For more specialized study, one might consult Jane Clapp's *Sculpture Index* (Metuchen, N.J.: Scarecrow Press, 1970), James McQuaid's *Index to American Photographic Collections* (Boston: G. K. Hall & Company, 1982), or other specialized references.

The most basic reference volume on iconography is James Hall's *Dictionary of Subjects and Symbols in Art* (London: J. Murray, 1974).

While this book is too large in scope to contain the most detailed information, it is a good beginning for discovering more about the subjects of paintings, prints, and sculptures, including some of the hidden meanings they may hold. Particular fields also have their own references, such as the three-volume study by Gertrude Jobes, *Dictionary of Mythology, Folklore, and Symbols* (Metuchen, N.J.: Scarecrow Press, 1961). Carl G. Jung's *Man and His Symbols* (New York: Doubleday & Company, 1964) should not be forgotten as an in-depth study of the human use of symbols.

For more detailed iconographic information on specific images, we must go to books on specialized themes. Much European and American art has Christian subjects; these are discussed in George Ferguson's *Signs and Symbols of Christian Art* (New York: Oxford University Press, 1954). Nor should we forget that marvelous old standby, *Butler's Lives of the Saints* (Westminster, Md.: Christian Classics, 1988), by Herbert J. Thurston and Donald Attwater. Many fields have their own iconographic manuals, such as Percy Preston's *Dictionary of Pictorial Subjects from Classical Literature* (New York: Charles Scribner's Sons, 1983), or Basil Stewart's *Guide to Japanese Prints and Their Subject Matter* (New York: Dover, 1979).

References for Artists

For studying individual artists, there are numerous books devoted to a single master. More broadly, the two best biographical dictionaries are in German and French. The former is the *Kunstler Lexicon* (Leipzig: E. A. Seemann, 1905–50), published in thirty-seven volumes; as might be expected, it is strongest in pre–twentieth-century artists. Benezit's ten-volume *Dictionnaire des Peintures* (Paris: Librarie Grund, 1976) is more up-to-date but not quite as complete. Naturally, it is especially useful for French artists. The *Artists Biographical Master Index* (Detroit: Gale Research Co., 1986) lists where biographies of artists can be found in more than seventy English-language indexes. One-volume biographical dictionaries include the larger *Biographical Dictionary of Artists* (London: Macmillan, 1983), which has 784 pages, and the more compact *Thames and Hudson Dictionary of Art and Artists* (New York: Thames and Hudson, 1985), at 352 pages. Edmund B. Feldman's *The Artist* (Englewood Cliffs, N.J.: Prentice Hall, 1982) discusses the status of the artist from prehistory to the present, including child and folk artists.

Many biographical dictionaries list artists by field, such as the *Macmillan Encyclopedia of Architects* (London: Macmillan Free Press, 1982), which has many extended essays in its four volumes. There are reference works for women artists, graphic artists, photographers, folk artists, interior decorators, and so on. Still other reference works focus on a certain period. For contemporary artists (and some art historians) in the United States, *Who's Who in American Art* (New York: R. R. Bowker, 1989) is useful, as is *Contemporary Artists* (Chicago: St. James Press, 1987), which contains biographies, exhibition listings, and some photographs. For American artists who worked between 1898 and 1947, *Who Was Who in American Art* (Madison, Conn.: Sound View Press, 1985) summarizes a great deal of information. There are also biographical dictionaries of artists in other countries—Lawrence Robert's *Dictionary of Japanese Artists* (New York: Weatherhill, 1976) is a good example. For those searching for an extended study of an individual artist, Wolfgang M. Freitag's *Art Books: A Basic Bibliography of Monographs on Artists* (New York: Garland, 1985) is an incomplete but still very helpful guide.

The Study of Patronage

Researching audience and patronage is occasionally fruitful within art-historical reference volumes. Biographies and monographs on artists may include some of this information, especially more recent studies. Even richer sources may be readings in economic, social, religious, and political history. These will often provide opportunities to understand the art from the patron's point of view. The powerful patron Lorenzo di Medici certainly influenced the course of Italian Renaissance art, as did Pope Gregory when he persuaded Michelangelo to paint the ceiling of the Sistine Chapel. Yet we sometimes treat artworks as though they had been created in isolation.

Beyond the effect of important individuals, we can learn much from a broader study of economic history. For example, the wealth of a European city during a particular age might not have only provided artists with patrons but also lead to the popularity of certain subjects and styles. If we find value in theories of class ideology as a determining factor in artistic production, we must read works on economics and history with a Marxist approach. Within the field, Nicos Hadjinicoleau's *Art History and Class Struggle* (London: Pluto Press, 1978) gives a broad view, while T. J. Clark's *Image of the People: Gustave Courbet and the 1848 Revolution* (London: Thames and Hudson, 1973) is one of several case studies by a very thoughtful art historian.

Social history might also show how artists were affected by the social order of their age. Among the different sources one might use are *The Courts of Europe: Politics, Patronage and Royalty 1400–1800*, ed. A. G. Dickens (New York: McGraw-Hill, 1977); Frances Haskell's *Patrons and*

Painters: A Study in the Relation between Italian Art and Society in the Age of the Baroque (New Haven: Yale University Press, 1980); and Niels von Holst's *Creators, Collectors and Connoisseurs: An Anatomy of Artistic Taste from Antiquity to the Present Day* (London: Thames and Hudson, 1967).

The Study of Art in Cultural Context

For the study of art in its total cultural context, to the question "What shall I read?" is the answer "Everything!" While this may seem beyond any mortal's power, it is both a challenge and an invitation. Everything about a society can illuminate its art, especially history, literature, religion, and philosophy but also science, politics, economics, music, theater, or any aspect of the era in question. By reading selectively, each art historian can carve out an intellectual territory and find inexhaustible riches within it, bringing new understanding even to familiar works of art. In effect, art historians can bring all their interests and experiences to the task of research and interpretation. The human potential for synthesis is what keeps art history alive, changing, and ever fascinating.

NOTES

1. Translation by Jonathan Chaves, from Stephen Addiss, *The World of Kameda Bosai* (New Orleans: New Orleans Museum of Art, 1984), pp. 47–48.

2. Translation by Stephen Addiss, from ibid., p. 39.

3. Translation by Jonathan Chaves, from ibid., p. 118.

4. *Object, Image, Inquiry: The Art Historian at Work* (Santa Monica, Calif.: J. Paul Getty Trust, 1988), p. 17.

5. Ibid., pp. 41–42.

6. Ibid., p. 55.

7. Ibid., p. 59.

8. Ibid., pp. 142, 143.

9. Ibid., p. 151.

10. Ibid., p. 71.

11. Anthony Hamber, Jean Miles, and William Vaughn, eds., *Computers and the History of Art* (London and New York: Mansell Publishing, 1989), p. 1.

12. Laura Corti, ed., *Census: Computerization in the History of Art* (Pisa: Scuola Normale Superiore; and Los Angeles: J. Paul Getty Trust, 1984).

13. W. McAllister Johnson, *Art History: Its Use and Abuse* (Toronto: University of Toronto Press, 1988), preface and p. 4.

14. Ibid., pp. 4–5.

15. Sylvan Barnet, *A Short Guide to Writing about Art* (Glenview, Ill.: Scott, Foresman and Co., 1989), p. 1.

16. Henry M. Sayre, *Writing about Art* (Englewood, N.J.: Prentice Hall, 1989), pp. 11, 14, 19.

17. Ibid., p. 72.

18. Paul Brazier, *Art History in Education: An Annotated Bibliography and History* (London: Heinemann Educational Books, 1985).

19. Lois Swan Jones, *Art Information: Methods and Resources* (Dubuque, Iowa: Kendall/Hall Publishing Company, 1991), pp. 119, 268.

5

Traditions of Teaching Art History: Are There Sound Foundations upon Which to Build?

Chapters 1 through 4 of this book are intended to orient the reader to the fascinations and complexities of the discipline of art history. For readers with a basic understanding of art history, these chapters open up new ideas about the breadth of issues and the range of methodologies that make up the discipline.

The remaining chapters are intended to help the reader contemplate the role art history can play in the education of America's youth. This chapter overviews traditions in art education that have influenced and continue to influence educators and the public as they ponder the teaching of art history.

How does one begin to consider the methods by which improvements can be made in teaching art history? Unlike computer graphics, art history is not a new subject to be included in the curriculum. Art history, or something like art history, has played a role in art education for at least a century.

In the late nineteenth and early twentieth centuries, art history, especially as a part of art appreciation, was considered helpful to moral development and improving one's social standing. In the middle years of the twentieth century, two trends emerged in art education that influenced the teaching of art history. First, the range of objects that might be studied was broadened beyond Western fine arts to include such items as consumer goods, domestic architecture, and, sometimes, art from non-Western cultures. Second, in the 1950s and 1960s, a strong focus on psychological development and creativity sometimes actually discouraged the teaching of art history as a part of art education. More recently, discipline-centered curriculum visions of the 1960s and discipline-based approaches beginning in the 1980s once again have promoted the teaching of art history as a significant component of art education.

Morality, Social Class, and Art Appreciation

Issues of morality and social class have been associated with teaching art history and art appreciation throughout the decades. As art history found its way into American universities in the nineteenth century, it was often linked to moral education.[1] And it was, of course, the privileged who had access to the moral lessons of a university art history education.[2]

During the time privileged young people were being exposed to the moral lessons of art history in universities, working-class people were sometimes introduced to art history through the more practically oriented approach of drawing classes. Historic ornament was a standard component of many drawing classes.[3] The study of ornamental detail on functional objects and in architecture from Western and non-Western culture was a recurrent component of the 1889 Prang art program, for example (fig. 9). The authors of that program called such study "ennobling."[4] Art-historical information was also being presented from a social and moral angle through the picture study movement.

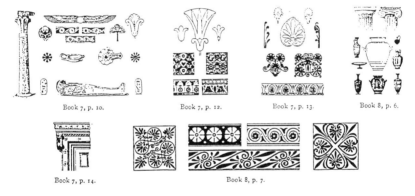

Book 7, p. 10.   Book 7, p. 12.   Book 7, p. 13.   Book 8, p. 6.

Book 7, p. 14.   Book 8, p. 7.

Fig. 9. "Examples of Historic Ornament," from *Teachers' Manual for the Prange Elementary Course in Art Instruction*, John S. Clark, Mary Dana Hicks, and Walter S. Perry (Boston: Prang Educational Co., 1889). The authors noted that these examples "are also very closely related to composition, furnishing very fine examples of space relations. They are to be especially studied with reference to beauty produced by spacing and proportion." Photo: Arizona State University Media Services.

Art appreciation, art history, and the picture study movement were intertwined throughout the first part of the twentieth century.[5] Proponents of art appreciation programs expected that studying valued artworks would yield enjoyment of great masterpieces and help mold moral people more capable of leading the "good life." Art-historical information was usually a significant portion of the content of art appreciation and picture study classes. One textbook author made her claim for art appreciation quite straightforwardly: "To be introduced in early years to the masterpieces of the ages, and to learn of the kingly minds who have ruled in this realm of beauty, is sure to develop an interest which will enlarge, enrich, and refine the future life of the pupil."[6] Some suggested that exposure to masterpieces had potential for improving one's standing and prestige in the community,[7] while others saw the appreciation of art as a gift that should be made available to all members of society.[8] For at least one state, North Dakota, picture study was a basis for moral education. Each month of the year was represented by a moral value: September—work; October—hope; November—gratitude; December—kindness; January—thrift; February—respect; March—courage; April—purity; May—duty[9] (fig. 10). In this case, the link between art appreciation and moral education was more than suggested, it was mandated.

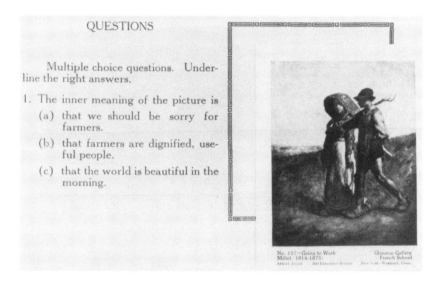

Fig. 10. "Questions," from *My Own Picture Book*, Theodore Pottle (Champaign, Ill., 1927). Photo: Arizona State University Media Services.

As one considers improvements in teaching art history in the elementary and secondary schools, one must recognize a wide range of values traditionally associated with knowledge and appreciation of the art of the past. Laura Chapman, in analyzing art education and the "cultural elite," concludes that "the process of acquiring knowledge about art thus remains a matter of privilege associated with membership in a social class in which such knowledge is valued and provided."[10] At the beginning of this century, art history was largely available to the "leisure classes" in colleges and universities, and Chapman finds the same to be true at the end of this century. Social class, morality, and art appreciation have been persistent issues traditionally associated with art history instruction. Substantial change in elementary and secondary teaching of art history seems unlikely to be brought about without our acknowledging and responding to these traditions.

A Broader Base and a Competing Agenda

From the 1920s through the 1940s, some art educators were advocating a broader base for art appreciation. In the fifties and sixties a focus on psychological development and creativity tended to displace interest in teaching art history. Early manual training approaches established a tradition of practicality in art education. During the Great Depression and afterward, a number of art educators expanded their scope of attention to include a wide range of genres, including folk art, crafts, city planning, consumer goods, and domestic architecture.[11] In many textbooks of this era, Western and non-Western works of art were introduced as exemplars of design principles that might be applied to objects in one's daily life. June King McFee's *Preparation for Art*,[12] published in 1961, took a strong stand for understanding the cultural bases of art education. She and many of her students might be credited with inspiring the multicultural emphasis that commands so much attention in the field of art education today.

Although art appreciation and cultural issues in art education were integrated into the literature and practice of some schools in the 1940s through the 1960s, another agenda for art education dominated those decades. As early as 1924, Eugene Neuhaus foreshadowed the agenda of the middle years of the century when he wrote that "the solution of important social problems is furthered by providing through the medium of art a release for the pent-up emotions of our people."[13] An interest in the psychological and developmental value of art activities was spearheaded by the inspirational leadership of Viktor Lowenfeld. Lowenfeld began to publish in the United States just after World War II, and his writings, revised posthumously, are still influential today.

Lowenfeld found a place for art history in his proposals for the art education of adolescents, and he offered some recommendations for teaching art appreciation.[14] But his philosophy of art education primarily centered on the potential of art activities to increase children's creativity and facilitate their development. He was also a strong advocate for the therapeutic value of art activities.[15] Fostering the growth and development of students free of adult interference was an explicit goal set forth by Lowenfeld. He wrote that "all modes of expression but the child's own are foreign to him. We should neither influence nor stimulate the child's imagination in any direction which is not appropriate to his thinking and perception. The child has his own world of experiences and expression."[16] If adult art is "foreign" and much teacher input is interference, it is not easy to imagine a strong place for art history instruction that could be compatible with Lowenfeld's philosophy. Some contemporaries of his were more extreme in their views. Ralph M. Pearson, for example, explicitly advocated an emotional versus an intellectual approach to art education.[17]

In the middle years of this century, when a child-centered approach dominated art education, some educators used art history to aid students in art production.[18] Historical artworks were selected primarily to support production, but the art history component of the art curriculum was spotty at best. Although there has always been some interest in teaching art history throughout the twentieth century, during the late 1940s, the 1950s, and the early 1960s, were not times of strong interest in teaching art history in elementary and secondary schools.

Momentum for Change

In a 1962 article in *Art Education*, entitled "Transition in Art Education: Changing Conceptions of Curriculum and Theory," Manuel Barkan argued for a refocus on works of art after years of neglect: "The study of art appreciation virtually disappeared from most schools, and many art teachers even argued strongly that looking at works of art was *detrimental* for children."[19] Barkan called for renewed attention to the development of instructional materials for teaching art history and criticism. Interest has slowly increased since Barkan's landmark article. Also in 1962, Ralph A. Smith proposed that the method of art-historical inquiry be taught as a component of art instruction.[20] In the 1970s, a number of prominent art educators, including Edmund Feldman, Elliot Eisner, Laura Chapman, Gilbert Clark, and Enid Zimmerman, incorporated art history into their structures for art education.[21] In 1978, Michael McCarthy wrote *Introducing Art History: A Guide for Teachers*, to assist secondary art teachers specifically in teaching art history.[22]

In the 1980s, the National Art Education Association set as its first goal the establishment of art programs that integrate the study of aesthetics, art criticism, art history, and studio art. The Getty Center for Education in the Arts also began its support of a comprehensive approach to teaching art, called discipline-based art education (DBAE), which stresses the study of art production, art criticism, art history, and aesthetics.[23] In the field of art education, interest in teaching art history has never been higher than it is today.

Most art educators agree that art history should be a component of the curriculum from kindergarten through twelfth grade.[24] Art teachers generally believe that art history should be part of the art curriculum, and many incorporate it into their teaching. However, the theoretical basis for that art history instruction is quite limited.[25]

Traditional Teaching Realities at the Elementary Level

Foremost among institutional realities affecting art history at the elementary level is the teacher responsible for the instruction. In some school districts, elementary art teachers are entirely responsible for the art program; in other districts, classroom teachers are responsible; and in some cases, responsibility for art instruction is shared between art specialists and classroom teachers.

When classroom teachers are responsible for art instruction, implementing an art history component requires considerable support. Classroom teachers are likely to have little or no background in art history, making them quite dependent on detailed curriculum support materials. On the other hand, classroom teachers are responsible for other areas within the elementary curriculum that can be coordinated with art history. For example, art history can fit naturally within a social studies program, where interdisciplinary connections with geography, cultural studies, and history can be made.

The wide range of responsibilities of the classroom teacher facilitates interdisciplinary study but can sometimes seem to pit one discipline against another. The school day is finite, yet there always seem to be new demands for added content, from writing across the disciplines to higher-order thinking skills to AIDS awareness to environmental education to fitness programs to more rigorous reading, writing, and arithmetic programs. Teachers interested in relieving the pressures of the school day may be inclined to favor a light-hearted, entertaining, nonthreatening, art program. Hands-on art production projects are traditional breaks in the academic regimen of the day or, in some cases, even rewards for good behavior. Of course, hands-on activities and personal involvement are possible in virtually all areas of the elementary curriculum, but the art program (along with other "special areas") has traditionally borne a large proportion of the burden for such activities.

Other circumstances arise when art teachers are responsible for the art program within the elementary curriculum. Virtually all art teachers have college course work in art history upon which to draw. They are more able to structure their own programs, drawing upon their more substantial education in art. Since a single art teacher often teaches all the children within a school building, that one teacher can implement a sequential curriculum virtually independently. On the other hand, many classroom teachers must be willing and able to cooperate if a sequential program across the grades is to be effective.

The load of classes serviced by one art teacher can vary tremendously from one district to another. One art teacher in one district might teach twenty to twenty-five classes, all in one building. In such circumstances art teachers might have their own art classrooms furnished with materials and equipment, including large reproductions, slide-projection facilities, video equipment, and textbook sets to support a program in art history. Other art teachers might be on call to serve twenty to twenty-five separate buildings, meeting each class of students only once in several months and carrying all the materials and equipment in their cars.

Art teachers can be quite isolated within the school system. When they travel from school to school, they sometimes slip through the bureaucratic structure, forgotten or neglected in the in-service and communication network. Being less numerous than classroom teachers, the work of art teachers may be less well understood than that of the majority of teachers. Unusual expectations can develop in such an environment. Art teachers are often expected to decorate school buildings, act as art supply quartermasters for all teachers in the building, and advise, if not execute, a wide range of visual projects from backdrops for plays to bulletin boards, posters, and parades. At the same time, the art program is often understood to be so nonverbal and noncognitive as to be appropriate for every type of student at all times. If art history content is to be included in an art program, traditional expectations may not be met.

Unfortunately, all too many districts served exclusively by art teachers either have no art supervisor or delegate administration of the art program to a principal or vice-principal who has no art background. Isolated as they are, art teachers need leadership if they are to develop or implement a sequential art program. It is difficult for an administrator who knows very little about art to provide such leadership. Administrators must often leave art teachers to negotiate their own art programs. The result of such a committee-negotiated art curriculum is often a loose structure of compromises written to allow wide options for all teachers. Without some specific agreements, any art history content within such an art curriculum is likely to be little more than a hodgepodge of unconnected supplements.

In some districts, the responsibility for teaching art is shared by classroom teachers and art teachers or by classroom teachers and an art supervisor. Some districts have detailed, sequential art programs taught alternately by the art teacher and the classroom teacher. When each teacher knows what the other teacher has taught and will teach, interdisciplinary coordination can be quite effective.

Art supervisors are usually spread very thin in a school district. Their responsibilities may be less supervision than in-service education, consultation, and demonstration teaching. When art teachers are not available, the importance of a clearly written art curriculum, a regular in-service program, and organized, effective instructional resources increases. Selecting, developing, refining, managing, and evaluating the curriculum, in-service programs, and resources are crucial responsibilities of an art supervisor.

Resources at the Elementary Level

If art history content is to be taught in the elementary schools, instructional resources must be available. Classroom teachers often prefer filmstrips, while art teachers prefer slides. Films, laser disks, videotapes, large and small two-dimensional reproductions, three-dimensional replicas, time lines, maps, artifacts, textbooks, and other materials are among the resources that might be required. Sometimes, art history resources such as filmstrips, slide and cassette programs, videotape sets, or textbooks are included as part of comprehensive commercial art-instruction packages. Since there are many more general classrooms than art classrooms, the market has tended to support the development of instructional materials to be used by classroom teachers.

Art museums continue to be sources for educational programs and instructional resources. Large urban museums such as the Philadelphia Museum of Art and the Metropolitan Museum of Art in New York City offer teaching materials and programs for teachers. The free educational services and reasonably priced reproductions offered by the National Gallery of Art in Washington, D.C., have supported art history teaching across the country for decades. At a local level, regional art and historical museums provide direct access to works of art as well as educational services tailored to regional needs.

As art history has become more vital to art programs, commercial publishers are developing and marketing a much wider range of resources with more substantial art history content. I have not attempted to review all the art history resources on the market but rather to discuss briefly a few selected textbooks.

More than half a century ago, an art history textbook series was available for the fourth, fifth, and sixth grades. V. M. Hillyer and E. G. Huey wrote *A Child's History of Art* in 1939.[26] It was a 443-page book with three parts: a history of painting for fourth grade, a history of sculpture for fifth grade, and a history of architecture for sixth grade. No such comprehensive art history text is available for elementary children today.

Two prominent art textbook series available today do, however, include some art history. Artworks are introduced from the first grade on and within a cultural and historical context beginning at the upper elementary grades. The sixth-grade text, from Guy Hubbard's *Art in Action* series, includes brief introductions to the art of many cultures and to many eras in Western art history. Laura Chapman's *Discover Art* series, like Hubbard's, makes liberal use of reproductions of artworks from around the world and across time.[27] Chapman's fifth-grade text builds art-historical understanding in a number of ways: through a series of lessons on American art, through several architecture lessons, and through graphic design and design history lessons. Her sixth-grade text has a strong art history component: roughly one-third of the sixty lessons focus on art history. (See chapter 7 for further discussion of developmentally appropriate art history instruction for various age levels.)

Traditional Realities and Resources in the Middle Grades

Traditional institutional circumstances affecting art history teaching at the middle and junior high school levels contrast markedly with those at the elementary school level. Middle school usually includes grades five through six or seven; junior high school usually includes grades seven through eight or nine. In most districts, a certified art teacher is responsible for the art program in these middle grades. Students can be expected to have more background knowledge and understanding of history and diverse cultures. Such background education can make the art teacher's task of putting artworks into their cultural and historical contexts much easier.

Generalizing about art programs in middle and junior high school is difficult since the structuring and scheduling of these programs is so varied. Some junior high art classes meet twice a week for a year; others meet once a week. Some classes span a year, some meet for a semester; and some are taught every day within one concentrated quarter. The junior high school exploratory approach tends to result in a segmented school day.

Special pressure is placed on these middle years of a school district's art program. In most schools across the country, these years are the last ones in which art is a required subject for all students and the only years during which art is taught by a certified art teacher. In most parts of the country, if students are going to receive a general education in art after elementary school, it will be in middle or junior high school.

Perhaps because of the scheduling diversity of middle and junior high school, the art history resources for this level have been spotty. Guy Hubbard's *Art in Action* series continues through the seventh and eighth grades.[28] It is richly illustrated with works from various times and cultures. In the majority of lessons the works are presented without information about the cultural contexts from which they come, though in the seventh-grade text some lessons introduce Egyptian, African, Native American, and Mexican art with some reference to cultural contexts. For example, the Mexican art lesson discusses pre-Columbian culture, the Spanish conquest, and some contemporary Mexican-American artists. Hubbard's eighth-grade text also includes a few lessons specifically focused on art history, including one on the Renaissance, one on Mexican painters, and several on architecture.

Gerald F. Brommer and George F. Horn have also written a pair of texts for middle and junior high school.[29] The first text includes a fifteen-page overview of Western art history; the second provides a more developed, twenty-seven-page presentation of Western art history and a short chapter on art with a multicultural perspective. Laura Chapman's junior high texts, *A World of Images* and *Art: Images and Ideas*,[30] include substantial art history information. *A World of Images*, for seventh graders, has three chapters that focus on art history. One chapter presents a global view of art, and the other two present an overview of Western art history from ancient times through the twentieth century. *Art: Images and Ideas*, for eighth graders, also provides three art history chapters—one gives a worldview of art; and the other two present American art from ancient to modern times, with attention paid to the art of Native Americans, Hispanics, African Americans, Asians, and women. In addition, Chapman includes multicultural time lines, art and culture maps, and sample forms for student research in art history.

Traditional Realities and Resources at the High School Level

High school art programs are usually taught exclusively by certified art teachers, with all courses offered as electives. For many years some high schools have offered separate art history courses for advanced placement college credit. These courses tend to be modeled after college art history survey courses. More and more states (over half the states in the United States at the time of this writing) have a fine arts or humanities course requirement for high school graduation. However, the regulations are in most cases sufficiently elastic to allow a broad range of courses to meet the requirement. Students in high school art classes generally tend to be students who are to some degree committed to art (usually the making of art), students who are difficult to schedule and are placed in art class as a convenience, or students who believe that art will provide a recreational or undemanding alternative to other course options. Accustomed to teaching such students, a traditionally trained (mostly studio) art teacher will find that a fine arts requirement will bring in a more representative cross-section of students. When not part of graduation requirements, art programs survive by being popular. Not being considered "academic" has made art courses attractive in the "marketplace" of competing high school electives. Such an atmosphere is not very conducive, however, to initiating an art history course or course component.

High school art history textbooks have been around for a long time. Ida Prentice Whitcomb's *Young People's Story of Art* was first published in 1906; Helen Gardner's *Understanding the Arts* was published in 1932. Other high school art history textbooks published later and still available today in revised editions include E. H. Gombrich's *The Story of Art*, H. W. Janson and Anthony F. Janson's *History of Art for Young People*, Gerald F. Brommer's *Discovering Art History*, and Gene A. Mittler's *Art in Focus*. Jack Hobbs and Richard Salome have included an excellent multicultural survey of art history in their high school text *The Visual Experience*. [31] The recent practice of adopting for college use Gombrich's *Story of Art*, originally written for high school students, evidences a decline in expectations of student performance.[32]

As concern for art history and multicultural education increases, publishers and curriculum developers must broaden their approach. Resources once called "art history" materials can be relabeled "Western art history" materials, resulting in a more focused and honest presentation of information. Supplementary materials addressing various interests such as women in art, non-Western art, the art of the disfranchised, and so forth, can also be developed. Such efforts may be attacked as tokenism or received as interim measures helpful in the transition to a broader philosophy of education. A third alternative is to integrate the art of the world through time into one program, understanding that no single history can ever finally address all the concerns of all interested parties. The need for intellectually sound and culturally sensitive resources for teaching art history is great enough to accommodate the best efforts of many inventive and thoughtful contributions.

The long-established traditions of teaching art history in the elementary and secondary schools of this country are a mixed blessing. On the one hand, these traditions make initial agreement on the importance of teaching art history relatively easy to achieve. On the other hand, they make agreement on the nature and purpose of art history instruction a much more difficult goal to reach.

NOTES

1. Mary Ann Stankiewicz, "Virtue and Good Manners: Toward a History of Art History Instruction," (paper presented at the College Art Association Annual Meeting, San Francisco, Calif., 18 February 1989); and Arthur Efland, *A History of Art Education: Intellectual and Social Currents in Teaching the Visual Arts* (New York: Teachers College Press, 1990).

2. S. Reinach, *Apollo: An Illustrated Manual of the History of Art throughout the Ages* (New York: Charles Scribner's Sons, 1922), p. x.

3. Mary Ann Stankiewicz, "Rules and Invention: From Ornament to Design in Art Education," in *Framing the Past: Essays on Art Education*, ed. Donald Soucy and Mary Ann Stankiewicz (Reston, Va.: National Art Education Association, 1990), pp. 89–101.

4. John S. Clark, Mary Dana Hicks, and Walter S. Perry, *Teachers' Manual for The Prang Elementary Course in Art Instruction, Books III and IV* (Boston: Prang Educational Co., 1889), p. 32.

5. L. L. Wilson, *Picture Study in Elementary Schools* (New York: Macmillan, 1899), p. ix.

6. Katherine Morris Lester, *Great Pictures and Their Stories, Book Eight* (New York: Menttzer Bush and Co., 1927), p. 125.

7. William G. Whitford, *An Introduction to Art Education* (New York: D. Appleton and Co., 1929), p. 30; and Bernice Starr Moore, *People and Art: A Textbook in Art Appreciation* (Boston: Allyn and Bacon, 1938), pp. 128–29.

8. Walter H. Klar and Theodore M. Dillaway, *The Appreciation of Pictures* (New York: Brown-Robertson Co., 1930).

9. Evan J. Kern, "The Study of Art Criticism in the Classroom," ed. Eldon Katter (Kutztown, Pa.: Kutztown University, 1984), p. 7.

10. Laura H. Chapman, *Instant Art, Instant Culture: The Unspoken Policy for American Schools* (New York: Teachers College Press, 1982), p. 3.

11. Harriet Goldstein and Vetta Goldstein, *Art in Everyday Life* (New York: Macmillan, 1932); Leon Loyal Winslow, *The Integrated School Art Program* (New York: McGraw-Hill, 1939); Ray Faulkner, Edwin Ziegfeld, and Gerald Hill, *Art Today: An Introduction to the Fine and Functional Arts* (New York: Henry Holt and Co., 1941); and Florence W. Nicholas, Mabel B. Trilling, Margaret Lee, and Elmer A. Stephan, *Art for Young America* (Peoria, Ill.: Manual Arts Press–Chas. A Bennett Co., 1946, 1952, 1960, 1962).

12. June King McFee, *Preparation for Art* (San Francisco: Wadsworth Publishing Co., 1961).

13. Eugene Neuhaus, *The Appreciation of Art* (Boston: Ginn and Co., 1924), p. 231.

14. Viktor Lowenfeld, *Creative and Mental Growth: A Textbook on Art Education* (New York: Macmillan, 1947), pp. 248–50; and Lowenfeld, *Creative and Mental Growth: A Textbook on Art Education*, 3d ed. (New York: Macmillan, 1957), pp. 33–34.

15. Lowenfeld, *Creative and Mental Growth*, 3d ed., p. 2.

16. Ibid., pp. 12–13, 14.

17. Ralph M. Pearson, *The New Art Education*, rev. ed. (New York: Harper and Brothers Publishers, 1953), pp. 33–42.

18. Henry Schaeffer-Simmern, *The Unfolding of Artistic Activity: Its Basis, Processes, and Implications* (Berkeley: University of California Press, 1948), p. 174; and Daniel M. Mendelowitz, *Children Are Artists: An Introduction to Children's Art for Teachers and Parents* (Stanford: Stanford University Press, 1953), p. 56.

19. Manuel Barkan, "Transition in Art Education: Changing Conceptions of Curriculum and Theory," *Art Education* 15, no. 7 (1962): 12–18.

20. Ralph A. Smith, "The Structure of Art-Historical Knowledge in Art Education," *Studies in Art Education* 4, no. 1 (1962): 23–33.

21. Edmund Burke Feldman, *Becoming Human through Art: Aesthetic Experience in the School* (Englewood Cliffs, N.J.: Prentice-Hall, 1970); Elliot W. Eisner, *Educating Artistic Vision* (New York: Macmillan, 1972); Laura H. Chapman, *Approaches to Art in Education* (New York: Harcourt, Brace, Jovanovich, 1978); and Gilbert A. Clark and Enid Zimmerman, "Professional Roles and Activities for Art Education," in *Research Readings for Discipline-based Art Education: A Journey Beyond Creating*, ed. Stephen M. Dobbs (Reston, Va.: National Art Education Association, 1988), pp. 78–97.

22. Michael McCarthy, *Introducing Art History: A Guide for Teachers* (Toronto: The Ontario Institute for Studies in Education, 1978).

23. Margaret Klempay DiBlasio, "Continuing the Translation: Further Delineation of the DBAE Fomat," *Studies in Art Education* 26, no. 4 (1985): 197–205.

24. Laura Chapman, "Teacher Viewpoint Survey: The Results," *School Arts* 78, no. 9 (1979): 3; and Laura Chapman and Connie Newton, "Teacher Viewpoint Survey," *School Arts* 90, no. 1 (1990): 41–45.

25. Ralph A. Smith, "The Changing Image of Art Education: Theoretical Antecedents of Discipline-based Art Education," in *Discipline-based Art Education*, ed. Ralph A. Smith (Urbana: University of Illinois Press, 1987), p. 23.

26. V. H. Hillyer and E. G. Huey, *A Child's History of Art* (New York: D. Appleton-Century Company, 1939).

27. Guy Hubbard, *Art in Action*, 6 vols. (San Diego: Coronado Publishers, 1987); and Laura H. Chapman, *Discover Art* (Worchester, Mass.: Davis Publications, 1985).

28. Guy Hubbard, *Art in Action: First Course* and *Art in Action: Second Course* (San Diego: Coronado Publishers, 1986).

29. Gerald F. Brommer and George F. Horn, *Art in Your Visual Environment* and *Art in Your World* (Worchester, Mass.: Davis Publications, 1985).

30. Laura H. Chapman, *A World of Images*, and *Art: Images and Ideas* (Worchester, Mass.: Davis Publications, 1991).

31. Ida Prentice Whitcomb, *Young People's Story of Art* (New York: Dodd, Mead and Co., 1923); Helen Gardner, *Understanding the Arts* (New York: Harcourt, Brace and Co., 1923); E. H. Gombrich, *The Story of Art* (London: Phaidon, 1950); H. W. Janson and Anthony F. Janson, *History of Art for Young People* (New York: Harry N. Abrams, 1987); Gerald F. Brommer, *Discovering Art History*, 2d ed. (Worchester, Mass.: Davis Publications, 1988); Gene A. Mittler, *Art in Focus* (Mission Hills, Calif.: Glencoe Publishing Co., 1986); Jack Hobbs and Richard Salome, *The Visual Experience* (Worchester, Mass.: Davis Publications, 1992).

32. Bradford R. Collins, "H. W. Janson, *History of Art* and E. H. Gombrich, *The Story of Art*," *Art Journal* 48, no. 1 (1989): 90–95.

6

The Nature and Educational Uses of Art History: What Is Art History and Why Should It Be Taught?

This chapter argues for the importance of including art history as a part of general education and considers different educational implications for teaching art history as information and as inquiry. Some justifications for teaching art history are rooted in its evolving nature; others are based on art history's significance among the arts and humanities; still others derive from art history's capacity to support learning in other areas of the curriculum. Goals are offered as each justification is considered in turn.

Justifications Drawn from the Discipline of Art History

Art History in a Visual Society

Some art historians have claimed, especially in recent years, that the essence of art history is broader than previously imagined and that the histories of advertising and of design are not peripheral but essential to understanding the history of art.[1] If this is so, then a powerful justification for teaching art history lies in its ability to help us understand and make choices in our visual culture.

In the last decades of the twentieth century, America has become a visual society. Everything from soap and clothing to ideas and politicians is visually sold to the public. It can be argued that, in the carefully managed performance that is a presidential media campaign, the image of a presidential candidate is as powerful as the candidate's words. The importance and sophistication of image in politics has increased steadily since 1960, when analysts credited John F. Kennedy's more appealing television image for his victory over Richard Nixon in their debate. The same powerful visual tactics are used by Madison Avenue to market everything from children's designer athletic shoes to automobiles.

It is not easy to separate one's voting, purchasing, or other decision making from the marketing techniques used to influence that decision making. Consider for a moment the Marlboro Man, an icon of successful advertising for more than twenty years. In recent years, a quite visible surgeon general's warning, presented in clear type in a white box on each Marlboro ad, informs consumers of dangers ranging from lung cancer to birth defects. Yet the image of the cowboy commands attention and product loyalty. Years ago, Marlboro had a verbal slogan, "The cigarette that won the West." The company has dropped the slogan but maintains the image. Cowboys, campfires, horses, saddles, and cattle are not very closely connected logically to either cigarette smoking or consumers' everyday lives. However, those visual images, not the explicit, frightening words of the surgeon general, seem to move many consumers to buy cigarettes—and not just any cigarettes, but Marlboros. So too can the visual marketing techniques of advertising be employed in an attempt to affect voting behavior.

There are several ways to gain perspective, that is, to distance oneself sufficiently in order to perceive more clearly. One way is to travel in space, another is to travel in time. When I first visited Arizona, I found it to be different from my home in Pennsylvania, and I was drawn to make comparisons. I realized that the streets in Pennsylvania are very narrow, that the sidewalks and alleys are amazingly clean, and that Pennsylvanians (at least as I am familiar with them) are less likely to greet a stranger on the street than are Arizonans. Having visited a different place, I was able to notice details and nuances that previously escaped me.

Visiting another time can assist us in a similar fashion. History is the discipline that helps us gain perspective through the study of the past. As new policies are developed in and toward what used to be the Soviet Union, we find ourselves looking back to earlier periods in history (to czarist Russia, to Stalin's Soviet Union, and to the cold war) to help us understand the choices of today. We can do something similar with art history. We might examine, for instance, World War I and World War II patriotic posters to gain some distance on the use of visual imagery to influence political decisions. We might examine Coca-Cola and Chevrolet advertisements from the 1950s to focus on visual marketing techniques used to promote consumer goods. Figures 11 and 12 provide examples of two types of designed objects from our ordinary experience that might be studied art-historically. Beautifully crafted ancient Incan architectural stonework leads one to see afresh the mass-produced, modular building techniques that dominate modern American architecture.

Like long-distance travel, history can provide a different set of circumstances that allows us, even stimulates us, to reflect on present circum-

Fig. 11. "Evolving 7-Up Bottle Designs," Mary Erickson Collection. Photo: Nicolas Bowen.

stances with clearer vision. A goal might be to teach art-historical inquiry. This goal, drawn from the discipline of art history, might be justified as a means to better understand visual culture. The distance that art history can provide can serve society as we prepare students to be responsible, autonomous citizens within that society.

Art History in a Multicultural Society

Traditional art historians and new art historians generally agree that art-historical inquiry should include a wide range of cultures from all parts of the globe. In the increasingly pluralistic culture that comprises the United States, the necessity of a multicultural approach to art history seems more and more evident, especially if we value the extraordinary artistic richness this pluralistic culture offers. The mass media are already

Fig. 12. "Popular Sheet Music Illustration, 1890–1950," Mary Erickson Collection. Photo: Nicolas Bowen.

powerful agents of cultural uniformity. Witness the transcontinental uniformity of the shopping mall. A shopping mall in Mesa, Arizona, is virtually indistinguishable from one in Reading, Pennsylvania. The same stores—McDonalds, GAP, GNC, Radio Shack—are there, only arranged a bit differently. One could be 2,500 miles east were it not for the regional addition of two Indian jewelry stores and a western wear shop. Great numbers of people from Nebraska to New Orleans to the Napa Valley dress like the same television and movie stars and walk and talk like the same media personalities.

If the richness of our artistic heritage is to thrive, we must study the arts, crafts, and architecture of nondominant as well as dominant cultures within our society. Pennsylvania German folk arts, Northwest Coast Native American carvings, Appalachian crafts, and ethnic street fairs contribute significant richness and diversity to the artistic heritage of America.

A multicultural approach to teaching art history is justifiable as well on democratic grounds. Unless we are prepared to return to an outmoded melting pot philosophy, we must recognize that the United States is not exclusively white, Anglo-Saxon, and Protestant and that diverse racial, ethnic, and religious groups strive for equal rights in this democracy. The artistic traditions of these diverse groups have a place in the art history taught in the public schools in this country. Thus two additional goals drawn from the discipline of art history might be: (1) that students learn that America's art is diverse and has many ethnic, cultural, and religious roots; and (2) that students learn to appreciate and support the multiple roots of America's artistic culture.

Art history education in a pluralistic democracy should reflect and serve the diverse cultures that comprise its population. Indeed, distinguishing American culture from other world cultures is becoming increasingly difficult. As Americans listen to Japanese radios, drive German, Swedish, and Yugoslovian cars, carry tote bags made in Kenya, wear shoes made in Italy, and dress in clothes made in India and Korea, one must recognize the increasing interdependencies among all cultures. As artworks from around the world serve as vehicles to understanding, art-historical studies can help students begin to develop as citizens of the world.

Art History and Our Cultural Heritage

Some art historians and educators argue for the necessity of maintaining contact with artistic traditions. America is a society in danger of losing much of its heritage. Educational reformers have much to say about cultural illiteracy. E. D. Hirsch cites studies showing that "two thirds of our seventeen year-olds do not know that the Civil War occurred between 1850 and 1900. Three-quarters do not know what *reconstruction* means. Half do not know the meaning of *Brown decision* and cannot identify either Stalin or Churchill."[2] When teenagers can name more brands of beer than presidents of the United States, one can only wonder at the degree of their ignorance about art history. How unconnected young people today must be from the history of ideas and feelings expressed through the art of the world. Accordingly, two additional goals drawn from the discipline of art history might be: (1) that students learn that art of the Western world has changed in many ways and for many reasons from ancient times to the present; and (2) that students learn that art has been produced all over the world—in Africa, Asia, Latin America, Europe, North America, and Oceania.

Justifications Drawn from Aesthetic Education and Humanities Education

Art History and Aesthetic Experience

Although definitions of aesthetic education vary, most advocates center their goals on increasing the student's capacity for aesthetic experience, with special attention given to fostering aesthetic experience with artworks. A goal of aesthetic education is the development of knowledge, skills, and attitudes that enable students to experience artworks (and sometimes other objects and events) for the sake of those experiences alone. Aesthetic experience is traditionally understood as an intrinsically rewarding experience, as distinct from extrinsic economic, religious, practical, scientific, or other values.[3] Some degree of aesthetic response can be achieved although students may have minimal background information. We can learn to enjoy stylistic characteristics of diverse artworks even though we know little about their cultural significance. Aesthetic enjoyment can be drawn from the colors, patterns, and forms of an African mask, a Persian miniature, a Japanese woodcut, or a northern Renaissance altarpiece. The formalist philosophy that dominated art education for much of this century accepts and promotes this kind of aesthetic response.

It can be argued that a narrow, formalistic sense of aesthetic appreciation limits young people's understanding of the nature and value of art. Formalism alone cannot provide the depth of aesthetic experience that a fuller understanding of cultural context can. In chapter 3, it was shown that the response to a Japanese painting can change dramatically when one understands its evocation of Zen meditation and persistence. One need not look to non-Western cultures or even to unfamiliar artworks to discover the importance of cultural context to art appreciation. Many are familiar with Rembrandt's *Syndics of the Cloth Guild*. They probably know that it is old and that it is Dutch because the costumes look dated and the image is used to sell a brand of cigars called Dutch Masters. But most people do not know the painting's significance as a manifestation of the rising seventeenth-century merchant class, equivalent to today's corporate photograph of a board of trustees. Rembrandt's use of light and his rich browns are marvelous to behold, but so are the businesslike manner and corporate values of seventeenth-century burghers a marvel to contemplate.

The degree to which aesthetic value should play a role in art-historical judgment is a hotly contested issue among art historians. Lorenz Eitner set the stage for the debate in his article "Art History and the Sense of Quality," in which he argued for the primacy of aesthetic quality: "The test of life in a work of art is its power to rouse our senses to a state of responsive happiness which communicates itself to our whole being: this power is the distinctive quality of the work of art." He concluded by claiming: "It is the irony of the situation that the quiet hoarding of the connoisseurs has more influence on the shape of art history, in the long run, than the theoretical ingenuity of historians."[4]

The position that aesthetic experience does and should shape art history is under attack by the new art historians. Tom Gretton articulates their viewpoint in his article "New Lamps for Old": "For most art historians 'art' does not designate a set of types of object—all paintings, sculptures, prints and so forth—but a subset arrived at by a more or less openly acknowledged selection on the basis of aesthetic criteria. But aesthetic criteria have no existence outside a specific historical situation; aesthetic values are falsely taken to be timeless."[5] Thus the very notion of aesthetic value is questioned by some. The implications for education are clear: "If understanding art is seen as good, then failure to understand is humiliating. Learning to understand, in as much as it involves accepting authority, reinforces subordination for one's own good, and in particular reinforces the notion that cultural authorities articulate not particular forms of social hierarchy but eternal values, the values of aesthetic worth."[6]

Early picture study and some art appreciation programs exemplified this notion of learning about selected artworks for one's moral and social good. For Gretton, aesthetic value is not an acceptable basis for selecting objects for art-historical study, and he warns against taking any approach that will ultimately "reinforce the notion that art is a transcendental value." Gretton comments that "the subset of images which we call art has become increasingly unimportant" and we should look to some alternative "image history" to replace the inadequate discipline of art history.[7]

Some art educators have voiced similar criticisms of aesthetic education. Vincent Lanier characterized aesthetic education as elitist on the grounds that it disdained or totally disregarded any art not accepted by museums and galleries.[8] Other educators, most notably Ralph A. Smith, have argued that aesthetic experience should be central to art education. Smith and Albert Levi argue that the choice for aesthetic experience is not a choice against democracy but a choice for excellence. Such diversity of opinion keeps art education exciting and open to new ideas.[9]

A Compromise

Is there no room for compromise between two such contradictory positions? Must the idea of aesthetic value be eliminated from art education in the name of social fairness? Perhaps there is no room for compromise right now, at the cutting edge of the art-historical debate. However, some sort of compromise that considers both sides of the issue would improve the present art history instruction in elementary and secondary schools. As long as public schools continue to exist in something like their present form, they will continue to maintain certain ideologies, such as the transmission of the culture's dominant, traditional values. In art history instruction, this belief translates into the transmission of traditional aesthetic values. However, we who work within the educational establishment need not be restricted from learning from the broader views of the new art historians. We can advocate attempts to include a range of aesthetic traditions from various Western and non-Western cultures and from various sectors of our visual heritage.

Goals proposed earlier in this chapter are drawn from the discipline of art history. Three more goals for teaching art history, drawn from the goals of aesthetic education, might be: (1) that students learn that aesthetic values vary from age to age and from culture to culture; (2) that students learn that it is possible to respond aesthetically to a wide range of visual objects; and (3) that students learn to understand and enjoy the art of many cultures, including their own.

Art History and the Humanities

Definitions of humanities education almost always include art history as an essential constituent discipline. The aims of humanities education include both coming to understand what it is to be human and coming to appreciate human values. If, as most commentators agree, the arts are major repositories for human values, then an understanding of their history is central to an education in the humanities. Controversy arises when the values of the established hierarchies of Western civilization are assumed to be the only values warranting inclusion in a humanities education. The arts of women, nondominant cultures, and non-Western civilizations have not always found their way into humanities education. Once again, schools can learn to improve art history instruction by considering the traditional as well as the newer conceptions of humanities education. Two goals for art history drawn from the goals of humanistic education might be: (1) that students learn to recognize artworks as manifestations of values held in different cultures at different times; and (2) that students learn to value art as an important realm of human accomplishment that can inform us about how we have come to be who we are.

Justifications Drawn from Other Educational Needs

In addition to justifications for teaching art history based on the discipline itself and on the broader fields of aesthetic education and the humanities, teaching art history can also be justified as supporting a broad range of areas across the curriculum.

Art History and Social Studies

Social studies is a major elementary and secondary school content area that can be effectively coordinated with art history content. Art history can be as much a part of history education as it is a part of art education. The National Council for the Social Studies (NCSS) Task Force on Early Childhood/Elementary Social Studies defines social studies as "the study of political, economical, cultural, and environmental aspects of societies in the past, present, and future." The task force further states that "active, curious children need, want, and are able to learn skills . . . so that they can make generalizations and integrate new information into a developing system of knowledge." Children should understand "how the multiplicity of cultures within society and the world has developed. Children need to recognize the contributions of each culture and explore its value system."[10]

Studying art history demands an interdisciplinary approach to learning that integrates information not only about artworks but also about the politics, religion, philosophy, economics, and social structure of various cultures. Studying Leonardo's notebooks or Raphael's painting *The School of Athens* is not just a study in visual style. These works embody the life and times of the Renaissance, a time of discovery and of science, a time to explore the idea of space. Painters explored space as they developed the system of linear perspective. Humanists explored the individual's place in the order of things. For better or for worse, Columbus explored space by sailing west to reach the east.

One might legitimately ask whether a distinction exists between history and art history. Much of what we understand of prehistory and early civilization is based almost entirely on paintings, sculpture, crafts, and architecture. Francie Alexander and Charlotte Crabtree, writing about California's new history—social science curriculum, argue that "teachers need to incorporate literature, *art*, music, primary documents and social history records that enliven these [historical] studies and increase the chances that students will enjoy and remember what they have learned."[11] Artworks are not only aesthetic objects but are marvelous "primary documents" of history.

The NCSS Task Force urges teachers not to teach only information acquisition but to use social studies education to teach skills such as "collecting, organizing, and interpreting data; thinking skills such as hypothesizing, comparing, drawing inferences; decision making skills such as considering alternatives and consequences; [and] interpersonal skills such as seeing others' points of view."[12] Art-historical inquiry can give students opportunities to develop such research, thinking, and decision-making skills.

Art History and General Education

Many areas of learning can be enriched by art history. The Pennsylvania Board of Education has adopted twelve quality goals of education that are presented as the central justification of education within the commonwealth. Every state, region, or district has some set of basic assumptions about its goals for public education. Pennsylvania's goals, though unique to the commonwealth, are not dissimilar from those set forth in various forms across the United States. Most of these goals are supported by art history instruction. For example, an analytic thinking goal in Pennsylvania is "the development of problem solving skills." To fulfill this objective, art history instruction might be tailored so that students learn how to ask questions, seek information, develop hypotheses, and draw conclusions about the meaning of artworks from other times and cultures. Another Pennsylvania goal is for students to understand others, to gain "knowledge of individual similarity and diversity."[13] Through art history students might learn that (as well as how and why) women, African Americans, Hispanics, and other ethnic groups have all produced significant and meaningful artworks.

Art history instruction can be used to reinforce a wide range of general education goals. Those goals can be drawn from the discipline of art history itself, from the goals of aesthetic education and humanities education, or, as noted above, from other general education goals. When integration across the curriculum is chosen as a priority within a district or school, art history has much to offer.

Teaching Art History as Artworks

Teachers have broad definitions for the phrase "teaching art history." At least three distinct approaches are taken: (1) teaching art history as artworks (a misconception); (2) teaching art history as information; and (3) teaching art history as inquiry.

A great number of art teachers simply teach about artworks, considering this to be "art history." Many art teachers use artworks to illustrate sensory elements, formal principles, subject matter selection, expressive power, and technical processes. A Rembrandt is shown to illustrate contrasting light and dark values; a Wyeth is used to illustrate compositional structure; an O'Keeffe is used to illustrate choice of subject matter; a Picasso embodies expressiveness; and a Van Gogh exemplifies technique. The name of the artist is probably introduced. Other factors such as the date of the work or the culture within which it was produced are less likely to be provided. These activities have as much, or more, to contribute to an art production or art criticism lesson as to an art history lesson. While showing artworks to young people can be part of an excellent art education, it is a misconception to call it teaching art history. Art historians would likely not recognize such instruction as teaching art history.

A number of art teachers do more than expose students to artworks of the past. Some present artworks chronologically and perhaps even cross-culturally. Tools such as time lines and maps help teachers and students relate isolated artists and works to times and places, thereby building a base for art-historical understanding.

Some art teachers introduce art-historical styles in their classes. Period styles are relatively easily listed and presented, and many art teachers provide such categories. Students learn general characteristics of Impressionism, cubism, or surrealism, though much less often medieval, Renaissance, or baroque styles. Years ago, when I taught high school, I set aside Thursdays for art history. I called Thursday "discussion day"; some of my students called it "disgusting day." I remember requiring that they be able to distinguish Doric, Ionic, and Corinthian styles of Greek architecture. I knew these distinctions were part of art history because they were in my college art history text. They were also relatively easy to list and present. However, I do not believe that I or my students understood why these distinctions were important. I taught my students how to identify an architectural style by looking at capitals on the tops of columns. The students learned very little, however, about the relationship of the capital to the columns or to the general proportions of the building and they learned even less about Greek architecture as a reflection of cultural beliefs. Nor were students introduced to the Greeks' conception of the Doric order as masculine and the Ionic order as feminine. Looking back to the discussion of Greek architecture in chapter 2, one might conclude that architectural orders are not what is most important; instead students should come to understand how classic Greek architecture was a celebration of Greek humanism (as opposed to the supernatural ideal of earlier civilizations).

Learning to recognize art-historical styles is an esoteric skill within the much larger discipline of art-historical scholarship. Taught in isolation, style recognition is likely to be boring and uninvolving. Teachers often attach some relevance to style recognition by teaching styles in the context of art production lessons. A better idea would be to place styles within their cultural contexts.

Teaching Art History as Information

A second way to teach art history is to teach it as information. Virtually all art teachers and a few elementary classroom teachers have taken art history courses in college. Most art teachers have had little more than introductory survey courses. The quantity of information students are routinely expected to recall is tremendous. This is especially true if one intends to teach art history within a general art curriculum that includes art production, criticism, and aesthetics. A review of chapter 2 will remind the reader of the range of objects that art historians have studied, from paintings and etchings to quilts and carvings, from jades and bronzes to mass-produced consumer goods, from ceramics to calligraphy, from manuscript illuminations to photographs and video images.

Selecting Artworks for Study

One way to cut through this volume of art-historical information is to settle on a list of important works. Teachers may not be able to teach everything they consider important in art history, but students should become familiar with such traditionally well-known names as Michelangelo, Rembrandt, Van Gogh, Picasso, and O'Keeffe.

Out of a commitment to tradition, some teachers have been eager to accept a canon of major artworks. But this canon has come under attack within the field of art history as Eurocentric, elitist, racist, and sexist. The works of nondominant classes are neglected while the works of the empowered continue to hold sway. For example, two feminist art historians propose that "the definition of craft as a low art form has been used to keep the female in her powerless place."[14]

New art historians have challenged the historical judgments that tradition presents as certainties. In the introduction to *The New Art History*, for example, the editors critically review the writings of a traditional art historian as "certainties [that] were not so much wrong as limited and uncomplicated."[15] Chapter 3 presents in detail the debate on art history's canons. Those charged with teaching art history in the elementary and secondary grades need accurate information, some fair way to limit that information, and some way to make that information comprehensible to young learners. They need information that is not so wrong, "limited," and "uncomplicated." Because there are few hours available for art history instruction in elementary and secondary education, art teachers must exercise clear principles for selecting the information to be provided.

Many teachers limit their choices to European and American artworks of the late nineteenth and twentieth century, seldom venturing more than 150 years into the past. Some teachers are fascinated by a particular period or culture and devote a great amount of time to that culture to the exclusion of others. Is the teaching of art history successful if a month is devoted to the work of Escher while Vermeer is never mentioned? Is art history instruction adequate when two weeks are spent on Ukrainian Easter eggs while Central and South American art is never seen? Though selecting art history content is difficult and controversial, teachers need guidance in making choices.

The art history component of an art curriculum might focus attention on a set of traditional and nontraditional canons. In the elementary grades, well-known and admired artists might be selected as exemplars of the traditional canon. If only two or three painters will be studied from the Renaissance, Leonardo, Michelangelo, and Raphael might be chosen over Del Sarto or Correggio. If only one or two Michelangelo sculptures will be studied, *Moses*, the *Pieta*, or *David* might be chosen over less well known works. Georgia O'Keeffe's *Rancho Taos* might be selected over her early watercolors. In areas such as graphic design, folk art, and crafts, similar traditional and nontraditional canons can be identified. The chairs and writing instruments in the Museum of Modern Art may constitute the traditional canon, while lawn furniture and BIC pens found at a yard sale might be included in a nontraditional canon. In a sequential art history program from kindergarten through twelfth grade, students made familiar with the traditional canons can also benefit from study of lesser-known artworks.

As the discipline of art history evolves, consensus may be reached regarding those artworks that are most significant from an art-historical perspective. In the meantime, educators should be guided in their selection by a clear understanding of why art history is being taught. Clear goals can serve as arbiters as the debate in art history and art education continues.

Textbooks can be helpful in establishing a range of works and cultures to be considered, especially in high school art history courses. However, such courses are not offered in many schools, and when they are, only a small fraction of all students enroll. If art-historical information is to become part of a general education, it must be taught as a segment within broad-based art courses. Since most high school graduates do not elect to take an art history or even a general art course, art-historical information must be introduced in elementary, middle, or junior high schools.

Providing a General Structure

The younger the learner, the greater the need for a limited and uncomplicated structure for teaching art history. One of the first questions to consider when planning the art history segment of an elementary or secondary art program is whether or not information should be presented chronologically. Some teachers have advocated a reverse chronological approach, but problems arise when one considers cultural influences on artistic change. Knowledge of earlier works and times is often necessary to understand later works and times. It is difficult to appreciate the revolutionary fervor of David's paintings without knowing the images of aristocratic decadence of the rococo painters. (In chapter 3, a chronological evolution of David's painting based on changes in the ideology of his patrons is outlined.) Similarly, it is difficult to appreciate the humanism of the Renaissance without understanding the religion-dominated culture of the Middle Ages. (A detailed discussion of this transition is in chapter 2.) A thematic approach to curriculum organization can cut through chronological structures. For example, in chapter 2 it is suggested that the artworks of agrarian cultures might be compared even though they might have been produced thousands of years apart.

An advantage of a chronological approach is the use of sequence. Sequence of instructional presentation can be used to reinforce sequence in historical time. However, other means such as time lines can also reinforce understanding of historical time sequence.

Perhaps the most important structuring device in elementary and secondary art history instruction is the narrative. Art history, like general history, is a story that is factual; and like history, there is more than one factual story. Art history is like science in its quest for an understanding of the facts; however, it is like art in its narrative form. Artistic qualities such as unity, balance, rhythm, and focal point apply to the writing of histories, or stories, of art. These artistic qualities can contribute to the understanding and involvement of students as they study a story of art.

I recently had the opportunity to devote several months to developing a storyline for a children's story of art. My goal was to write a narrative that presented an overview of Western art history and an introduction to non-Western art history for grades one through six. The story was to be simplest at the beginning and become more complex through the years. It was to coordinate with the elementary social studies curriculum. Each grade's segment was limited in length in acknowledgment of the broad-based art program within which it was intended to be taught. I found the task invigorating. Tying all the strings of the narrative together was the closest I ever expect to come to novel writing. An outline of the curriculum "A Story of Art in the World" is provided in appendix 1.

The storyline of "A Story of Art in the World" attempts to open up the traditional canons with multicultural lessons and with lessons outside the canon of fine art. With some exceptions, each lesson has three parts. (Two sample lessons from the curriculum are provided in appendix 2.) The first part attempts to immerse the students in a culture or era. In the second part, key works (often from the traditional canon) are examined as artworks and as cultural artifacts. In the third part, students are led to apply concepts from the lesson to their own lives (often with a focus on nontraditional canons). For example, in "The Great House of Egypt," students are introduced to ancient Egyptian culture through a discussion of farming along the Nile. In the second part of the lesson, in which selected paintings, sculptures, and architecture are examined, children are shown how clothing, furniture, and size were used in art to show who was important. To conclude, children are asked to notice visual clues that people sometimes use today to show that they are special.

The third part of each lesson focuses on questions that apply ideas from the lesson to the lives and interests of students. A number of these activities direct students toward art-historical inquiry. Several activities are specifically intended to engage students in inquiry. The next portion of this chapter takes a look at the possibilities of teaching students to inquire art-historically. Art-historical inquiry is considered in terms of three issues: how facts can be established; how historical interpretations are developed; and how narratives or explanations are developed that account for change through time and across cultures.

Teaching Art History as Inquiry

Replicative and Generative Inquiry

Two distinct types of art-historical inquiry can be undertaken in the classroom; replicative and generative. Replicative inquiry is rediscovery of accepted knowledge. Generative inquiry is inquiry that has never before been undertaken.¹⁶ Both can be valuable processes within an art history program. The classic high school term paper is a prime example of replicative research. Students are asked to locate, read, analyze, ponder, and synthesize what others have concluded about a subject, and then they are asked to share their conclusions and synthesis in the form of a written or oral report.

Interesting activities have been developed by teachers to help students come to understand traditionally accepted information in art history. A high school art teacher concluding a lesson on Renaissance painting shows pairs of slides contrasting High Renaissance and baroque paintings. The students are asked to compare and contrast the two sets of slides. Actively analyzing and comparing, they reach conclusions about general characteristics of painting in the two periods. This exercise is a marvelous way to engage students actively in thinking about art history. The students' conclusions are predictable, like the results of a chemistry "experiment" following procedures outlined in a high school laboratory manual.

Another example of replicative inquiry in art history instruction involves sorting reproductions into stylistic groupings and placing them in chronological order. The students "discover" styles and sequences that are well accepted in the field of art history. If a student "discovers" that Impressionism occurred after cubism, the replicative "experiment" went wrong. Replicative inquiry is an excellent instructional method for teaching art history. Although new information is not generated, established information is introduced indirectly.

Generative inquiry in art history leads into the unknown and is therefore generally more difficult but potentially more rewarding. The process is engaging and participatory, and the results are not predictable. In generative inquiry, students are challenged to ask new questions about artists and artworks of the past,¹⁷ or they are challenged to inquire about more-familiar, less-studied visual artifacts such as advertising design, fashion, local art, or popular art.

Is teaching generative art-historical inquiry a worthwhile goal within an art program? Is the acquisition of information sufficient for a complete understanding of art history? Is history adequately taught if students are unable to raise historical issues? Is science adequately taught without experimentation? Education is more than the acquisition of knowledge. Skills and attitudes are also part of the content of education. This issue is raised at the very outset of this book in the context of art-historical scholarship: "one is never to believe experts without thinking for oneself." The axiom holds not only for art historians but for all of us.

Students should learn to think for themselves about art history for several reasons. First, they will have an inaccurate understanding of the discipline if they understand nothing of its methods. Minimally, students should come to realize that the art-historical information presented to them was established as a result of the curiosity and investigation of art historians.[18] Art historians think for themselves and sometimes disagree with each other to reach conclusions. Their thinking and disagreement help us all to better understand artworks from the past and from other cultures.

Students should also learn to think for themselves about art history simply to meet the general goals of education. Art-historical inquiry requires higher-order thinking skills that are too seldom present in the elementary and secondary curriculum. Authentic generative inquiry is intrinsically more interesting and can therefore be a means of increasing student motivation. Understanding the method, not only the information, that characterizes a discipline can empower students to move beyond the limitations of their curriculum. When planning instruction in a discipline that is as information intensive as art history and in courses that are as short on instructional time as art courses, fostering inquiry is doubly important. When tough choices must be made about which artworks, periods, and cultures to study, encouraging art-historical inquiry can enable students to investigate neglected areas independently. This empowering may instill in the students an encompassing curiosity about visual objects and an interest in how people of other times and other places saw the world. It can also serve them outside the formal structures of schooling as they face their own worlds.

Three Categories of Inquiry

Art-historical inquiry can be defined as establishing facts, interpreting meaning, and accounting for change.

These statements make different sorts of claims. Much of what art historians attempt to do is to establish basic facts about works. They make claims about what an artwork looked like when it was produced; about how an artwork was made, what subjects are depicted, and how the work is formally organized; and about who made the artwork, for whom, when, and where. All such claims are factual claims. An artwork either did or did not have certain qualities when it was made; it was either made by a certain process or it was not; and so forth. We know that art historians have sometimes been wrong in their factual claims. However, what they attempt to establish are matters of fact.

One might categorize art historians' basic factual claims into three groups: imagined restoration, description, and attribution. Imagined restoration is the process of determining how an artwork appeared when it was produced. Description is the process of examining an artwork in great detail and reporting one's findings. Attribution is the process of examining evidence in and outside the work that leads to a conclusion about who produced the work, for whom, when, and where.

Art historians make additional claims that are interpretive, not factual. Art-historical interpretation is the process of making sense of an artwork within its own context. Art historians must learn to remove themselves from the here and now and to imagine themselves there and then to interpret an artwork. An art-historical interpretation states what an artwork was about for the artist who made it, for contemporary viewers who saw it, and within the context of the culture in which it was produced. Art-historical interpretations include claims about the contemporary meaning or significance of an individual artwork that are not factual but are inextricably involved with human values. Interpretive claims are judged on their comprehensiveness and credibility.

Art historians also make claims that may be called accounts or explanations. With the accumulation of many factual and interpretive claims, patterns and divergences emerge among artworks of different times and places. Art-historical styles are identified in order to describe similarities and differences. Art-historical accounts attempt to explain why these differences and similarities occurred. Some accounts focus on particulars, as narrative art histories do. Other accounts focus more on generalizations, as theoretical art histories do. There have been and will continue to be multiple art-historical accounts of the same historical or cultural changes.

How one art historian came to make claims (or conclusions) in all three categories is discussed in chapter 4. In that chapter Stephen Addiss describes his own art-historical inquiry process as he studied the art of Kameda Bosai, a Japanese artist and calligrapher of the Edo period.

In the factual category, Addiss writes about three parts of his research in Japan. He calls one of those parts "seeing artworks," which serves as a basis for descriptive notes of "original impressions." He describes Bosai's calligraphy as having been given "a sense of rhythmic life by [his] alternations of heavier and lighter strokes, thicker and thinner lines, and straight and curved shapes." He describes the subject matter of a Bosai painting as "a scholar-poet crossing a bridge beneath high mountains, with a lonely pavilion near the peak." Addiss uses his descriptive notes of original impressions when he compares photographic reproductions of Bosai's work. In addition, Addiss establishes basic facts about a number of works. By studying signatures and seals, he is able to attribute some works to Bosai and to identify others as imitations of Bosai's work.

To prepare himself to interpret Bosai's work historically, Addiss did background reading in Japanese history, culture, and the art of the Edo period before leaving the United States. In Japan, he retraced the route of a journey made by Bosai, stopping at farms where Bosai might have stopped and passing mountains and rivers that might have "encouraged" Bosai in his landscape painting. Addiss learned much about Bosai's life and world that led him to conclude that Bosai's work "is deeply embedded into the values of traditional Japanese literati culture." In the exhibition catalog that was the culmination of his inquiry, Addiss wrote comments that he intended to be helpful for viewers attempting to understand or interpret Bosai's work.

Addiss also explains changes in Bosai's work over time. His narrative account of Bosai's life and work includes, for example, an explanation of the effects of Bosai's journey on his calligraphy and painting. Art historians do not always draw conclusions about facts, interpretation, and explanation in all their studies, nor does inquiry in these three categories need necessarily to be pursued in the sequence presented here. Addiss has done some work in each category, working back and forth from one type to another as he studies the life and art of Bosai.

Teaching through Establishing Facts

Teachers might engage students in generative art-historical inquiry in their own classrooms. As noted earlier in this chapter, some art historians challenge the selection of objects that can be considered appropriate for art-historical investigation. Donald Kuspit characterized the present state of art-historical scholarship this way: "If [the discipline of art history] is to develop, to get a move on, the distinctions between the art-historical and the extra-art historical, what is proper and improper art history, must give way. . . . The whole decorum and topography of art history must change. It must understand itself to exist in a field of humanistic operations, as one of many cross-fertilized investigations."[19]

Art teachers are not as bound by "decorum and topography" as art historians are, and in many cases, they have established traditions of broadened "topography." In art classrooms, crafts, advertising, package design, and product design are commonly studied alongside the more traditional painting, sculpture, and architecture. In their continuing search for ways to relate art to the lives and interests of students, teachers have broadened the range of objects studied in art classes. However, this focus is usually taken only in art production classes. Jewelry, magazine ads, album covers, containers, book illustrations, and other objects are used to stimulate production of similar objects. They are seldom exploited as objects for art-historical inquiry.

Factual investigations might be undertaken with ordinary objects such as toys, books, and clothing. To appreciate the task and significance of imagined (or real) restoration, students might be given an old doll, a broken toy car, or a worn-out baseball cap. They might speculate on how the object appeared when it was new. This is the same process that art historians must undertake when they study the Parthenon as it appears today. Before drawing conclusions about Van Eyck's *Arnolfini Wedding Portrait* (fig. 13), art historians must be confident that it has not deteriorated or been altered through the centuries.

The skills of detailed observation can be practiced with ordinary objects. Students can list any subject matter they find, identify the materials from which it is made, speculate about how the parts were put together, and list the object's colors, shapes, textures, and use of space. As observations are put into words, students are learning to be descriptive. Description is a basic skill of art-historical investigation. As art historians begin their studies of artworks, they make detailed observations. Tiny details, like the fruit on the window sill or the decoration on the mirror in the Van Eyck painting, are carefully considered.

Attribution, or the establishment of basic information about a work, can also be undertaken with ordinary objects. Students might attempt to date a magazine advertisement by talking with older people or making comparisons with other ads from dated magazines. Old toys, kitchen utensils, or children's books might have original packaging materials, labels, or title pages that give clues about who manufactured an item or when and where it was made. Evidence might be available in the form of other artifacts, old documents, or memories of contemporary witnesses. Art historians attribute works to particular artists and establish dates of production through examination of similar evidence. Some paintings long assumed to have been painted by Rembrandt have been "de-attributed" in recent years by renewed art-historical inquiry. The history of ownership of the *Arnolfini Wedding Portrait* helps determine when and under what circumstances the painting was produced.

Teaching through Art-Historical Interpretation

The skills of art-historical interpretation can be practiced with everyday objects. For example, the regalia of a full-fledged hippie couple of the 1960s might seem absurd to today's young people. How could anyone have ever thought that sandals, leather-fringed jackets, love beads, handmade muslin dresses, and macrame vests were "cool"? What sort of statement did hippies make as they put together their look? These are questions for art-historical interpretation. They require that today's young people set aside today's fashions and values and attempt to place themselves in the sixties. They must come to understand that the parents of

Fig. 13. *The Marriage of Giovanni Arnolfini and Giovanna Cenami,* by Jan Van Eyck. Reproduced courtesy of the Trustees, The National Gallery, London.

hippies were the World War II generation and that many young people of the time were breaking traditional taboos about sex, careers, drugs, and music. This was also a time when Americans were sharply divided on the Vietnam war. Just as the 1980s yuppie "dress-for-success" look was intended to communicate upward mobility, the 1960s hippie look was sometimes a declaration of independence with antiwar overtones. Supposedly, the sixties look is coming back into fashion as a nostalgic look of rebellion. This neo-hippie fashion revival will surely complicate the task of interpreting the clothing styles of that era—just as during the Italian Renaissance or the French neoclassical era, when interpreting ancient Greek and Roman art was made more complex by their contemporary revival.

Popular culture shifts rapidly—no current example will be current for long. Perhaps studying the white shoes and polyester suits of the 1970s disco look can provide a genuine challenge for young people's historical interpretation skills. Are there symbols to be found in the disco look? Students must use the same skills if they are to come to understand historical artworks. If students are unable to step out of the here and now and imagine themselves there and then, they will see Van Eyck's *Arnolfini Wedding Portrait* as a picture of a man and a pregnant woman in funny clothes with their pet dog. (A more thorough discussion of art historians' study of subject matter, or iconography, is presented in chapter 3.) The significance of the dog, mirror, bed, woman's figure, and clothing will be lost on students without some skill in art-historical interpretation.

Teaching through the Development of Art-Historical Explanations or Narratives

As with art-historical attribution and interpretation, students can learn to account for visual change by using familiar objects. A collection of old soda bottles, sheet music, neckties, costume jewelry, or children's books can exemplify a visual change through time that demands explanation (recall figs. 11 and 12). Many young people are collectors, and their own collections might be studied. Others are connoisseurs of visual change in their own areas of interest, such as skateboard stickers or MTV videos. Students can look for style groupings within their chronologically sequenced collections. They can invent names for and establish basic characteristics of each style. They might investigate whether there have been any revivals through the years. They might discover when change is gradual and when it is dramatic. They might also find that, during some time periods, more than one style exists.

After describing visual change, some attempt can be made to explain it. Art-historical explanation cannot be undertaken without some knowledge of the times in which the objects were produced. Reading assignments, social studies classes, and conversations with parents and neighbors can provide some of that knowledge. Students might report their findings as general principles of visual change or as event-to-event narratives of change. Arnold Hauser accounts for changes in art through the millennia by tracing changes in society. Heinrich Wolfflin explains changes in styles of painting by proposing a theory of alternating baroque and classical tendencies. Hans Belting cautions that the scholar's conception of art history may dictate that scholar's interpretation of historical events.[20] Students will be better prepared to appreciate the significance of changes in art history if they are made aware of the notion of change closer to home.

Sources of Art History Content

When we think of what can be taught about art history, we tend to think first of teaching information. In the preceding section I have attempted to show that students can also learn inquiry processes. Information and inquiry are interrelated. As we gain information, we are able to ask new questions that lead to further inquiry. This often yields new information that in turn leads to new inquiry.

Identifying what is to be learned in the area of art-historical inquiry requires that we identify not only information but also skills and attitudes. If students are to learn the process of art-historical inquiry, then they need to be able to carry out certain tasks—that is, they need to learn skills. Such skills include describing and contrasting visual change; supporting conclusions; imagining life in another time or culture; constructing historical interpretations; and proposing explanations that account for change. There are also attitudes associated with art-historical inquiry— inclinations, tendencies, beliefs, values. Some attitudes that might be encouraged in art history instruction are appreciating the views of others; valuing art as a realm of human accomplishment; and valuing one's own ability to make sense of the visual world. A list of art history skills and attitudes appears in the form of instructional objectives in appendix 3.

The educational content that might be drawn from the discipline of art history is broad indeed. As art history is made part of the art curriculum, many factors must be considered. The next chapter examines children's development, a primary factor as we select art-historical content for elementary and secondary schools.

NOTES

1. Tom Gretton, "New Lamps for Old," in *The New Art History*, ed. A. L. Rees and F. Barzello (Atlantic Highlands, N.J.: Humanities Press, 1988), pp. 63–74; Donald B. Kuspit, "Conflicting Logics: Twentieth-Century Studies at the Crossroads," *Art Bulletin* 69, no. 3 (1987): 117–32; Russel Nye, *The Embarrassed Muse: The Popular Arts in America* (New York: The Dial Press, 1970); and Adrian Rifkin, "Art's Histories," in *The New Art History*, pp. 157–63.

2. E. D. Hirsch, Jr., *Cultural Literacy: What Every American Needs to Know* (New York: Vintage-Random House, 1988), p. 8.

3. Monroe Beardsley, *Aesthetics* (New York: Harcourt Brace, 1958); and George Dickie, *Aesthetics: An Introduction* (Indianapolis: Bobbs-Merrill, 1971).

4. Lorenz Eitner, "Art History and the Sense of Quality," *Art International* 19 (May 1975): 80.

5. Gretton, "New Lamps," p. 64.

6. Ibid., p. 76.

7. Ibid., pp. 69, 72, 73.

8. Vincent Lanier, "Six Items on the Agenda for the Eighties," *Art Education* 33, no. 5 (1980): 20.

9. Albert William Levi and Ralph A. Smith, *Art Education: A Critical Necessity* (Urbana: University of Illinois Press, 1991), p. 4.

10. NCSS Task Force on Early Childhood/Elementary Social Studies, "Social Studies for Early Childhood and Elementary School Children Preparing for the 21st Century," *Social Education* 53, no. 1 (1989): 15, 16.

11. Francie Alexander and Charlotte Crabtree, "California's New History–Social Science Curriculum Promises Richness and Depth," *Leadership* 6, no. 1 (1988): 12 (emphasis added).

12. NCSS Task Force, "Social Studies," p. 16.

13. *Regulations of the State Board of Education of Pennsylvania*, chap. 5, sec. 5.201 (Harrisburg: State Department of Education, Jan. 1988).

14. Thalia Gouman-Peterson and Patricia Mathews, "The Feminist Critique of Art History," *Art Bulletin* 69, no. 3 (1987): 334.

15. Rees and Borzello, *The New Art History*, p. 4.

16. The examples and persistent interest of Thomas Laudenslager, art teacher at Palisades High School in Doylestown, Pa., contributed to the formation of this distinction.

17. Virginia Fitzpatrick, "Teaching Art History as Inquiry," *Ohio Art Line* 14, no. 3 (1989): 12.

18. Kerry Freedman, "Recent Theoretical Shifts in the Field of Art History," *Art Education* 44, no. 6 (1991): 40–45.

19. Kuspit, "Conflicting Logics," p. 117.

20. Arnold Hauser, *The Social History of Art* (New York: Alfred A. Knopf, 1951); Heinrich Woelfflin, *Principles of Art History: The Problem of the Development of Style in Later Art* (New York: Dover Publications, 1932); and Hans Belting, *The End of Art History?* trans. Christopher S. Wood (Chicago: University of Chicago Press, 1987).

7

Art History and Educational Levels: When Can Art History Be Taught?

The Need for Research

On a recent busperson's holiday, I observed the teaching of art history in several regions of the country. I observed an art teacher teaching about ancient Egypt and Egyptian art in western New York State. I worked with a bilingual teacher in a suburb of Chicago teaching her fifth graders about artworks from many ages and cultures. In an elementary art room outside Philadelphia, I observed an art teacher whose curriculum for grades one through five includes an overview, in the first grade, of art history beginning with prehistoric art. In another Pennsylvania school, I observed a dynamic high school honors class in the history of art and music. In Virginia, I followed traveling art history teachers who taught a wide range of lessons coordinated with nonart subject areas, from early Virginia history in a fourth-grade class to French architecture in a high school French class to Muslim decorative patterns in a high school world cultures class. In Omaha, I watched as third graders were shown how evolving race relations help us understand the paintings of Horace Pippin.

Having sought out and consulted many practicing teachers who are committed to teaching art history at various school levels, I am encouraged by my discoveries. Inspired by their commitment and guided by their own good sense and informal classroom "experimentation," teachers have succeeded in introducing art-historical ideas to learners of all ages. However, these teachers have not had the benefit of empirical research about art-historical learning at different developmental levels. I am aware of no published research that systematically addresses children's developing understanding of art history through childhood to adolescence.

As art history becomes an integral part of art instruction at the elementary and secondary levels, one should expect to find more research interest. In the meantime, two general areas of research should prove helpful for planning for art history instruction: research focusing on understanding learning in the social studies; and research in children's developing understanding of art and aesthetic experience. Social studies research can tell us about children's developing understanding of time, space, and history but does not attend to artworks as unique forms of historical evidence that are valuable in their own right. Developmental studies in art can tell us about children's changing responses to artworks but have little to say about children's understanding of artworks within their historical and cultural contexts. Developmental studies in art are less likely than developmental studies in history to reflect the role of art education in child development since art education is virtually nonexistent at some levels in some regions of the country. Moreover, art history instruction is probably the exception rather than the rule in young people's elementary and secondary education.

When one applies conclusions from related developmental research to understanding art history, certain qualifications should be made. We must realize that descriptive research is not prescriptive. Describing the abilities of children who have had no exposure to art history is not the same as describing the developmental limitations of children in understanding art history. Describing what children do is not the same as describing what children can do. If ten-year-olds in France do not speak English, it is not because they are not mature enough to learn; rather, it is because they have not been taught. Howard Gardner found that children's skills in style categorization could in fact be increased with training.[1]

David Henry Feldman has underlined the significance of educational intervention in his comparison of nonuniversal versus universal development theory.[2] Descriptive studies give some indication of what one can expect untutored children to do at various ages. However, one will not know what children are capable of doing until there are studies of children who have had art history instruction.

The remainder of this chapter considers the teaching of art history at elementary, early secondary, and upper secondary grade levels. Each level is considered from the point of view of developmental research and then with an eye toward classroom applications.

Teaching Art History in the Elementary Grades

Research in the Development of Historical Understanding

Teaching art history in the elementary grades seems difficult, if not impossible, to some teachers. We know that historical concepts are difficult for children, who have lived through only a few short years themselves, to grasp. I remember developing my first idea of "history" very early. I thought about the possibilities and concluded that history must be a valley or ravine, probably one with trees in a winter landscape. My first memory of the word "history" is its use in "Rudolph the Red-Nosed Reindeer": according to that Christmas song, Rudolph would "go down in history." I could think of only one place into which a deer might go down and that was a ravine. How can one expect children to understand art history if they cannot even grasp the meaning of the word "history"? One should not draw overly broad conclusions from the fact that children do not understand the word "history" or historical dates. Morals can be taught without reference to the words "morality" or "ethics." Children understand narratives that tell stories through time even though they may not be able to define the word "history."

Studies of historical learning conducted by Roy N. Hallam in the 1960s are often cited to justify delaying the introduction of history until after the primary grades. Hallam's studies are built on Jean Piaget's theory of cognitive development. An overview of that theory, based on Patricia H. Miller's analysis, includes the following four stages: (1) sensorimotor period (roughly birth to two years) in which the child moves "from single reflexes . . . to an organized set of schemes"; (2) preoperational period (roughly two to seven years), in which the child uses "symbols in an increasingly organized and logical manner"; (3) concrete operational period (roughly seven to eleven years), in which "the child acquires certain logical structures"; and (4) formal operations period (roughly eleven to fifteen years), in which a young person can apply mental operations "to purely verbal or logical statements, to the possible as well as the real, to the future as well as the present."[3] Hallam's findings suggest that historical understanding does not keep pace with Piaget's stages. He concludes that in history, young people's concrete operations stage starts from twelve years and four months to thirteen years and two months; and formal operations do not begin until sixteen years and eight months to eighteen years and two months.[4] Martin E. Sleeper cites evidence that children do not understand chronological dates until about the age of eleven and do not "understand interpretation and hypothesis in history" until adolescence.[5]

In recent years traditional assumptions about the inappropriateness of teaching history in early childhood have been challenged theoretically and empirically. John B. Poster advocates a more careful look at the different senses of "time" that may be required for historical understanding, noting such alternatives as "social time," "literary time," "personal or interior time," "physical or clock time," as well as "historiographical time."[6] In a study by Lorraine Harner, children from three to seven years old were found to be able to use past and future tenses appropriately.[7]

According to Robert P. Craig's research, children between the ages of four and eight "hold quite specific concepts of time."[8] They can order actions in sequence and relate sequences in a temporal fashion.

Other scholars have taken a more cognitive approach to explaining historical understanding in young people. These scholars tend to build on or argue for refining or rethinking Piaget's cognitive theory. Martin L. Hoffman has looked at the development of role-taking abilities, abilities that presumably are necessary for historical understanding. He proposes that Piagetian studies have assessed advanced cognitive or verbal operations rather than role-taking abilities.[9] Kerry J. Kennedy argues that the Piaget-Hallam model lacks understanding of the influence of information-processing capacity on historical understanding.[10] Jerry R. Moore, James L. Alouf, and Janie Needham have considered historical reasoning skills beyond oral and written language. They propose four successive levels at which thought can be represented: through sensorimotor actions, through symbols and images, through signs and words, and finally through logical thought.[11] According to them, one must consider these levels of cognitive development to understand how children comprehend historical content.

Perhaps the social studies researcher whose work is potentially most insightful for guiding the study of art-historical understanding is Linda S. Levstik. She argues that conclusions about development may not apply similarly across domains; that narrative may play a significant role in children's historical understanding; and that "if . . . early learning does not occur, the optimal teaching time for some concepts may pass." Levstik lists four categories of concepts: social perspective, civic understanding, economic understanding, and space and time.[12]

Parson's Research in the Development of Aesthetic Experience

Michael J. Parsons is the art education researcher whose developmental studies seem to offer the most evidence for planning developmentally appropriate art-historical instruction. Parsons's five-stage theory of developing art understanding is used as the basic reference throughout this chapter. The following statements outline the essential characteristics of each of Parsons's stages:[13]

1. Favoritism
"The primary characteristics of stage one are an intuitive delight in most paintings, a strong attraction to color, and a freewheeling associative response to subject matter."

2. Beauty and Realism
"The dominant idea of stage two is that of the subject. Stage two is organized around the idea of representation."

3. Expressiveness

"The organizing insight of stage three has to do with expressiveness. We look at paintings for the quality of the experience they can produce, and the more intense and interesting the experience the better the painting."

4. Style and Form

"The new insight here is that the significance of a painting is a social rather than an individual achievement. It exists within a tradition, which is composed by a number of peoples looking over time at a number of works and talking about them."

5. Autonomy

"The central insight here is that the individual must judge the concept and values with which the tradition constructs the meanings of works of art."

Parsons's study involves subjects ranging from preschoolers to college art professors, and he carefully limits his claims about the generalizability of his stages to particular age groups.[14] He is concerned with his subjects' cognitive understanding of art. Parsons's findings are based on discussions of eight paintings, seven of which are modern. One might hope that his theory one day will be tested with art forms from varying cultures and time periods.

Although Parsons would caution us about tying stages and ages, he seems to attribute stage 2 understanding to most children by the time they enter elementary school. At stage 1, according to Parsons, young children enjoy most paintings. They are quite happy to spend extended periods of time identifying and locating colors, shapes, subject matter, and other details in artworks. At stage 2, children's interest in subject matter intensifies. They want to know what is depicted and they want a painting to be realistic. According to Parsons, children at stage 2 have a difficult time understanding abstract art, since it seems purposeless to them. Further, children at stage 2 tend to admire technical skill.

By the intermediate grades, children are developmentally prepared for somewhat more sophisticated art history instruction. Although Parsons does not discuss historical-cultural influences on understanding until stage 4, there is some evidence that upper elementary school children can begin to grasp how context affects the appearance and meaning of artworks.[15] It is important to remember that Parsons is describing what untutored children do, not what they might be able to do if taught.

Howard Gardner cautions us not to limit learners' experience based strictly on a stage theory of artistic development: "The past decade has not been friendly to the strong version of the stage hypothesis. It turns out that young children are capable of many operations once withheld from them; and that, under certain circumstances, adults must pass through stages of learning paralleling those realized by the young child." Gardner goes on to caution that more advanced learning may never occur if left until adulthood: "It is the fool-hardy optimist who, confident that certain symbolic skills can be easily acquired by the adult, would withhold crucial symbolic experiences from children."[16] Gardner is not writing specifically about art history understanding, but we may extrapolate his point to art-historical understanding. Art-historical information and inquiry should be presented at a developmentally appropriate level of sophistication in the elementary grades. There is a need for research into what art-historical understanding children of different developmental levels can attain with appropriate instruction.

Classroom Applications

Because young children have difficulty remembering lessons from earlier years in school, it makes sense to build review into the art history component of any elementary art program. A permanent visual display in the art room or elsewhere in the school can be used as a reference to aid students in recalling works and cultures studied in earlier grades.

Art history instruction in the primary grades should take advantage of some of what researchers tell us about teaching young children. Lessons should use concrete activities, dramatics, and narratives. Students' attention should be directed toward subject matter and technical production processes. A detailed sample lesson plan on prehistoric painting with a narrative written for the primary level is provided in appendix 2. That narrative can be compared with the analysis of prehistoric art in chapter 1 to underscore developmental differences between primary children, who are the intended audience of the lesson, and educated adults, who are the intended audience for this book.

Art history instruction in the intermediate grades can exploit storytelling as children are introduced to artworks of other times and cultures. Activities planned for the intermediate grades should involve active tasks using concrete objects, such as postcard reproductions, maps, and time lines.[17]

Teaching Art History in the Early Secondary Grades

Developmental differences between elementary grades and secondary grades blur. Much of what research suggests about teaching art history in elementary school applies quite well to middle or junior high school. If children have had some art history instruction in the elementary grades, one should be able to expect a bit more comfort, at minimum, or sophistication, at maximum, as those students continue their art-historical study in secondary school. If middle or junior high students have had no art history or even art criticism or art appreciation in their elementary art program, one should expect to plan lessons at a lower level.

Middle school or junior high and beginning high school are crucial levels in art history instruction. In many regions of the country, all students are required to take art instruction only in grades one through eight. And in many regions of the country, certified art teachers are charged with the responsibility of teaching art in only the last two or three of those years. An increasing number of states are implementing a fine-arts graduation requirement in high school. Therefore, beginning level high school art courses may be some students' only or last opportunity to learn about art history as part of their secondary education.

Research in the Development of Historical Understanding

Let us consider first what social studies educators conclude about developmental research and history education. Christian Laville and Linda W. Rosenzweig, writing on developmental dimensions of teaching and learning history, characterize the developmental circumstances of beginning secondary education as follows: "History teachers have a fundamental responsibility to facilitate students' progress from concrete operations to formal operations. By using the tools of concrete topics and data, and inductive teaching techniques [building knowledge up from particulars rather than down from generalizations]—especially in the early years of secondary school—they can structure instruction to meet the cognitive developmental needs and characteristics of their students."[18] After having analyzed the developmental research literature on teaching and learning in history, Laville and Rosenzweig conclude that history is not too abstract for beginning secondary students to understand, but that teaching methods must bridge the transition from concrete to formal operations.

Adolescents can also employ higher-order thinking skills in their understanding of art. Planning art history instruction for elementary and secondary grades should not be a matter of placing some artists, works, eras, or cultures at one level and others at another. Prehistoric, Byzantine, and modern art do not belong more to one level than another. According to Sleeper, the "simple truths" presented in elementary school are seen as more complicated and even questionable in adolescence.[19] To accommodate this increased sophistication, the way that art-historical content is presented, not necessarily the content itself, should vary from one level to the next.

History teachers teaching history may well be faced with a more difficult problem than that facing art teachers who teach art history. The essential element of history is the historical event. The essential element of art history is the art-historical object. Unlike the historical event, the art-historical object is not an action of long ago that no longer exists today. The art-historical object very often still exists in a physical form available for direct examination in the present. These objects can be seen in museums or brought into the classroom, or they may be shown in the classroom in the form of photographs. Although historical documents and artifacts can be brought into the history classroom, the historical event cannot. The fact that art history centers on objects makes beginning to learn art history, by its very nature, more concrete than beginning to learn history.

One might use Moore, Alouf, and Needham's four-level theory of historical reasoning to propose that art history has a built-in developmental advantage over history. Their theory identifies increasingly developed historical reasoning levels beginning with sensorimotor actions, then images, then words, and finally logical thoughts. At level 1, art history has the advantage of centering on concrete physical objects that can be experienced through sensorimotor actions. Unlike ideas and historical events, artworks and artifacts can be seen, touched, walked around or through, and sometimes (as in the case of mobiles) manipulated in space. At level 2, art provides rich possibilities because much of art history is about images, that is, representations of things and ideas in visual form. As one considers art history instruction beyond the elementary school, one can expect to move into the more abstract verbal and logical modes of historical reasoning that Moore, Alouf, and Needham identify in levels 3 and 4. One should be able to expect that older students are better able to use language to describe, analyze, and interpret the objects and images of art history and that they can begin to reason out possibilities that were unimaginable at an earlier age.

Parsons's Research in the Development of Aesthetic Experience

Parsons seems to suggest that his third stage of understanding should be achievable in adolescence. However, one must always remember that education may play a role in moving students from one stage to the next. Some students may never grow sophisticated in stage 3 understanding and will perhaps never experience stage 4 and 5 understanding without the challenge of education aimed at those higher levels.

Parsons's stage 3 centers on expression. He recognizes a move toward increased abstraction. He concludes that for a person at this stage of understanding, the subject is not a physical thing but rather an idea or theme. The emotional power of a work and the ideas being expressed replace concern for realism.[20] Parsons finds persons at stage 3 to be more interested in puzzling out the meanings of works than are persons at a lower stage of understanding who would simply dismiss those works as meaningless. Parsons suggests that persons at stage 3 are on the threshold of learning to interpret paintings.

Adolescents are more able than children to distance themselves and understand the point of view of others. Beginning to understand that people may experience many things (not just paintings) differently is essential to beginning to be able to interpret artworks historically. One must understand that people of other times and cultures experienced their world differently and that their artworks reflect those different experiences. With this understanding, students can begin to learn to interpret artworks within historical and cultural contexts.

Classroom Applications

In the beginning years of secondary school, one should expect considerably more comprehension of history and art on the part of young people. Since, according to Parsons, expression is a key factor in adolescents' understanding of art, it could become a major focus in art history instruction. Studying expressiveness in modern and contemporary art movements seems a reasonable choice for these years. Since adolescents at Parsons's stage 3 are more tolerant of abstraction, modern and contemporary art seem doubly appropriate.

If young people are to develop a comprehensive understanding of art history, other eras and cultures in addition to modern Western art should be studied. Expressiveness in art extends throughout time and across cultures. The traditional masks of various areas in western Africa differ dramatically in their expressiveness. The quiet reserve of the bronzes of the Ife of Nigeria contrasts sharply with the highly abstracted and embellished wooden masks of the Kuba of Zaire. The dramatic baroque art of the Counter-Reformation in Europe contrasts with the relative calm of the High Renaissance. Whether the art is from Japan, Alaska, Greece, or France, it possesses an expressiveness that can serve as a focus for study.

Similarly, abstraction is a feature of artwork from many cultures. Abstraction was highly developed in the ancient cultures of Central America. Mayan and Aztec stone carvings offer powerful examples of abstraction. Abstraction was highly developed in the Middle Ages in eastern and western Europe. The mosaics of Byzantium epitomize eastern abstraction, while manuscript illumination, like that in the *Book of Lindisfarne,* are representative of Western abstraction.

Parsons has found that, in addition to their interest in expressiveness and tolerance for abstraction, adolescents at stage 3 are interested in puzzling out the meaning of artworks. In modern art, one might select surrealism as a movement rich in puzzles. Any secondary level art teacher can testify to students' fascination with decoding an Escher drawing. Such interest might be extended to the works of Dali and Magritte.

As with expressiveness and abstraction, puzzles are not limited to the art of modern Western culture. Deciphering the symbolic meanings of Indian paintings and stone carvings is an engaging puzzle demanding some knowledge of Hindu and Buddhist religions. Similarly, deciphering the Italian Renaissance frescoes of Michelangelo demands knowledge of Christianity and, specifically, Renaissance Catholicism. Unraveling such mysteries can be intellectually challenging to adolescents who are fascinated by puzzles.

In the beginning secondary years, students should be able not only to appreciate a wide range of artworks but also to begin to understand them in their cultural contexts. Adolescents can begin to understand the implications of multiple points of view. This understanding is crucial to the process of art-historical interpretation. Whereas elementary school children can be taught about a sequence of eras in Western art history and introduced to non-Western art history, adolescents can more fully appreciate why works from different times and places look different from each other. Adolescents can more fully understand that life-styles, values, and beliefs have varied in different times and places.

Art-historical interpretation can be developed in adolescents through activities focused on art-historical inquiry. Students in secondary school can examine familiar objects and events to understand changing points of view. Secondary school students are keenly aware of subtle stylistic changes in popular fashion. They are connoisseurs of music videos and athletic shoes. Some students are even aware of regional stylistic differences. A few years ago, a colleague of mine moved with her two teenagers from Maine to Pennsylvania. Both the girl and the boy needed new sneakers, but they could not buy them until after they had done some regional style research. They could not be sure that what was fashionable last spring in Bangor, Maine, would be acceptable this fall in Berks County, Pennsylvania. Before making their purchases, they made a foray to a popular local mall, not to select their favorite shoes, but to study what young people were wearing on their feet. Imagine what those young people might think of the square-toed, clunky platform shoes of the early 1970s. Expeditions into closets and attics will yield a whole range of outdated shoe styles. Students can look at contemporary artifacts such as magazines and movies in an attempt to establish a shoe chronology. But, more important, students can interview their older siblings, parents, or other relatives and neighbors to try to understand how it was possible to like those old shoes. Album covers, popular music, cars, and any other artifacts from the seventies, sixties, or fifties could be used to enrich students' appreciation of difference.

Understanding the meaning of a 1957 Chevy for one's middle-aged uncle or a store-bought dress for one's depression-era great-grandmother is beginning to understand differences in historical and cultural meaning. Such understanding is what is needed to interpret artworks art-historically. Skills in art-historical interpretation are needed to understand totem poles not as movie props but as symbolic objects representing the traditions of highly sophisticated, permanently settled Native Americans who lived in wooden houses on the northwest coast of America before and after the arrival of white settlers. Skills of art-historical interpretation are needed to understand the political and revolutionary importance of David's propagandistic portraits of Napoleon.

In middle or junior high school, students study the history of the United States, Western civilization, and world cultures. Adolescents should have a more sophisticated understanding of historical time and geography as well as a more sophisticated understanding of art. With such understanding, students in the beginning secondary grades are capable of understanding a basic overview of Western art history as well as an introduction to non-Western art.

Teaching Art History in the Upper Secondary Grades

Parsons's Research in the Development of Aesthetic Experience

According to Parsons, students' understanding of art at stage 4 is dominated by their attention to medium, form, and style. He finds that at stage 4 people begin to see style as characteristic of a time and place. They understand that artists can express ideas of other times. In addition to being more culturally aware, persons at stage 4 are also more capable of suspending judgment. Parsons describes these students as being "willing to look again, talk some more, and withhold judgment. It is reasonable to spend time on the views of others, even if at first they have little meaning."[21] Such increased cultural awareness and increased tolerance should greatly enhance students' prospects in coming to understand art history. If, at stage 3, adolescents begin to understand the point of view of others, at stage 4 this ability is even more advanced. With an increase in the capacity to understand others should come an increase in the capacity to interpret art-historically, that is, to understand artworks within their own cultural contexts.

Parsons's studies have led him to conclude that education is necessary to students' developing an understanding of art. He claims that "few people will reach a stage four understanding without more serious schooling in the arts than usual."[22] The challenge of teaching art history in senior high school, and perhaps also at the college level, is to teach a more developed understanding of art history. Parsons's stages 4 and 5 give us some ideas about the more advanced levels of art understanding that students might gain through higher-level art history instruction.

At stages 4 and 5, according to Parsons, people begin to develop a much more sophisticated sense of history, or what was referred to in chapter 6 as the ability to explain or narrate history. Historical explanation or narrative refers to an understanding of how and why artworks change through time and across cultures. Parsons describes an individual at stage 4 as understanding that "a tradition may be stable and slow to change, as may the society that it reflects"; or, by contrast, as is the case with American art, that a "tradition . . . is . . . everchanging, varied, full of movements, a rich mixture of styles and values, with a fast-moving history." He describes a person with a stage 5 understanding as having an even more advanced sense of history, "aware of history as a stream of continuing change that affects himself and his contemporaries."[23] As this sense of history is developed, students should be increasingly capable of understanding and perhaps even proposing accounts to explain art-historical change.

Classroom Applications

A variety of possibilities exists for advanced high school art history instruction, especially if preceded by elementary and beginning secondary art history instruction. A humanities course might be organized around the study of selected eras or cultures such as the Renaissance, the Enlightenment, or traditional Japan. Advanced high school students might be expected to work more independently to develop their own historical accounts of art of the past. More contemporary art-historical issues focused on the twentieth century might include the ebb and flow of abstraction; interrelationships between fine-art movements and commercial graphic design history from the 1890s to the 1990s; the changing role of the mass media in art and culture; or the impact of military, political, and environmental conflicts on art.

An analysis of the literature of developmentalists seems to suggest that, though art history may be comprehensible throughout elementary and secondary education, the nature of that comprehension will vary tremendously as we move through the grades. The three general categories of art-historical inquiry outlined in chapter 6 (establishment of facts, historical interpretation, and narratives or explanations) may be helpful in considering what might be taught at what developmental level. Although art-historical interpretation, explanation, and narrative have some place in the elementary grades, the preponderance of art history objectives at that level (especially the primary grades) are most effectively focused on matters of art-historical fact. To some extent, in the beginning grades of secondary school, students can be expected to begin to understand art-historical interpretation as well as art-historical facts. As we move to the more advanced levels of senior high school, students can begin to understand art-historical explanations and narratives as well as historical interpretations and facts. Surely the best art history program in the elementary and secondary schools addresses art-historical learning throughout the grades at increased levels of sophistication as the student grows more capable of art-historical understanding.

NOTES

1. Howard Gardner, "The Development of Sensitivity to Figural and Stylistic Aspects of Paintings," *British Journal of Psychology* 63 (1972): 605–15.

2. David Henry Feldman, "Developmental Psychology and Art Education: Two Fields at the Crossroads," *Journal of Aesthetic Education* 21, no. 2 (1987): 245.

3. Patricia H. Miller, *Theories of Developmental Psychology*, 2d ed. (New York: W. H. Freeman and Company, 1989), p. 45.

4. Roy N. Hallam, "Thinking and Learning in History," *Teaching History* 2 (1972): 342.

5. Martin E. Sleeper, "A Developmental Framework for History Education in Adolescence," *School Review* 84 (November 1975): 97.

6. John B. Poster, "The Birth of the Past: Children's Perceptions of Historical Time," *History Teacher* 6 (1973): 588.

7. Lorraine Harner, "Children Talk about the Time and Aspect of Actions," *Child Development* 52, no. 2 (1981): 501.

8. Robert P. Craig, "The Child's Construction of Space and Time," *Science and Children* 19, no. 3 (1981): 37.

9. Martin L. Hoffman, "Empathy, Role-taking, Guilt, and Development of

Altruistic Motives," in *Moral Development and Behavior: Theory, Research, and Social Issues,* ed. Thomas Lickona (New York: Holt, Rinehart and Winston, 1976), p. 129.

10. Kerry J. Kennedy, "Assessing the Relationship between Information Processing Capacity and Historical Understanding," *Theory and Research in Social Education* 11, no. 2 (1983): 1–22.

11. Jerry R. Moore, James L. Alouf, and Janie Needham, "Cognitive Development and Historical Reasoning in Social Studies Curriculum," *Theory and Research in Social Education* 12, no. 2 (1984): 56.

12. Linda S. Levstik, "Conceptual Development in Social Studies" (Paper presented at the Association of American Publishers Conference, March 1988, Palm Beach, Fla.), pp. 10, 16; Levstik, "Historical Narrative and the Young Learner," *TIP* 28, no. 2 (1981): 114–19; Linda S. Levstik and Christine C. Pappas, "Exploring the Development of Historical Understanding," *Journal of Research and Development in Education* 21, no. 1 (1987): 14.

13. Michael J. Parsons, *How We Understand Art: A Cognitive Developmental Account of Aesthetic Experience* (Cambridge: Cambridge University Press, 1987), pp. 22, 23, 24, 25.

14. Ibid., pp. 3–12.

15. Jennifer Pazienza, "Modes of Historical Inquiry" (Ph.D. diss., Pennsylvania State University, 1989), pp. 115–244; and Mary Erickson, "Art Historical Understanding in Early Childhood" in *Visual Arts and Early Childhood Learning,* ed. Christine Thompson (Reston, Va.: National Art Education Association, forthcoming).

16. Howard Gardner, *Frames of Mind: The Theory of Multiple Intelligences* (New York: Basic Books, 1985), pp. 314–15.

17. Al Hurwitz and Michael Day, *Children and Their Art: Methods for the Elementary School,* 5th ed. (New York: Harcourt Brace Jovanovich, 1991), pp. 354–66.

18. Christian Laville and Linda W. Rosenzweig, "Teaching and Learning History: Developmental Dimensions," in *Developmental Perspectives on the Social Studies.* Bulletin 66, ed. L. W. Rosenzweig (Washington, D.C.: National Council for the Social Studies, 1982), p. 62.

19. Sleeper, "Developmental Framework," p. 105.

20. Parsons, *How We Understand Art,* p. 94.

21. Ibid., p. 143.

22. Ibid., p. 117.

23. Ibid., pp. 115, 147.

8

Curriculum:
How Can Art History Teaching Be
Organized and Taught?

If we are convinced that art history should be a part of young people's education and that art history is comprehensible in various ways to elementary and secondary school students, then we can begin to consider the effective organization of learning based on the discipline of art history. Before considering various curriculum structures, let us examine goals, objectives, and scope of content. Chapter 6 addressed rationales for teaching art history and suggested a number of goals and objectives.

Goals

Listed below are four goals that are based on the discipline of art history:

1. Students learn how to use art-historical inquiry as a means of better understanding our visual culture.

2. Students learn that America's art is diverse and has many ethnic, cultural, and religious roots.

3. Students learn that the art of the Western world has changed in many ways and for many reasons from ancient times to the present.

4. Students learn that art has been produced all over the world—in Africa, Asia, Latin America, Europe, North America, and Oceania.

Additional goals for teaching art history begin to extend beyond the discipline of art history into broader areas of education:

5. Students learn that aesthetic values vary from age to age and from culture to culture and that it is possible to respond aesthetically to a wide range of visual objects.

6. Students learn to recognize artworks as manifestations of values held in different cultures and at different times.

Goals for teaching art history can be further influenced by goals of general education (as based loosely on Pennsylvania's quality goals of education). Students should learn how to communicate effectively; how to be good citizens; how to think critically and analytically; to appreciate and understand their environment; to develop their self-esteem; and to understand others in this country and around the world.

Before specific curriculum development can begin, major goals should be selected. Goals most closely related to art history, such as the first six listed above, could be used to provide a general direction that can be modified, revised, and extended to meet additional goals such as general education goals.

Objectives

While major goals remind us of our purpose and stand as beacons to guide our decisions, specific objectives are necessary to translate major goals into teachable segments that together propel us toward those goals. Chapter 6 is a source for many specific learning objectives. The chapter concludes with an argument for attitude and skill objectives listed in appendix 3. The outline of "A Story of Art in the World," in appendix 1, suggests a wide range of knowledge objectives. As every teacher knows, objective writing means different things in different districts. Ever since the accountability movement of the 1970s, objectives have been a major focus for educational reform. Behavioral objectives are mandated in some districts, while other styles of objective writing are used elsewhere. The form for objective writing used in this book is based on distinctions made by the educational philosopher Israel Scheffler, who identifies three types of teaching and, by implication, three types of learning. Simply put, these are knowledge, skill, and attitude acquisition.[1]

Different instructional methods are necessary to ensure achievement of different types of objectives. Different methods of evaluation are necessary to determine whether each type of objective has been achieved. Because each type of objective requires its own instructional method, each type also demands different time and energy commitments. Knowledge tends to be most easily taught and learned; skills tend to require more time; and attitudes require a dedicated, continuing effort. Therefore, a curriculum generally might be expected to include more knowledge than skill objectives and more skill than attitude objectives.

The next section illustrates how different types of specific objectives in art history lead to quite different implications for instructional activities as well as different methods of evaluation.

Teaching for Art-Historical Knowledge

The following is a sample knowledge objective that might be used to guide lesson planning. Students learn that Egyptian artists used size to show importance in their art. This objective identifies information that can be presented through such straightforward and traditional methods as lecture, discussion, illustration, or reading. For example, students might be shown reproductions of Egyptian tomb paintings or monumental sculpture. They could then be informed of the identities of the major figures represented. As the relative status of each person is discussed, the relative size of its representation could be measured and compared with the representations of other persons.

Evaluation of knowledge acquisition tends to be rather simple and straightforward.[2] In traditional tests, true or false, recall, or multiple choice questions can be asked. For example, students should be able to select the correct response from a series that includes the following alternatives: Egyptian artists showed important people to be larger than other people; Egyptian artists showed important people higher up in the painting than other people; and Egyptian artists showed important people to be more red than other people.

In a less formal way, students' learning might be assessed by a review in a later class session. Students might simply be asked what they remember about Egyptian art and specifically what they can recall about distinguishing important from less-important people in Egyptian art. Students' verbal responses would provide some evidence of their learning.

Teaching for Art-Historical Skills

Skill objectives cannot be taught or evaluated by the same means as knowledge objectives. A rudimentary objective might be that students learn how to describe visual artifacts or art works from the past. This skill, which is crucial to art-historical inquiry, is also essential to learning about art criticism and other aspects of art. Skills must be practiced to be learned.

One can learn that a skill exists by seeing an example of that skill demonstrated, but if one is to acquire that skill, one must practice it individually. Hearing a teacher describe an artwork in great detail can teach students that description is a skill and that some people can describe very well, but such learning is knowledge acquisition, not skill acquisition. If students are going to learn how to describe visual artifacts or artworks, they must each have an opportunity to practice describing. Practicing a skill usually requires considerable time and often equipment.

In a class discussion, the teacher might show a large reproduction and, through recitation, teach the class to describe the image. However, only those students who are reciting have the opportunity to practice the skill. A more effective means of teaching a skill is to provide each student with an artwork to describe in writing. Or students can be paired and provided with duplicate sets of reproductions. Each student in turn describes one of the works in detail, while the other student attempts to identify which reproduction the student is describing. This last activity requires a differently structured classroom and different resources. However, in this activity every student in the class has the time and opportunity to practice describing.

Evaluating whether a skill objective has been achieved cannot be accomplished through the same means as evaluating knowledge acquisition. A multiple choice or true/false test item may test whether students can recognize a good description but not whether they can describe. Students' individual written descriptions can be used to assess their skill acquisition. One-on-one teacher-student discussions of an artwork or teacher checklists of students' oral responses will likewise provide evidence of a student's skill. Less formally, classroom discussion can provide sketchy evidence about those students who respond (but not, of course, about those who do not). When planning instruction in teaching art history, it is important to decide whether knowledge or skill acquisition is the desired outcome, since methods appropriate for achieving one are inappropriate for achieving the other.

Teaching for Art-Historical Attitudes

Finally, let us consider an art history attitude objective: that students learn to appreciate art as a way of understanding the point of view of persons of other cultures and times. Methods for teaching attitudes are usually quite complex and often less direct than teaching skills or knowledge. Telling students that something is good, important, or worth valuing is not always an effective method to change students' attitudes toward that thing. Through the authority of the classroom situation, the teacher can oblige students to behave as if they value something, but if the behavior is not voluntarily continued outside the constraints of the classroom, the students have not acquired the attitude. In addition to explaining the value of something, teachers can model their own valuing and reinforce valuing behavior when students exhibit such behavior.

To learn to appreciate art as a way of understanding the point of view of persons of other cultures and times, students require some prior knowledge and skill. Students must know that artworks have been produced in other cultures and times and that artworks can help us to understand the point of view of artists and their cultures. To value the point of view of others, it is necessary to learn how to identify one's own point of view and how to contrast it with the point of view of someone from another time or culture. If the attitude objective is to be reached, it must inspire a whole series of prerequisite learning experiences. As one teaches for knowledge of the arts of Egypt, the Middle Ages, and the nineteenth century, one is building a foundation for teaching toward the attitude objective. As students role-play artists and viewers of other times and as they learn how to interpret works art-historically, they are building the prerequisite skills for achieving the attitude objective. Acquiring the prerequisite knowledge and skills is necessary but not sufficient to guarantee that the attitude is learned. The teacher might propose reasons why it is important and worthwhile to understand other peoples in an effort to convince students of the significance of the attitude. In addition, the teacher might positively reinforce any student who exhibits interest, curiosity, or respect for art as it manifests the point of view of other peoples. And, finally, the teacher should model the appreciative attitude by sharing personal enthusiasm and interest in how artworks reflect their times or cultures. Attitude objectives are not primarily identified and taught in specific lessons; rather, they are identified as significant and used to guide all instruction.

Like knowledge and skills, attitude objectives have their appropriate means of evaluation. Testing the students' prerequisite knowledge and skill is not sufficient. Measuring attitude change is a difficult process at best. To evaluate whether students have acquired an attitude, they must be observed to be acting freely in accordance with the attitude. Such observation cannot be mandated, for then one is observing the control of the teacher rather than the attitude of the student. Despite the difficulty of measuring attitudes, attitudinal learning is nonetheless a significant part of art history learning. For example, an important component of art-historical understanding is curiosity about artworks from other times and cultures or appreciation and enjoyment of artworks within their historical-cultural contexts.

To build the art history component of an art curriculum, one must identify the major art history goals for the curriculum and then the specific objectives that, taken together, build toward those goals. To plan effective strategies for reaching specific art history objectives, one should identify the type of learning to be acquired. Having determined what specific knowledge, skills, and attitudes are to be learned, one can proceed to plan appropriate instructional strategies as well as appropriate evaluation techniques.

Scope

Early in the curriculum development process comes the definition of scope, that is, the determination of the range of content to be taught. What should be included? Chapter 6 outlined the potential scope of art history teaching, which should include an introduction to art from around the world, an overview of Western art history, and an introduction to art-historical inquiry processes. In addition, a wide range of works should be considered art-historically, including the traditional fine arts, folk art, graphic design, popular art, and consumer products of visual interest. Others might conclude that the scope of art history learning in elementary and secondary education should be somewhat differently defined. In any case, the scope *must* be defined. Curriculum planning without attention to scope can result in learning that does not culminate in a unified understanding of art history. Just as we plan a balanced scope in the art production component of the art curriculum, we should consider a balanced scope in art history. We would not consider an art production component to be adequate in scope if only two-dimensional processes were explored or if processes were selected based solely on convenience and student interest. The same is true for art history content. We may want to consider a changing balance between knowledge and skill as students move through the grades, increasing the skill learning with older students. We might change the scope of learning from one grade to another to distribute content throughout the grades. However, the changing scope of content should not be haphazard. Students will not build a sense of art history as a whole if lessons are selected solely on such grounds as application to art production or immediate student interest.

Sequence

Once the scope of a curriculum has been roughly defined, the development of sequence can begin. Learning within an elementary and secondary art curriculum can be sequenced in many different ways. While no full analysis of curriculum sequencing is attempted here, a range of possibilities are presented. Among the ways that content can be sequenced are by mutual agreement; through a developmental decision; as a unifying concern; as a practical consideration; or through a decision based on the discipline being taught. In the following section each of these is addressed in turn.

One way the curriculum can be sequenced is by mutual agreement on the part of those responsible for the kindergarten through high school art program. Without such an agreement, teachers cannot be sure what students were taught in previous years. Without some agreed-upon sequence, learning is too often haphazard and redundant. Favorite works by artists such as Van Gogh, O'Keeffe, or Wyeth are used extensively, while those of other artists—perhaps Constable, Cassatt, and Tanner—are less likely to be shown. Introductory ideas such as warm and cool colors or basic description skills might be taught again and again if teachers believe that they must always begin at the beginning. Teachers cannot build to higher levels if they cannot assume certain foundations.

A second way that the curriculum can be sequenced is in accordance with what we know of students' developing understanding. In chapter 7, Parsons's development stages were outlined as mileposts for content sequencing. Parsons has generally identified a shifting focus of attention from favorites and color to subject matter to expression to form to judgment, as individuals move from early to later stages of development. If color is a strong attraction for primary children, art history lessons using artworks with brighter colors might be selected for the early grades. If understanding the point of view of others is a more highly developed skill, then lessons in art-historical interpretation should be planned for students who have reached a higher level of art-historical understanding. While some research is available to indicate how children respond without art history instruction, more must be done to determine how art history instruction can affect learning at various developmental levels.

A third way that the art history component of an art curriculum might be sequenced is to provide unity within the curriculum. A multidisciplinary unit might be organized around themes such as work or women. (Shorewood Fine Art Reproduction has developed sets of reproductions based on themes such as "City and Country," "Who Am I?," "Living by a Code," and "We Each Have a Dream.") In a unit developed around a theme, art-historical issues that contribute to the unit theme can be identified. For example, Diego Rivera, Grant Wood, Soviet proletarian art produced under Stalin, and the photographs of Dorothea Lange might be studied together with paintings by Pieter Breughel in a unit focusing on work. Contrasting historical ideals of female beauty by artists such as Van Eyck and Rubens might be compared to twentieth-century depictions of flappers, movie stars, or fashion models as depicted in Sears catalog ads, movie posters, magazines, or sheet music illustration (recall fig. 12). In a unit on various conceptions of women in society, these different Western ideals of beauty might be compared with those of non-Western cultures such as India, Japan, or Africa.

A fourth way that curricular sequence can be determined is by a variety of practical considerations. A concentrated unit on art history might be planned to coincide with an annual field trip to an art museum.

The history of landscape painting and drawing might be planned in early spring, just before it is warm enough to venture into the open air for drawing and watercolor sketching expeditions. The art curriculum and its art history component might be sequenced to take advantage of established units in nonart areas of the curriculum. If careful observation is being emphasized in a primary science curriculum, the description of artworks from the past might be planned to reinforce observation skills. If motion is the phenomenon being studied in a junior high science class, futurism might be a sensible period to investigate in art history. If westward expansion is the focus of a fifth-grade history class, then the art of Native Americans such as the Sioux, the Haida, and the Pueblos and the art of European-Americans such as Bingham, Catlin, and O'Sullivan might be studied in an art history unit.

Fifth and finally, the art history component of an art curriculum might be based on sequences drawn from the discipline of art history. Art history lessons can be arranged chronologically at one or several levels within the elementary and secondary art curriculum. Of course, there can be more than one possible chronology. A high school photography class could include a chronologically sequenced history of photography unit. A sixth-grade unit could focus on transitions in art in China. A junior high crafts class could include a chronological survey of metalwork and furniture design through the ages.

Implications for curriculum sequencing can be drawn from art-historical information and from art-historical inquiry. One might plan a sequence of increasingly sophisticated inquiry lessons beginning with the establishment of facts, moving on to art-historical interpretation, and concluding with the development of art-historical explanations or narratives. Some art-historical facts must already be established to begin art-historical interpretation. Art-historical explanation or narrative must be built on facts and interpretations of many works over a period of time.

Lesson Planning

After preliminary decisions have been made about goals, objectives, scope, and sequence, curriculum development can continue through the planning of lessons and units. Objectives provide a bridge between the basic principles set forth in goals, scope, and sequence and the more specific, detailed planning of lessons and units. The traditional way to organize a curriculum is to break it into units and then to break the units into lessons. Let me begin by focusing on the individual lesson plan.

Lesson Plan Components

Lesson plans can take many forms. Traditional components of most lesson plan formats are objectives, activities, resources, and evaluation techniques. A sample lesson on prehistoric painting is provided in appendix 2. That lesson was referred to in chapter 7 as an illustration of developmentally appropriate art history content and instructional activity for the primary grades. A second sample lesson on Chinese painting is also given in appendix 2. Both plans include objectives, activities, resources, and evaluation. In addition, because the plans are quite detailed, they begin with overviews to remind the teacher of the direction the lessons take. The lessons also include vocabulary lists and are followed by a series of suggestions for possible lessons in other art disciplines, with the assumption that these lessons might be part of a multidisciplinary curriculum. These suggestions identify potential connections that might be exploited in building a unit from a series of coordinated lessons. Finally, the lessons conclude with student narratives, a component that is not at all traditional. These narratives are included to provide the teacher with basic information about the art of the era or culture to be studied, written at a language level appropriate for the students for whom the lesson is planned. When an appropriate textbook or other instructional materials are available, such a narrative is not necessary. A narrative is also not necessary when the teacher is sufficiently knowledgeable about the art-historical content to flesh out the ideas outlined in the objective and activity components.

Both the prehistoric and Chinese lesson plans are intended as parts of the curriculum "A Story of Art in the World" outlined in appendix 1. The activities listed for each lesson are divided into three sections: introduction, development, and conclusion. The three categories of these activities are intended to serve rather specific purposes within each lesson. The introduction activities in both plans are intended to provide students with basic information about other times and places—in these plans, about prehistoric times and ancient China. The development activities in both plans focus students' attention on specific artworks from the cultures being studied. A few key works are identified for detailed investigation and are examined as cultural objects and as art objects. In the prehistoric lesson, possible purposes for cave paintings are considered, and the paintings are examined with attention to subject matter and production process. In the Chinese lesson, Sung dynasty paintings are considered as avenues toward peace and happiness. The effects of scale and value are also examined within these paintings. In each lesson, the concluding activity is intended to draw some relationship between ideas in the lesson and issues in the students' own lives. As it happens, both the prehistoric lesson and the Chinese lesson focus on nature. In the prehistoric lesson, students are helped to distinguish objects in nature from objects made by people. In the Chinese lesson, since it is assumed that students can already distinguish between objects made by nature and by people, students instead are asked to consider the beauty of natural objects.

The three sorts of activities illustrated in the prehistoric and Chinese lesson plans have three purposes: to immerse students in another time or place so that they can begin to appreciate a culture different from their own; to encourage students to observe carefully and reflect on key works, both culturally and aesthetically; and to help students discover that art from other times and places has some relationship to their own lives and interests. These three sorts of activities need not necessarily be followed in the order presented or slavishly adhered to in every lesson. Nor do they exhaust all the sound approaches that might be taken to planning art history instruction. However, they present an essential approach that should be employed with some regularity within the art history component of an art curriculum.

Sequencing Lessons

The reader may well have noticed the sequential relationship of the prehistoric and Chinese lessons. A glance at the overview of "A Story of Art in the World" in appendix 1 reveals that the prehistoric lesson is followed by a lesson on Egyptian art and then a lesson on Greek art. The Chinese lesson is intended to follow the Greek lesson. Some advantages of a sequenced curriculum can be found in these lessons. In setting aside the basically chronological sequence of the lessons, one can see other sequencing principles. The Chinese lesson's concluding activity on nature builds on a simpler understanding of nature presented in the prehistoric lesson. One of the objectives in the Egyptian lesson, sequenced between the prehistoric and Chinese lessons, addresses the use of size to signify importance in Egyptian art; this knowledge is reinforced in the Chinese lesson. A reference to the Greek lesson that directly precedes the Chinese lesson is made through a *Discus Thrower* comparison.

As noted earlier, different curriculum sequences can be established by using different combinations of sequencing principles. Students are likely to find new knowledge more interesting when it reinforces and builds on knowledge with which they are already comfortable. Increased educational efficiency and effectiveness are possible with careful sequencing.

Unit Planning

Let us move our attention now to the many ways in which lesson plans can be organized into units. Unit plans are constituted of coordinated lesson plans organized around some central idea. Lessons within a unit reinforce each other, build on each other, and foster the transfer of learning from one content area to another. Units within a balanced art curriculum can be structured in a number of ways, depending on the model of interdisciplinary integration assumed within the curriculum.

Three distinct models of integration among the art disciplines have been proposed, to which Eldon Katter has recently added a fourth.[3] A food metaphor is used to illustrate these four models.

Segregated Units

The first model of integration is the segregated, or supermarket, model. In this model, integration is analogous to different pea products within a supermarket. We find frozen peas in the frozen food department, canned peas in the canned goods department, dried peas in a third department, and so on. The pea products are in different departments; they are handled differently and not cross-referenced in any way. The segregated art curriculum is common in colleges and universities. Studio courses are taught in the fine arts department; art history is taught in the art history department; aesthetics is taught in the philosophy department; and art criticism might be taught in the English department, art education department, or whatever department develops an interest in criticism (if, indeed, it is taught at all). Some high school art history courses reflect this segregated model. A distinct art history course may be offered without curricular connections to other art courses offered in the high school.

Coequal Units

A second model for integration is the coequal, or peas-in-a-pod model, in which the distinctive components (or disciplines) are each carefully and separately attended to. For example, in a coequal curriculum, there might be a unit devoted to art criticism, another to art history, another to aesthetics, and a fourth to art production. The components line up like peas in a pod. In a coequal curriculum, a program or a course holds together separate courses or units that otherwise are quite distinct. The curriculum component "A Story of Art in the World," given in appendix 1, is designed as a coequal part of a multiyear art curriculum. It is intended to be abbreviated enough to fit within the time constraints of an elementary art curriculum. It also acknowledges possible relationships that might be constructed across the art disciplines, but it was developed essentially as a distinct curriculum component.

Assimilated Units

A third model for integration is the assimilation, or split-pea soup, model. In an assimilated curriculum, the components lose their individual identities and mix together to form an organic whole. For example, in an assimilated curriculum, students might be involved in a production project initiated with references to artworks of the past that culminates with a critique of student work based on a variety of standards of aesthetic value. The components are so fragmented and diffused that they are as unidentifiable as peas and carrots in split-pea soup. This is a common model of interdisciplinary integration in elementary and secondary art curricula. Michelangelo and Leonardo drawings might be added to the mix of a high school drawing unit to exemplify and inspire excellence in drawing. However, the Renaissance works in such a unit may not be considered at all within their art-historical context. They may be labeled by period, culture, artist, and date, but other art-historical information may be completely absent. In such a lesson, the ideas and ideals of the Renaissance, perhaps even the subject matter of the drawings, are ignored, while the technical skills of the artists are highlighted. Although the studio goals of such a unit are clear, art history goals are insignificant or unrecognizable.

Amalgamated Units

A fourth model for integration is the amalgamated, or stir-fry, model of integration. In an amalgamated curriculum, the components work together in a variety of ways with a variety of emphases, all the while maintaining their individual identities. The components maintain their integrity, each flavoring the whole like snowpeas and carrots in a stir-fry. The amalgamated model of integration is perhaps the ideal model for integrating art disciplines within a curriculum. Amalgamated units can be constructed using a number of different types of central ideas such as a theme, a function, a formal concept, a technical issue, a culture, or a work of art.

In chapter 1, a number of issues were presented that can be used as ideas around which to build amalgamated units. One might use a function of art as a central idea—for example, the function of art in early agrarian cultures. Such an idea could cut across centuries and continents. Other functions could also serve as unit ideas, such as art as social comment, as container, or as ritual object.

A formal issue can serve as the central idea for an amalgamated high school unit. For instance, Heinrich Woelfflin's formally defined distinction between classical and baroque styles in painting can provide the central idea for a unit. An art history lesson can look at prime examples of the pendulum swings from classical to baroque style in the Renaissance and beyond. A criticism lesson could investigate the formal characteristics of Woelfflin's classical and baroque styles in contemporary painting. A lesson in aesthetics could examine whether notions of style can be lifted from their contextual roots. In a production class, students could produce a painting either in the classical style (using linearity, planar structure, closed form, multiplicity, and absolute clarity of subject) or in the baroque style (using painterliness, recession, open form, unity, and relative clarity of subject).[4]

An amalgamated unit, such as a ceramics unit within a high school crafts course, might be organized around a medium or technique. In a production lesson within such a unit, students could design and build a ceramic container. In an art criticism lesson, students might look at slides of contemporary ceramic pieces and discuss the significance of such work. They might even read articles or reviews in *American Craft.* In an aesthetics lesson, students could examine distinctions between the concepts "art" and "craft." Student ceramic projects, museum pieces, and molded bunnies and elves made in community ceramics classes could be examined. Karen A. Hamblen has proposed discussions of such contested concepts as a strategy for introducing aesthetics into the art classroom.[5] An art history lesson within such a unit might examine the evolving importance of function in the history of American ceramics or the spiritual significance of ceramic tea services in traditional Japanese culture.

An era such as the baroque can serve as the central idea for an amalgamated unit. In an art history class, two cultural issues might receive attention: the exploitation of ancient Native American cultures to fund the arts of colonial powers; and the contrasting baroque styles of Catholic and Protestant regions of Europe. Much of the opulence of baroque architecture was made possible by the profits made from Europe's colonies in Africa, Asia, and the Americas. The mystery and grandeur of religious paintings helped support the Counter-Reformation in Catholic Europe, while the shift from religious to secular subject matter (such as portraits, still lifes, and landscapes) reflected the loss of the Church as a major patron of the arts in Protestant Europe. Baroque developments in composition and lighting might provide the basis for a production lesson. In an art criticism lesson, comparisons might be made between the drama of baroque paintings and drama in contemporary neo-expressionist art. In an aesthetics lesson, students might consider whether expressiveness is a defining characteristic of art.

Finally, an amalgamated unit can be organized around one artwork such as the sixteenth-century Netherlandish painting by Pieter Brueghel entitled *Harvesters*. An art history lesson could investigate changing representations of farming throughout Western art history: in harvesting and herding scenes depicted in Egyptian tomb paintings; in farm scenes used to illustrate months of the year in the Limbourg Brothers' fifteenth-century book of hours; in idyllic nineteenth-century English country landscapes painted by John Constable; and in agricultural subjects in later art such as Rosa Bonheur's *Horse Fair* or Grant Wood's Iowa landscapes. Another art history lesson could examine agricultural subjects in non-Western art, such as representations of the corn god in Mayan sculpture; ancient corn, rain, sun, and cloud kachina dolls in the U.S. Southwest; an appliqued cotton wall hanging from Dahomey, West Africa, depicting a coconut harvest; and a Japanese scroll painting depicting peasants in a country landscape. An art criticism lesson could be developed around Sue Coe's recent series of paintings called *Porkopolis*, a biting commentary on contemporary "factory farming." A production lesson developed around Breughel's *Harvesters* could focus on how artists get ideas from the world around them. Possible subjects include: "People Working Together," "Where Food Comes From," and "People and the Natural Environment." An aesthetics lesson might ask the question, Is it ever really possible to understand what an artwork means to someone else?

Summary

Many variables must be balanced when organizing art history teaching. Identifying significant, clear goals and establishing the scope of content to be taught are first priorities. Selecting principles to be used in sequencing art history content must also be considered early in the curriculum-planning process. After goals are established, specific objectives intended to lead to those goals can be identified. Specific objectives provide the core for planning lessons, including instructional activities, resources, and evaluation procedures. Somewhere in the curriculum organization process, principles must be selected for organizing groups of lessons into units. Many different, sound organizational structures can be developed, depending on decisions made at each step of the curriculum-planning process. Integration of art history with other art disciplines is one of the most complex issues to be considered when planning a balanced curriculum. The next chapter continues to analyze that issue.

NOTES

1. Israel Scheffler, *The Language of Education* (Springfield, Ill.: Charles C. Thomas, 1960), pp. 105–6.

2. Michael D. Day, "Evaluating Student Achievement in Discipline-based Art Programs," *Studies in Art Education* 26, no. 4 (1985): 237.

3. Mary Erickson and Eldon Katter, "Integrating the Four Components of a Quality Art Education," *NAEA Advisory*, Fall 1988.

4. Heinrich Woelfflin, *Principles of Art History: The Problem of the Development of Style in Later Art* (New York: Dover Publications, 1932), pp. 14–15.

5. Karen A. Hamblen, "Exploring Contested Concepts for Aesthetic Literacy," *Journal of Aesthetic Education* 20, no. 2 (1986): 67–76.

9

Integration: Where Does Art History Fit into the Art Curriculum?

As art educators work to develop broad-based, balanced art curricula, they encounter the challenge of integration among art disciplines. Although some debates continue in the field, many art educators agree that four art disciplines are important sources of content for elementary and secondary art education. Those disciplines are art criticism, art history, art production, and aesthetics. These disciplines, especially art history, are informed by other disciplines such as anthropology, archaeology, mythology, and social psychology, but the core art disciplines remain the main focus of art educators.

This book has focused on art history. A few teachers, especially at the high school level, have the opportunity to plan courses based on just one discipline. By far, most art courses in elementary and secondary art programs do not provide such opportunities but instead require that all art education, regardless of its source discipline, be included in one integrated course, usually one course per grade level. Time allotment in these courses is not sufficient to further subdivide into distinct minicourses, one in each art discipline. Content from all art disciplines must somehow be effectively and efficiently integrated into a whole.

There is considerable debate about how multiple art disciplines should be integrated within a single art curriculum. A number of alternatives exist. Some present sound solutions and others do not. In their enthusiasm to reflect current thinking in the field, some art educators have examined their present practice, discovered some activities that bear some resemblance to nonproduction art disciplines, and labeled those relationships art history, art criticism, or aesthetics. Showing students a reproduction of an artwork might be called art history. Conducting a class critique of students' work might be called art criticism.[1] Aesthetic perception exercises might be called aesthetics. Although these classroom activities may be sound art education, it is misleading to claim that they teach art history, criticism, or aesthetics. It may not be important that primary school children be able to distinguish one art discipline from another, but those who develop the curriculum should be able to. If teachers claim that their curriculum is based on an art discipline, some of the subject matter content within the curriculum should reflect characteristic concerns of that discipline. This chapter presents some possibilities for integration between art history and other art disciplines, possibilities that identify learning content based on characteristic concerns of the art disciplines.

Integrating Art History and Art Production

Let us consider first the relationship between art history and art production. The reader will recall that in chapter 6, art history teaching was categorized as "teaching art history as artworks," "teaching art history as information," and "teaching art history as inquiry." Artworks from the past have been used in many art production lessons for many years. Artworks are used as exemplars of sensory qualities, of formal structures, of technical processes, as expressive achievements, and as precedents in depiction of subject matter. When artworks of the past are presented outside their historical contexts as illustrations of art concepts and principles, they can be excellent instructional aids. However, curriculum planners should realize that when artworks from the past are thus used, they are contributing to learning about art production but may not be contributing in any significant way to learning about art history.

How, then, can the discipline of art history, not just artworks, relate to the discipline of art production? It may be helpful to make some distinctions within the artistic production process. These distinctions are based loosely on the writings of Monroe Beardsley and Laura Chapman.[2] One can conceive of the artistic production process as having four phases: idea generation, development, use of media, and judgment of completion. Art-historical information can be helpful in understanding each of these phases.

Idea Generation

How might idea generation be enhanced through art history? The history of art is rich with insights into the influences of culture on artistic idea generation. As power structures shift, the influence of societal forces on art changes. We can observe, for example, the virtually complete control of the medieval church; the middle-class patronage of baroque artists in the north; the traditional pressures exerted by the French academy;

the advertising expectations for Toulouse Lautrec's posters; the social agenda of the WPA artists during the Great Depression; and the concerns of Congress about the artistic ideas currently supported by the National Endowment for the Arts. There have always been less-obvious societal influences on the ideas that artists find significant. Feminists and neo-Marxists have focused attention on the influences of gender and status on artistic production throughout history. One need only contrast the low status of the anonymous medieval artisan with the royal status of the emperor-artist Hui Tsung to recognize that societal notions about art and status varied dramatically in the twelfth century in different regions of the world. Even though artists of other times and cultures may not always have consciously intended to present values within their cultures, they seem invariably to have done so.

Students in a secondary-level art production class might find it valuable to identify contemporary influences on the ideas they find interesting in their own artistic production. They can attempt to identify patrons for their own art such as the school and social groups as well as family and friends. They can attempt to determine to what extent their artistic ideas are influenced by teachers, family and friends, the designers of consumer goods, mass media decision makers, and others. Students learning about art production should understand that throughout the ages and across the globe, artists, with occasional exceptions, have used their knowledge of art history as a starting point for their own art. Renaissance artists were inspired by the artwork of ancient Greece and Rome. Chinese painters were inspired by generation after generation of landscape painters. Today's Northwest Coast Native American artists use tribal traditions in their art. Like the revivalist architects working one hundred years ago, postmodern architects borrow ideas for their buildings from a rich storehouse of historical styles.

In some eras, like the early to High Renaissance, particular problems captured the attention of generations of artists. Problems in the representation of solid form and three-dimensional space on a two-dimensional surface were attacked gradually as artists learned from the study and experimentation of those who preceded them. In other eras, such as the past forty years in America, some artists have used the art of the immediate past as a stimulus against which to react. The looseness of the abstract expressionists was followed by the rigidity of op art and hard-edge painting. Pop artists reacted against the exclusivity of the fine-art world. As students learn about artistic production, they should learn that a treasure house of ideas lies ready to be discovered among the issues and problems faced by artists before them.

Artistic Decision Making

After ideas for an artwork have been selected, how might art history contribute to the development of that artwork? Usually, we have only the completed work to examine, which manifests, but does not necessarily reveal, the decision-making process of its maker. Happily, preliminary sketches and drawings for some major works still exist that exhibit the choices with which an artist was faced. Michelangelo and Picasso are just two of many artists who reveal much of their decision making through their preliminary sketches. X-rays and restorations sometimes reveal choices made by artists as they produced their work. Sometimes other documents, such as Van Gogh's letters to his brother or correspondence surrounding the commissioning of a portrait by Rembrandt, exist that can shed light on the artistic decision-making process. In more recent years, modern technology has made even more information available, like the films of Diego Rivera at work.

If historical evidence is not always available about the evolution of individual artworks, there is very often historical evidence of shifting artistic choices within the overall oeuvre of one artist. By studying the work of one artist, such as Francisco Goya or Jacob Lawrence, as it evolved throughout that artist's lifetime, one can learn much of the artist's changing influences, interests, and artistic choices. Individual works themselves can reveal dramatic differences in artists' modes of production. One need only contrast the copious drawings and cutouts of Matisse with the much less numerous, laboriously constructed paintings of Seurat to recognize the range among ways of working. Students learning about artistic production should understand that artists make decisions as they work and that artists sometimes accept or reject those decisions. Students should understand that artists sometimes plan their work in great detail and at other times execute a work spontaneously— that is, there are many different modes of artistic production.

The Use of Media

How might art history contribute to a better understanding of the use of media in artistic production? Students can consider art-historical examples of a remarkable range of artistic media from bark baskets of eastern woodland Native Americans to assemblages of metal, wood, horn, shells, and beads made by the Songe people of central Africa; from traditional sand painting of the Navajo to egg tempera painting in the Gothic era in Europe. The precision stonework of the Inca or the extraordinarily crafted bronzes of Shang-dynasty China also provide models of excellence that might inspire students to become masters of their media.

Diverse uses of a single medium, are thoroughly exemplified in art of the past. Consider, for example, the application of oil paint by Rubens, Van Gogh, Helen Frankenthaler, and Richard Estes.

The examples offered so far use historical works illustratively. Art-historical information can also provide insight into the use of media in artistic production. Art history offers examples of dramatic changes in art brought on, at least in part, by the introduction of new media. Consider the influence of the invention of oil paint in the fifteenth century, the impact of the invention of photography on art in the nine-teenth century, or the influence in the past century of steel construction on architectural design. As students consider the use of newer media such as plastic, neon, video, and computers in their art, they might reflect on media revolutions of the past. At the same time, they can consider the millennia-long, global continuity of traditional media such as wood, fiber, ceramics, charcoal, and paper.

The Judgment of Completion

A final phase of artistic production can be called the "judgment of completion." Can art history help students learn how to determine when their artworks are complete? Artists must learn to be critics of their own work. The history of art illustrates clearly that different standards have been used to judge success in different times and cultures. The Romans attempted to adopt the standards established earlier in their captive province, Greece. Medieval artists were more concerned with spiritual power than realistic representation in their art. Sensuousness was set as a standard of beauty in rococo painting. Political persuasiveness, in very different forms, was the standard of excellence for the Napoleonic propa-ganda of David and the satire of Daumier. Established European and East Coast standards were rejected by painters in the 1930s such as Thomas Hart Benton and Grant Wood, who chose to depict regional pride and independence. The fact that Henry Ossawa Tanner discontinued painting genre scenes and devoted much effort to religious paintings suggests to some that he may not have valued his genre paintings highly within the body of his work.

Art history provides not only a tremendous range of standards for judging whether a production process has been successfully completed but also dramatically illustrates the transitory nature of art judgments through time. Art judged a failure in one era is sometimes judged to be a great success in another. Consider the Renaissance estimation of medie-val architecture as crude, hence the name "Gothic" after the barbarian Goths; or the rediscovery, centuries later, of a long-forgotten artist such as Georges De La Tour; or today's interest in African art objects once characterized as little more than crude curiosities. Occasionally, one can identify works that an artist of the past was unable to complete, such as Michelangelo's *Rondanini Pieta*. Such a work can inform students of the persistence of the problem of completion, even for established, experienced artists. Students studying the production process should learn that a decision must be made about when an artwork is complete and that artists throughout time have faced such judgments.

We know that artworks from the past and information about those works can be helpful in teaching about art production. Let us now turn to art-historical inquiry as it might relate to the teaching of art production.

Art-Historical Inquiry and Art Production

Students learning about art production can learn much from the application of art-historical inquiry to their own artistic development. Let me illustrate with two sample activities: a production analysis exercise and a peer art history exercise. A production analysis exercise is an activity in which students reflect historically on the production of one of their own artworks. Such an analysis can be organized around the four phases of artistic production outlined above: idea generation, development, use of media, and judgment of completion. The exercise can be assigned either before or after an artwork has been produced. If the exercise is assigned prior to the beginning of an art project, students can keep a running sketchbook-log in which they note inspirations, trial-and-error experiments, thumbnail sketches, sources for ideas, false starts, working drawings, teacher comments, in-process notes, and the like. If the exercise is assigned after the work is completed, the students must use their memories to recall ideas and decisions made as they progressed. The production analysis might be reported in the form of a short paper or oral report given on the occasion of a final critique, or the analysis might be reported on a worksheet submitted with the artwork. A sample production analysis worksheet can be found in appendix 4. Historical reflection on students' own work should help increase their consciousness of artistic decision making and at the same time increase their awareness of their place within the larger art world and the culture of which it is a part.

A peer art history exercise is another application of art-historical inquiry to artistic production. In this exercise, each student is assigned a classmate as a subject artist. This exercise should be especially effective in a senior-level portfolio class. The task of each student as art-historical researcher is to use a classmate's portfolio as the beginning evidence for building an art-historical account of that classmate's artistic development. The portfolio can be supplemented with other historical evidence requested by the researcher, such as sketchbooks and work produced earlier in the subject's life, both in and out of school. The researcher might choose to interview the subject-artist and perhaps others, such as classmates and teachers. Issues to be considered might include early influences, dramatic changes, pressures, rewards, viewer reception, career high points, interpretations of key works, and explanations of changes within the artist's career. The peer art history can be reported either orally or in written form, either to the class as a whole or only to the teacher and the subject-artist. Such an exercise should help young artists develop objectivity and some appreciation for a variety of shared issues within their own art community.

Art Production Supporting Learning in Art History

All the relationships presented thus far have focused on how art history can aid in the teaching of art production. Can this relationship be reversed? Can instruction in art production aid in the teaching of art history? Absolutely. All the activities suggested above can be used to help students better understand art history. Whenever a concept in art history is related to the immediate production experience of a student, that concept is made more relevant to the student's life and immediate interests. Comparing the artistic production processes of artists of other times and cultures with students' own artistic production brings concreteness to what might otherwise seem to be very distant and abstract historical situations. Such comparisons act as analogies to aid students' understanding. Applying art-historical inquiry to students' own artistic production offers students opportunities to practice art-historical inquiry skills. Such inquiry exercises develop independent investigation, hypothesizing, evaluation of evidence, argument building, and other higher-order thinking skills, all of which are required in art-historical inquiry. Such exercises should also foster attitudes such as curiosity, independence, and an interest in asking questions, all of which are essential for art-historical inquiry.

Integrating Art History and Art Criticism

Distinguishing Art Criticism from Art History

The distinction between the work of the artist and the art historian is easy to draw, but such a distinction is not so easily drawn between the work of the art critic and the art historian. Art historians traditionally have academic credentials in the field. They tend to be employed in university art history departments or in art museums. Art critics can come to the field from a variety of backgrounds. They may be employed by universities or perhaps more often by newspapers and magazines.

Unlike art historians, art critics do not necessarily have a clear-cut academic area or department in which to be trained or with which to be identified. Critics may study or teach in art, English, journalism, or American studies departments, or wherever professors interested in criticism can be found; then, too, they may develop their skills on the job in a journalistic setting.

Much of what art critics do is very similar, if not identical, to what art historians do. Art critics can sometimes write art history, and art historians can sometimes write art criticism. Howard Risatti distinguishes the two disciplines quite simply: "Art criticism tends to focus on modern and contemporary art rather than art from other periods. Unlike art history, which by definition is concerned with art in a historical context, criticism is concerned with art within the context of the present."[3]

Art-Historical Information and Art Criticism

How is the information of art history related to the information of art criticism? Art historians do not use knowledge of contemporary art to explain the art of the past. Although the focus of art criticism is on contemporary art, art critics often make comparisons between today's art and art of earlier times. Such comparisons might be useful to teachers in their attempts to integrate art content within an art course. If students are acquainted with basic art-historical information, they might be asked to draw parallels between the work of contemporary artists and works produced in other times and places. For example, Keith Haring's calligraphic symbols might be compared to Chinese calligraphy, Aztec symbols, or Egyptian hieroglyphs; contemporary neo-expressionist painting might be contrasted with abstract expressionist and German expressionist painting.

Art-historical information is traditionally systematized into a network of information organized chronologically and by cultures. Art criticism information tends not to be as systematically organized. Both art-historical and critical information is published in book and periodical form. However, art criticism is usually found in periodicals because it is most often focused on current events in today's art world. Traditionally, when educators have drawn educational content from art history, they have tended to focus first on information. When they draw content from art criticism, they have tended to focus first on inquiry process.

Inquiry in Art Criticism and Art History

Art-historical and art-critical information can easily (if arbitrarily) be distinguished by the date of production of the artwork being studied. The processes of art-historical and art-critical inquiry cannot so easily be distinguished. In chapter 6, I discussed the three components of art-historical inquiry: the establishment of facts, the historical interpretation of meaning, and the explanation or narration of change. There is a tradition in art education, stimulated by the writing of Edmund Burke Feldman, that divides art criticism into four processes: description, analysis, interpretation, and evaluation. This four-step process is very much in use as a guide for teaching art criticism today.[4]

Some art educators studying the teaching of art criticism caution teachers about the limitations of the Feldman model. George Geahigan notes that contemporary art criticism has a looser structure, a broader contextual base, a less formalist orientation, and more concern for audience reception than does the Feldman model. The same concerns Geahigan describes in contemporary art criticism can be found in contemporary art-historical scholarship. In fact, art criticism's broader contextual base and concern for audience reception would seem to bring that discipline closer to art history. Geahigan argues that art criticism and art history should "work together in tandem, not be parceled out into two completely separate entities."[5]

I shall attempt to demonstrate Geahigan's point by comparing my three-step analysis of art-historical inquiry processes with art education's traditional four-step art criticism process. It is important to remember that the steps identified in these disciplines are not evident in all cases of art history or art criticism and that no set sequence of steps is followed in either discipline. Nonetheless, as art educators attempt to plan instruction in art education, they may find it valuable to isolate phases within a larger process in order to plan activities aimed at developing specific skills drawn from the very complex disciplines of art history and art criticism.

Description and Analysis

Let us consider first the skills of description and analysis, which are often taught as fundamental processes of art criticism. Both these skills are needed as part of the "establishing facts" phase of art-historical inquiry. At the factual level of inquiry, art history often requires additional steps not usually required in art criticism. Before art historians can describe or analyze artworks, they must determine whether the work on view today has changed in appearance from the work that was produced at some earlier time. I have called this process "imagined restoration." Because art critics generally deal with newer artworks that have not been changed over a period of decades, centuries, or millennia, imagined restoration is not a common problem in art criticism. Attribution is another basic fact-establishing process often required of art historians but seldom required of art critics. Determining who produced an artwork and when, where, or for whom it was produced may require great effort on the part of art historians. Such basic facts are usually readily available to art critics studying recently made artworks.

Setting aside imagined restoration and attribution, the basic fact-gathering processes of description and analysis are the same for art critics and art historians. Practicing these skills can benefit learning in one discipline as much as the other. Skills in description and analysis in either discipline depend upon the development of an art vocabulary. Terms such as "landscape," "color intensity," "negative space," "stridency," and "impasto" assist students in perceptual discrimination. Increasing students' ability to maintain their attention on an artwork and to discriminate its visual qualities is essential to both disciplines.

Interpretation

A primary skill in art criticism and art history is that of interpretation. In outlining art-historical inquiry processes, I qualified interpretation in art history as "historical interpretation." Interpretation in either discipline is focused on determining what an artwork is about or what it means. Postmodern art criticism and art history tend to de-emphasize the significance of form as the essence of meaning in an artwork. In recent years, contextual issues, always of considerable interest to art historians, have gained increased attention in both disciplines. Politics, economics, class, gender, and other contextual factors are called upon more and more often as evidence in the interpretation of contemporary and historical artworks. Because art historians are basically involved with art from other times or cultures and art critics tend to interpret artworks made relatively recently, the demands of interpretation differ in the two disciplines. For the most part, art critics can use their familiarity with the culture they live in as a basis for interpreting artworks made in and for the same culture. Art historians, on the other hand, cannot rely on their own culture as a basis for historical interpretation. Art historians attempt to interpret artworks in their own contexts. For example, to interpret a medieval ivory carving or a Persian miniature, art historians must become familiar with cultures quite different from their own. It may be true that we cannot ever completely set aside our own culture; however, it is true that we can increase our knowledge of another culture. Art historians attempt to interpret artworks in light of this increased knowledge.

Art programs in elementary and secondary grades should focus significant attention on meaning in artworks, whether those artworks are contemporary or historical. Students should understand that artworks are more than the result of technical processes and more than formal organizations. They should understand that artworks are meaningful. Both art criticism and art history can lead to this understanding.

Judgment

The last of the traditional art-critical phases is evaluation or judgment. For some, evaluation is the culmination of the art criticism process. For others, evaluation is less significant than interpretation. Evaluation plays a different role in art criticism than in art history. An evaluation of an artwork or exhibition is often the conclusion of the art criticism process for a critic. An evaluation and evidence to support that evaluation are very frequent components of critical writing. Many pieces of art-historical writing do not include evaluative conclusions at all. Whereas evaluation is often the conclusion of the art criticism process, evaluation is more often the beginning of the art-historical process. A critic or reviewer is often willing (and may even feel obliged) to consider any exhibition being presented in the community. An art historian is less likely to begin with an exhibition than with an evaluation. An art historian might reach the evaluative conclusion that some work, artist, period, or art form is important art-historically but is inadequately understood. For instance, Stephen Addiss offers a personal evaluation in chapter 4 as part of his decision to investigate Bosai. Addiss says that the informality and freedom of Bosai's landscape paintings and the wild dance of his calligraphy appealed to him. At a more scholarly level, he concludes that no research had been completed on Bosai and his work. These evaluations initiated rather than culminated his art-historical inquiry process.

In an educational setting, evaluation can be set aside in favor of general art-historical understanding. Visual objects from another time might be investigated art-historically to help students understand how values are manifest in visual forms and how visual transformations occur through time. Objects such as automobiles, telephones, record album covers, T-shirts, or make-up fashions can be selected for art-historical study. Students may well be motivated to consider the meaning of objects so closely related to their own lives.

Converging Disciplines

One process of art-historical inquiry that remains to be considered in relation to art criticism is explanation or narration—that is, the process of accounting for change through time. Explanations or narratives are built on facts and historical interpretations of many artworks produced at different times or in different cultures. Since art criticism tends to focus on an individual work or exhibition, explanation or narration is not usually a concern of art critics. When art critics begin to connect the art of today with art from the past, art criticism and art history begin to merge.

A great deal of overlap exists between the inquiry processes of art history and art criticism. Issues related to different times or different cultures are characteristic concerns of art history and not characteristic concerns of art criticism. A number of skills related to description, analysis, and interpretation are common to art history and art criticism, making transfer potential between the two disciplines great.

Integrating Art History and Aesthetics

Aesthetic Education

The fourth art discipline commonly proposed as a source for content in art education is aesthetics. Educational prescriptions based on aesthetics have varied widely through the years. For about a quarter of a century, there has been an interest area within education called "aesthetic education." At least two quite distinct senses of aesthetic education exist. One views aesthetic education as instruction in the arts with a central focus on aesthetic experience. The second views aesthetic education as instruction that focuses on aesthetic experience as educational method rather than content. In this broader sense, educational activities may be proposed for any content area of the curriculum, from mathematics to social studies. Activities are planned with the intention that students experience the content as aesthetic, that is, intrinsically rewarding.

Both senses of aesthetic education are much broader than art education. The first sense of aesthetic education encompasses most of what is usually considered art education as well as education in music, dance, theater, and sometimes literature. Aesthetic perception and aesthetic experience have been important concepts used to justify and structure aesthetic education in this first sense. Activities are proposed in which students are guided in their perception of the arts with the aim of enriching the aesthetic dimension of their lives. The second sense of aesthetic education is broader still. It calls for nothing less than a rethinking of the whole educational enterprise, transforming all learning into aesthetic experience.

Aesthetics as Philosophy

The analysis of aesthetics presented here is based on a different notion of aesthetics, a notion of teaching aesthetics rather than aesthetic education. In this chapter, teaching aesthetics refers to teaching based on that branch of philosophy called aesthetics.[6] Teaching aesthetics has broad parameters.

The branch of philosophy called aesthetics is by no means limited to the study of visual artworks. Traditionally, aesthetics has addressed all the arts as well as any other object or event that might be considered beautiful or that might provide an aesthetic experience. Marilyn Stewart identifies four basic issues in aesthetics. She describes aesthetics as dialogue (or "reasonable discussion") on the nature and significance of art, beauty, aesthetic response, and criticism.[7] A fifth set of issues for dialogue in aesthetics concerns relationships between aesthetic and other values. The work of the aesthetician and the art critic is sometimes difficult to distinguish. For the purposes of this analysis, I shall define the art critic as primarily interested in specific artworks and the aesthetician as primarily interested in general issues about art.

Is there information in aesthetics, or is aesthetics all about the inquiry process? When planning instruction in aesthetics, one tends first to consider dialogue or the philosophical inquiry process rather than information. There is, of course, a history of dialogue on issues in aesthetics. People have thought, speculated, reflected, and argued about issues in aesthetics in different cultures around the world for a very long time (see chapter 2 for a discussion of that thought in several cultures). Art educators might consider informing students about some of the conclusions reached by thinkers of other times and places. If such information were to constitute a portion of elementary or secondary art education, then art history information could be effectively coordinated with aesthetics information.

Let us consider each of the five areas in aesthetics identified above and art-historical information that might be integrated with study in those areas. For non-Western aesthetics, I rely heavily on Richard L. Anderson's *Calliope's Sisters: A Comparative Study of Philosophies of Art.*[8]

The Nature and Significance of Art

Reflection on the nature and significance of art has a long history in Western philosophy, from ancient Greece to the Renaissance to today. Some non-Western cultures also have long histories of reflecting on art. For example, the history of Japanese speculative thought contains concepts that apply to art beginning with Shintoism, Esoteric, Amida, Zen Buddhism, and Japanese Confucianism. What counts as art has changed through the years in different cultures. Wine and oil containers of ancient Greece are housed in art museums with Renaissance paintings and sculptures and with documentation of contemporary conceptual art performances. Very different ideas about the nature and significance of art are evidenced by those objects. In chapter 4, an aesthetic issue was introduced: the Western notion of calligraphy as a minor art form compared with Chinese and Japanese conceptions of calligraphy as "the pinnacle of all art forms." Consider the educational value of presenting and comparing William Blake's work in chapter 2 to the Guerrilla Girls poster in chapter 3 and to the Bosai calligraphy piece in chapter 4. Each artwork manifests a different culture's idea about the nature of art. Activities that focus on the nature and significance of art can be planned to teach about art history as well as aesthetics.

The Nature and Significance of Beauty

A second area of interest in aesthetics is the notion of beauty. What is considered beautiful has varied widely through time and across cultures. To raise issues about beauty, a teacher might introduce body decoration and adornment from different times and places. Baroque costume, hairdos, and facial powder might be compared to today's clothing, hair, and make-up fashions. Personal beautification in today's industrial, consumer-oriented Western culture might be contrasted with personal beautification among the foraging San people of southwestern Africa. The San are nomadic and carry everything they own with them as they move through the Kalahari Desert, yet they devote considerable effort to beautifying themselves with ostrich egg jewelry, tattoos, hair ornaments, and body painting. The study of beauty, a significant consideration in today's popular culture, can be used to increase art-historical understanding as well as an understanding of aesthetics.

The Nature and Significance of Aesthetic Experience

A third area of interest in aesthetics concerns the concept of aesthetic experience, which is generally understood here to be an experience worth having for its own sake. As religion became a less-dominant force in Western art and as photography usurped some of the traditional documentary functions of painting and drawing, modern art built its reason for being more and more firmly on the notion of aesthetic experience. In recent years, some commentators, particularly those involved in postmodern cultural theory, have argued that there is no such special experience at all. But, as some recent publications clearly indicate, debate about the existence and value of aesthetic experience goes on.[9]

Although the term "aesthetic experience" is a Western one, non-Western cultures have valued the experience of the beautiful. Traditional Navajo culture, moreover, has placed a strong emphasis on experiencing the beautiful. Anderson writes that "Navajos believe that the world was created in a state of beauty, balance, and harmony, held in dynamic balance with ugliness, chaos, and evil."[10] Because the Navajo believe that beauty is found in process, not in products, some of their most sophisticated art—sandpainting—requires hours to make but exists in its finished form for only a few minutes. Classroom discussion of aesthetic experience could surely be initiated by consideration of the different aesthetic experiences stimulated by Navajo sandpainting, on the one hand, and French Impressionist painting, on the other. Students might ask whether experiencing beauty in the harmony of the world shares characteristics with experiencing artistic harmony. Such activities, focused on understanding aesthetic experience, can support instruction in art history and aesthetics.

The Nature and Significance of Art Criticism

A fourth area of interest to aestheticians is the nature and significance of art criticism. Teachers might set contemporary art criticism in context by presenting examples of controversial art criticism: the panning of the Impressionists in the late nineteenth century or the neglect, until recently, of folk art. Essential to any analysis of art criticism is identification of criteria used to judge artworks. Any review of the history of art would reveal changing evaluative criteria. Criteria used today (or at any other time in Western art history) might be contrasted with criteria used in some non-Western cultures. For example, Anderson identifies nine traditional criteria that the Yoruba of west Africa use to evaluate statuary: a good Yoruba carving should not be too real or too abstract; it should have clarity of form and line; it should also have a smooth surface, roundness, delicacy, and proper positioning of parts of the figure; it should exhibit craftsmanship; it is usually bilaterally symmetrical and expressive of calm dignity; and, finally, it should depict an individual in the prime of life, neither very young nor old.

Students might be asked to propose their own criteria for evaluating art or to identify the criteria appealed to within the writings of some contemporary art critics. A dialogue on the nature and significance of art criticism is likely to encompass more than a discussion of evaluation. As indicated in the previous section of this chapter, art criticism also employs description, analysis, and interpretation. A dialogue on art criticism might investigate the similarities and differences between critical analysis and historical analysis. Comparing critical and historical interpretations might be particularly informative.

Art and Other Values

A fifth area of interest to aestheticians is the relationship between aesthetic and nonaesthetic values. Recently, debates about the relationships between art, obscenity, and the common good have flooded the news media. Art has always had connections with other values. Religious values have been integrated with aesthetic values throughout most art history, Western and non-Western. No study of medieval art can avoid consideration of the religious values that dominated that historical era. Anderson describes aboriginal Australian aesthetic beliefs: "Through art mortals can come into immediate, intimate, and genuine contact with the all important spirits of the Eternal Dreamtime."[11] Does this description also approximate the beliefs of the medieval peasant in a Gothic cathedral or a Buddhist monk contemplating a painting of bamboo? Information about art from other times and cultures can be used within the classroom setting to illustrate propositions in aesthetics, both Western and non-Western.

Stewart proposes that education in aesthetics may be rooted in a history of aesthetics, but the essence of teaching aesthetics should be in "reasonable discussion" or dialogue. She would have art educators engage students in dialogue about issues in aesthetics. In the preceding section, I have attempted to show how the history of art can be used to stimulate dialogue in five areas of interest. Stewart identifies additional issues in aesthetics raised by cross-temporal and cross-cultural comparisons. Are there universals in art? What does it mean to say that a work is original? Is the value of a work tied to its historical relevance? She agrees that art history can support study in aesthetics but also argues further that the study of aesthetics can support the study of art history. She proposes that engaging students in dialogue about aesthetics develops students' capacity to wonder about art. Stewart suggests that this experience in wondering might enhance students' interest and understanding of what people of other times and places thought and believed about art.[12]

Summary

Developing art curricula for the elementary and secondary grades is a complex task that can be approached from different perspectives and can therefore yield quite different results. Integrating the constituent art disciplines is a major challenge for any such curriculum development effort. Some ideas for integration come quickly to mind. Others can be understood and evaluated only with considerable knowledge of constituent art disciplines, as they draw significant content from these areas. Still others exploit superficial or trivial interdisciplinary relationships. The aim of this chapter has been to demonstrate significant interconnectedness among the art disciplines that, in a coordinated plan, can lead to deeper and fuller understanding of art. The aim of this book has been to present an introduction to the discipline of art history, which can serve as a foundation for art educators as they develop and plan art education for young people.

NOTES

1. Terry Barrett, "A Comparison of the Goals of Studio Professors Conducting Critiques and Art Education Goals for Teaching Art Criticism," *Studies in Art Education* 30, no. 1 (1988): 22–27.

2. Monroe C. Beardsley, "On the Creation of Art," in his *The Aesthetic Point of View*, ed. M. J. Wreen and D. M. Callen (Ithaca: Cornell University Press, 1982); and Laura H. Chapman, *Approaches to Art in Education* (New York: Harcourt Brace Jovanovich, 1978).

3. Howard Risatti, "Art Criticism in Discipline-based Art Education," *Journal of Aesthetic Education* 21, no. 2 (1987): 219.

4. Edmund Burke Feldman, *Art as Image and Idea* (Englewood Cliffs, N.J.: Prentice Hall, 1967). See also Jerry Tollifson, "Tips on Teaching Art Criticism," *NAEA Advisory*, Summer 1990.

5. George Geahigan, "Integrating Art History into the Art Curriculum" (Panel presentation with Mary Erickson, David Ebitz, Eldon Katter, Jon Sharer, and Marilyn Stewart, National Art Education Association Conference, 8 April 1990, Kansas City, Mo.).

6. E. Louis Lankford, "Making Sense of Aesthetics," *Studies in Art Education* 28, no. 1 (1986): 49–52; and Robert L. Russell, "Children's Philosophical Inquiry into Defining Art: A Quasi-Experimental Study of Aesthetics in the Elementary Classroom," *Studies in Art Education* 29, no. 3 (1988): 282.

7. Marilyn Stewart, "Integrating Art History into the Art Curriculum" (Panel presentation with Mary Erickson, David Ebitz, George Geahigan, Eldon Katter, and Jon Sharer, National Art Education Association Conference, 8 April 1990, Kansas City, Mo.).

8. Richard L. Anderson, *Calliope's Sisters: A Comparative Study of Philosophies of Art* (Englewood Cliffs, N.J.: Prentice Hall, 1990).

9. Marcia Muelder Eaton, *Basic Issues in Aesthetics* (Belmont, Calif.: Wadsworth Publishing Company, 1988).

10. Anderson, *Calliope's Sisters*, p. 111.

11. Ibid., p. 71.

12. Stewart, "Integrating Art History."

Epilogue

Both art history and art education are currently at exciting stages of development. Art history is witnessing the introduction of many new methodologies—including Marxist, feminist, deconstructionist. At the same time, traditional approaches to art-historical inquiry, such as stylistic analysis and iconography, continue to develop. The result is a new variety of approaches that enable art historians to examine both familiar and unfamiliar art from wider perspectives than ever before.

Art history has also been enlivened by a widening of the art canon. While previously the primarily European great masters occupied most scholars, there is now interest in world art of every period and style, including cave art, folk art, and popular culture. Additionally, a wider range of art is available to the general public in many countries. In Japan there are now exhibitions of Austrian drawings, American quilts, and Bulgarian icons, while in the United States, Buddhist art from Bhutan, bark paintings from Australian aborigines, and South American textiles have recently been exhibited.

What does this mean for the field? First, it shows that both researchers and the general public are open to a wide range of arts and therefore to many conceptions of art. When seeing the work of so many different cultures, one finds it impossible to maintain a narrow focus on what is worthwhile. Certain works of art, often called masterpieces, have an especially strong appeal and communicate with great power and depth. These masterpieces may be identified in the art of every culture. Nevertheless, we must remember that although any single scholar or viewer may have distinct preferences, we are all the richer for the variety of artistic experiences now accessible to us.

This expanded range also means that art history is no longer the province of a few highly trained specialists. While professional standards for university professors and museum curators have gradually risen, there is room for everyone to study art history. It may require a special background to decipher the inscriptions on Chinese paintings, but study-

ing the art of one's own community or heritage requires only curiosity. Our understanding of the art of any culture or historical period
can grow from being examined by a fresh eye. We each bring to art our
own sensibilities, and therefore each of us has something unique to
contribute.

Differing backgrounds and interests also provide interesting perspectives.
For example, a ceramic dish decorated with birds and flowers will be seen
differently by people interested in ornothology, plant biology, gardening,
gastronomy, pottery techniques, and the environment. A mountain climber
has a fresh view of landscape paintings, and someone who can make his
or her own clothes looks anew not only at textiles but also at paintings,
photographs, and prints of different historical periods. In fact, we all
bring our own backgrounds and interests to every artistic experience,
from visiting a museum to leafing through a magazine.

Art history, then, has opened itself to every culture, time period,
media, and person. What of art education? There has never been as much
potential in the field as there is now. The opportunity to go beyond the
limitations of the past to include art history, art creation, aesthetics, and
art criticism in the curriculum means that art education can dramatically
broaden its base. Just like art history, it can traverse all cultures and time
periods, which also opens it up more fully to the here and now. We can
study not only the *Mona Lisa* but also film history; not only medieval
cathedrals but also American homes; not only ancient Greek sculptures
but also the works of contemporary Hispanics, blacks, and Native
Americans; not only Picasso but also the artists in our own town; not
only oil paintings but also the designs of ceramics and bottles; not only
others but also ourselves.

We offer this challenge: Is there anyone reading this book who does
not have, or cannot imagine, an area of visual interest that would be
exciting to study? Has there ever been a powerful visual experience that
has added meaning to your life? Have you never been curious to learn
more about some textile, photograph, print, poster, painting, vase, ornamental object, doll, wallpaper design, sculpture, film, or design from
popular culture? Can you formulate a plan on how to follow up on this
interest? If you are a teacher, how can you incorporate your own interest
in visual inquiry into your classes? Even more vital, how can you convey
the excitement of *having* a field of inquiry to students, who all have their
own individual visual interests?

It is not so important that we share our own visual delights, although
that is surely stimulating, but that we encourage each other, no matter whether we are five or eighty-five, to develop our own visual
potential. We hope that this book has encouraged you, and we invite

your further participation in the process of art-historical study as part of your own appreciation and teaching of art. We hope you will not only participate yourselves, but also encourage others; this is a field for us all.

Appendix 1

Elementary Art History Curriculum Outline for "A Story of Art in the World"

Unit 1: Art before History
Before people grew crops or domesticated animals and before people had invented writing, art was a central part of their lives.
    Prehistoric Art
    The Art of Hunters and Gatherers

Unit 2: Art in the First Cities
With the domestication of agricultural plants and animals, people were able to make permanent settlements. Separate ancient civilizations developed in rich agricultural areas around the globe.
    The Art of Ancient Iraq and Egypt
    The Art of Ancient China
    The Art of Ancient India
    The Art of Ancient Meso-America

Unit 3: Our Place in the World
People have always tried to find order and harmony in their lives by thinking about how people fit into the world.
    Classical Greek and Roman Art
    Indian Buddhist Art
    Confucian and Taoist Art in China

Unit 4: Religion around the World
People throughout time have used art as a way to relate to powers outside themselves.
    Gods in Art (Oceania, Africa, Native America)
    Byzantine Art
    Islamic Art
    Medieval Art

Unit 5: When Cultures Meet
As different cultures meet each other they clash, compete, or learn from each other.
    Mayan Art of Meso-America
    Incan Art of South America
    Renaissance Art
    Conflict in Baroque Art

Unit 6: The Art of Powerful Families
In many cultures power has been in the hands of a few families who have used art to express that power.
    The Art of Powerful European Families
    The Art of Powerful African Families
    The Art of Powerful Native American Families

Unit 7: Art and Revolution
In times of revolution art is often used to carry strong messages. The art of the day is often replaced by a new art or by newly reappraised art of the past.
    Art and the Pueblo Revolt
    Art and the American Revolution
    Art of the French Revolution
    Communist Revolutionary Art

Unit 8: Art and Technology
The development and refinement of new materials and processes have lead some cultures to new directions in art or even new art forms.
    Ancient African and Chinese Bronzes
    Printmaking in China and Japan
    Painting after the Camera
    Modern Building Techniques
    Computer and Video Art

Unit 9: Art and the Individual
Especially in Euro-America beginning in the Renaissance, the individual (as opposed to the group) has been valued increasingly.
    Naive Art
    Post-Impressionism
    Expressionism and Fauvism
    Surrealism
    Abstract Expressionism
    Dada and Conceptual Art

Unit 10: Art and the Global Village
As mass communication and high-speed transportation bring ideas together from around a planet that seems more and more fragile, people are reexamining traditional as well as cross-cultural values.

Traditional Arts Today
Popular Arts and the Consumer Economy
Intercultural Art

Appendix 2

Lesson Plans and Narratives for
"A Story of Art in the World"

The Oldest Art We Know

Lesson Overview

Through an introductory imagination activity, children are helped to appreciate how different life was in prehistoric times than it is today.

Prehistoric paintings and sculpture are examined in detail with attention directed to subject matter and production processes. The purposes of prehistoric art are discussed.

Students are asked to distinguish natural objects from objects made by people in the world around them.

Objectives

Knowledge

1. Students learn that people have made art for a very long time.
2. Students learn that nature can be the subject matter of art.
3. Students learn that artists of long ago made their own art materials from things they could find.

Skills

4. Students learn how to identify subject matter in detail.

Activities

Introduction

Teachers begin the lesson with an extended "what if" exercise in which they help children imagine what life was like for people living in prehistoric times. A simple narrative introduction titled "Life in the Cave" follows this lesson plan.

Suggestions   Teachers might consider darkening the room and gathering students on rugs on the floor to simulate the cave. A lamp, the shade of which is covered with a red cloth, might be used to simulate a camp fire. If possible, the thermostate might be turned down temporarily to lower the temperature in the classroom.

Questions and Discussion   Have you ever been way out in the country, away from towns and houses? In big parks, we can sometimes get away from houses and cars and people.

Have you ever been camping? Maybe you have slept outdoors at night with no electricity for lights. Maybe you have cooked hot dogs over a camp fire. Maybe you have pulled your clothes around you tightly as the sun went down and it got chilly. Then maybe you can begin to understand how different it was to live so very long ago.

Development

The lesson continues with a discussion of specific prehistoric artworks focusing on three issues: the natural subject matter, the handmade tools and materials, and the magical function of the works. Focusing on one work at a time, students are asked to name the subject matter, for example, a horse, a cow, or a bison. Students are asked to point to the item as they name it. Specific details about each animal, such as mane, ears, horns, eyes, antlers, spots, hoofs, mouth, and legs, should be identified. Students should continue to point to each detail as it is identified. Students are asked to reflect on how the paintings and carvings were made. Finally, discussion can turn to the question of why the paintings were made. A simple narrative titled "Art in the Cave" follows this lesson plan.

Suggestions   Teachers might illustrate cave paintings on interior walls and ceilings by drawing or painting pictures on the inside of a cardboard box or on the inside surfaces of a brown paper sack. A toy figure of a person might be used to indicate scale. Students might be asked to tell about any experiences they have had underground in a cave, tunnel, storm cellar, subway, or the like.

The teacher might bring in several bones to show how they might be carved or blown through like a straw. A piece of partially burned firewood, or even a burned wooden matchstick, can illustrate the marking potential of charcoal. The teacher might use a variety of rock or soil samples to illustrate possible sources of color.

Questions and Discussion   What could you draw or paint with if you didn't have a brush, pencil, or crayon? Have you ever made a mark on the sidewalk or on a rock with another rock? What would you draw on if you didn't have paper? How could you carve a bone if you didn't have a metal knife?

Do you know anyone who has a kind of magical object, like a lucky rabbit's foot or a lucky penny? Some people think four-leaf clovers are lucky and black cats are unlucky. Why did the people in the cave paint animals but not trees and water? (Animals were not so easily found and killed.)

Look very carefully at these paintings and carvings. How many kinds of horns do you see? Are all the animals' tails alike? Can you see the animals' eyes, noses, necks, ears? Which animals are big and which are small? Are they all the same color?

Conclusion

The lesson concludes with students learning to distinguish natural from people-made objects in the world around them. A simple narrative titled "Nature and People" follows this lesson plan.

Suggestion   A collection of objects might be categorized by children into two boxes: one marked "natural," the other marked "people-made." This sorting exercise could be done either with actual objects or with photographs of objects.

Questions and Discussion   Do we live close to nature today? Is everything in your home, like chairs, tables, boxes, and toys, made by a person? Do you have any natural objects in your home, like plants, animals (pets), seashells, or rocks?

What do you like to draw or paint? Do you show the people and things you know best, the people and things that are around you? Did you ever draw your family, your house, your school, or your friends?

Evaluation

When asked whether painting is a new invention or something that people have done for a very long time, children should be able to answer that people have made paintings for a very long time.

Given a choice between things in nature and things made by people when asked what cave people painted long ago, children should be able to answer that cave people painted things from nature.

Given a choice between "bought in a store" and "made themselves" when asked where cave people got their art materials, children should be able to answer that cave people made their materials themselves.

Shown a painting with clear-cut subject matter, children should be able to point to and name accurately subject matter in general and in detail.

Materials and Resources

Reproductions or slides of prehistoric art works:

Horses, Bull and Stags. Superimposed polychrome cave painting. Lascaux, Dordogne, France. Late Paleolithic age, ca. 14,000–13,500 B.C.

Reclining Bison. Polychrome cave painting. Altamira, Spain. Late Paleolithic age, 15,000–10,000 B.C.

Bone Staff, Ivory Woman's Head, and Bone Horse's Head. Musée des Antiques Nationale, Saint-Germain-en-lay, France. Prehistoric art, 20,000–10,000 B.C.

A variety of rock and soil samples of different colors.

Several bones.

A piece of partially burned firewood or a burned wooden matchstick.

A collection of small natural objects and objects made by people, or a collection of photographs of natural and people-made objects.

Two boxes: one marked "natural"; the other, "people-made."

Key Vocabulary Words:

cave
magic
natural
people-made

Interdisciplinary Integration

Production

Drawing, painting, or modeling from nature would be a good follow-up production activity. Drawing animals would be a very direct follow-up activity. It is recommended that children be guided in carefully looking at and describing natural objects in preparation for such production activities.

Criticism

Children would be better prepared to understand the content of this lesson if they had experience describing artworks prior to this lesson. Specifically, they would benefit from practice in describing subject matter detail and technical aspects of artworks, that is, how the artworks are made.

Philosophy of Art

As children begin to gain experience with different kinds of artwork, they can wonder together about whether art has a purpose or whether all art has the same purpose.

Student Narrative: Life in the Cave

We're going to learn about people who lived long, long ago before you or your teacher or your parents or your grandparents were born. After the time of the dinosaurs, but still hundreds and hundreds of years ago, people lived a hard life. The people of those days did not have many of the things we have today. They didn't have television, stereos, radios, or electricity; they didn't have airplanes, cars, trains, or buses; they didn't have schools, stores, or playgrounds; they didn't have furniture, stoves, refrigerators, or even a house. There were no cities or towns. People lived together with their families and perhaps a few other families. They lived in homes made of branches, bones, rocks, and anything they could find. Sometimes they lived in caves, hollow places under the ground. They had to find someplace like a cave to stay warm at night. People kept warm and cooked food over an open fire.

To stay alive, people way back then had to find their own food and make their own clothing. They found food that grew wild around them. They ate nuts, berries, roots, and seeds from plants. They also learned to hunt and kill animals to eat. They had no guns to shoot the animals. They made their own spears and knives from stone, branches, and animals' horns. Animals can run fast, and people long ago had no trucks or motorcycles to drive and no tame horses to ride. Hunters had to understand animals very well to be able to find them and kill them. When an animal was killed, the people used everything they could from the animal. They ate the meat, made tools and other things from the bones, and made clothing from the skin.

Student Narrative: Art in the Cave

Not so long ago, a little girl went along with her father to explore a cave he had found. The girl looked up at interesting shapes on the ceiling of the cave. After a while, she saw that the shapes were paintings of animals. She found some of the oldest paintings in the world. This is a photograph of one of the paintings she saw (*Reclining Bison*). This is a painting of a bison, which is an animal a lot like a buffalo. Some time later, several boys playing in another cave found more of these old paintings. This is a photograph of some of those paintings (*Horses, Bull and Stags*).

People long ago had to get along without many things that we have today. These paintings are made on the rock surfaces of cave walls and ceilings. Some say plants and hair were used to spread color. Colors came from different colors of earth and ground-up stone. The people in the caves also drew with charcoal made from burnt wood. Some say smooth areas were sprayed by blowing powdered colors through a hollow bone, like blowing through a straw. Bones were carefully carved with sharpened stones. This is a picture of a carving of a horse's head made of bone (*Bone Horse's Head*).

The paintings we have been looking at were found very deep in caves. They were found in places that are difficult to get to, not where the cave people spent most of their time. They were not made to make the cave look nice, the way we might have wallpaper to make the living room look nice. Some people think they were made as a kind of magic. The cave people thought that if they could paint the animals very well, then maybe the real animals they needed to hunt would be easier to catch. The paintings of animals might make the hunters lucky in finding and killing real animals. The cave people sometimes threw spears at the paintings as if the paintings were real animals, almost like practicing for the hunt. It was difficult and dangerous to live in a cave so very long ago. The people there might try almost anything to make sure they would have something to wear and food to eat. Cave people got most of their clothing and food from animals. They watched those animals very carefully so they could hunt them. By watching the animals carefully, they knew just how the animals looked. It is only because the cave people looked at the animals very carefully that they were able to draw them so beautifully in their caves.

Student Narrative: Nature and People

Cave people painted the animals of nature that were around them. Natural things such as trees, rocks, and animals are not made by people. People make other things such as houses, cars, clothes, and chairs. When you draw the things around you that you know best, you are like the cave painters of long, long ago who drew the animals that lived around them and that they learned to know very well.

Chinese Landscapes

Lesson Overview

The lesson begins with an introduction to Asia and a simple introduction to Confucianism.

Chinese landscape paintings are examined with a focus on the importance of nature and the use of light and dark and shades of gray.

Children are asked to reflect on the beauty of nature around them as they consider Chinese nature studies.

Objectives
Knowledge

1. Students learn that size can sometimes tell us what is important in a painting (review).

2. Students learn that there was a time in China when artists depicted nature in their paintings.

Skill

3. Students learn how to distinguish various shades of gray within a painting.

4. Students learn how to distinguish natural objects from objects made by people (review).

Activities
Introduction

The teacher introduces Asian culture with a brief discussion of Confucianism. A simple narrative introduction titled "China and Confucius" is provided at the end of this lesson plan.

Suggestions   A globe or map of the world should be used for geographic references.

Objects from Asia, especially China, might be brought to class to help children begin to build experience related to a distant culture.

Development

The teacher shows Sung dynasty landscapes with attention given to their representation of the greatness of nature and their use of scale and shades of gray to show space. A simple narrative titled "Nature Is Important," provided at the end of this lesson plan, focuses attention on several Chinese paintings.

Suggestions   The teacher might illustrate a range of grays with torn sheets on increasingly lighter paper (gray or brown) placed one on top of the other.

Questions and Discussion   Can you find the people in the painting, the bridges, the buildings? What natural objects can you find in the painting? Which objects are larger, the people and the things the people make or natural objects? Point to a very dark place in the painting. Point to a very light place in the painting. Point to a place that is a medium gray in the painting.

Conclusion

The teacher reinforces the Chinese interest in nature through examination of intimate nature studies. A simple narrative titled "Looking at Nature" is provided at the end of this lesson plan.

Suggestions   The teacher might show and discuss a few carefully selected small, natural objects such as shells, nuts, rocks, or leaves.

Children might be asked to bring to school one object from nature and one object made by people. These objects could then be sorted by the class as a whole.

Evaluation

Given a choice of Canada, India, Mexico, China, and the United States when asked to identify areas within Asia, the students should be able to select India and China as Asian.

Given a choice of people, nature, sports, and machinery when asked to identify a major interest of Chinese painters of long ago, students should be able to identify nature as an interest in Chinese painting.

Given a collection of objects made by nature and by people, students should be able to sort them into natural and people-made categories.

Materials and Resources:

Reproductions or slides of Chinese and other artworks:

Tuning the Lute and Drinking Tea. Attributed to Chou Fang (ca. 780–810 A.D.). Tenth- or eleventh-century copy after T'ang dynasty design.

Travelling amid Mountains and Streams: Hanging Scroll. National Palace Museum, Taipei, Taiwan. By Fan K'uan (990–1030 A.D.). Sung dynasty.

Bare Willows and Distant Mountains. Museum of Fine Arts, Boston. By Ma Yuan (1190–1225 A.D.). Sung dynasty.

Rain Storm. Baron Kawasaki Collection, Kobe. By Hsia Kuei (1195–1224 A.D.). Sung dynasty.

The Five-colored Parakeet. Museum of Fine Arts, Boston. By Emperor Hui Tsung (1082–1135 A.D.). Sung dynasty.

Persimmons. Ink on paper, Ryukoin Temple, Kyoto. By Mu-Ch'i (early thirteenth century A.D.). Sung dynasty.

Bamboo: Album Leaf. National Palace Museum, Taipei, Taiwan. By Wu Chen (1280–1354 A.D.). Yuan dynasty.

The Discus Thrower. British Museum, London. Roman copy after Myron, ca. 460–450 B.C.

Globe or map of the world.

Several shades of gray paper (or several shades of brown or blue paper).

A collection of small natural objects such as shells, nuts, or leaves.

Objects made in Asia, especially China.

Key Vocabulary Words

nature

size

light

dark

Interdisciplinary Integration

Production

Experience with monochromatic color schemes or various shades of ink wash would be valuable prior to this lesson. A follow-up lesson might involve careful observation and then drawing or painting a small natural object.

Criticism

The effects of light and dark contrast might be examined in artworks from other time periods, such as Rembrandt's paintings and Impressionist paintings.

Philosophy of Art

Since both this and the preceding Greek lesson (from "A Story of Art in the World," not included here) focus on important subject matter, one might wonder about whether a painting with important subject matter is necessarily better than a painting with a less important subject.

Student Narrative: China and Confucius

There have been cities and countries in different parts of the world for a very long time. While the Egyptians and later the Greeks lived by the Mediterranean Sea, there were also old cities and countries like India, Japan, and China, in Asia. Asia is the largest piece of land in the world.

One of the oldest and largest countries in the world is China. A teacher named Confucius lived long ago in China. He taught people rules about how to get along together. He had rules about people in families, people in towns, and people in the whole country. Confucius's rules helped people know how to act with specific people, for example, how a child should obey a parent or how a nobleman should obey the emperor.

Confucius said that good music was important in people's lives. This painting (*Tuning the Lute and Drinking Tea*) shows women enjoying time together following Confucius' rules of order and listening to good music.

Student Narrative: Nature Is Important

There were some Chinese people who thought that there was more to life than rules and order. Some of these people (called Taoists) believed that there was another way to peace and happiness. They believed that being close to nature was the way. One of the greatest painters of this time was Fan K'uan. Fan K'uan lived all alone in the mountains so that he could find peace and happiness.

This is a painting made by Fan K'uan (*Travelling amid Mountains and Streams: Hanging Scroll*). Nature was very important to him. Size can sometimes tell us what is important. See the packhorses in the lower right and the temples below the waterfall in the forest? They are very tiny. The people and the things that people make look very small in this painting. The things made by nature, such as the mountains, trees, rocks, and waterfall, are bigger and more important in the painting.

The artist uses lots of light and dark and gray in his painting. The trees and rocks below are darker than the road where the packhorses are. The sky is lighter than the high mountain.

Let's look at two more paintings from China (*Bare Willows and Distant Mountains* and *Rain Storm*). Both paintings show trees, a river, a bridge, a person, and faraway mountains. Like Fan K'uan, each artist used dark and light and shades of gray in his painting.

Student Narrative: Looking at Nature

The classical Greeks showed in their art that they thought people were very important. In their sculpture, the Greeks depicted people as perfect (*The Discus Thrower*). The Chinese had different ideas. They thought nature was very important and very beautiful. Chinese artists of long ago showed nature to be so big that you could get lost in it. Sometimes we can show how important we think nature is by looking at little things. There was a Chinese emperor long ago who loved nature. He studied it very closely. He made a painting of a bird on a branch (*The Five-colored Parakeet*). Another painter showed his interest in nature by making this simple painting of six fruits (*Persimmons*). Still another Chinese painter found beauty in a few leaves on a branch (*Bamboo: Album Leaf*).

Like that Chinese emperor, we can show an interest in the beauty of nature around us. Have you ever seen something from nature that you could look at for a long time because it was pretty or interesting? We can find natural beauty in big things like clouds at sunset or canyons and mountains. Sometimes the beauty of nature is very small, like a raindrop on a flower, sunshine on a leaf, or snow falling on pebbles.

Appendix 3

Art History Skills and Attitudes as Instructional Objectives

Skills

1. Students learn how to describe visual artifacts or artworks from the past.

2. Students learn how to identify change within their own lifetime (art history "readiness").

3. Students learn how to compare and contrast visual qualities as a basis for speculating about when artifacts or artworks were made.

4. Students learn how to support conclusions about when artifacts or artworks were made (by examining documents, other artifacts, or artworks, or by interviewing witnesses).

5. Students learn how to propose what alterations in an artwork or artifact would be required to make it look new (imagined restoration).

6. Students learn how to imagine living in a different time or different culture to understand how an artwork can be interpreted in its own context.

7. Students learn how to construct a history that explains visual transition through time.

Attitudes

1. Students learn to value the art-historical process as a way of coming to know another time and place.

2. Students learn to appreciate art as a way of understanding the point of view of persons of other cultures and times.

3. Students learn to appreciate historical preservations as efforts to maintain a community's visual heritage.

4. Students learn to value art as an important realm of human accomplishment that can inform us about how we have come to be who we are.

5. Students learn to value their own capacities to make sense of their own visual environment.

Appendix 4

Production Analysis Worksheet

Idea Generation

What ideas did you use in your work (for example, subject matter, qualities of materials, feeling tone, sensory qualities, formal relationships, messages)?

Where did these ideas come from (for example, teacher, other art, ordinary world, personal or social events, family, or community traditions)?

Why do you suppose you found these ideas interesting (for example, long-established tastes or preference, fascination with the new, or personal commitment)?

Development

What decisions did you make in progress (for example, change in subject matter, medium, technique, format, size, meaning, expression, or composition)?

Why did you make these decisions (for example, concern for expressiveness, composition, realism, or function)?

Use of Media

What medium and technique(s) did you select? Why?

What technical problems did you confront as you worked? How did you solve them? Did you change your method of working at any point? Why?

Completion

Is the work complete (capable of standing on its own as a work of art)?

What standards are you using to determine whether the work is complete (for example, realism, expressiveness, functionality, formal organization, or craftsmanship)?

How well did your work meet those standards? Give evidence in the work for each of the standards that you have selected.

Bibliographic Essay

Chapter 1: Art before Art History

A good general survey of the art of prehistoric people is T. G. E. Powell, *Prehistoric Art* (New York: Oxford University Press, 1966). Powell divides his chapters into the arts of hunters, cultivators, metal-workers, and a "barbarian nation" (the Celtic peoples). For the Paleolithic era, Randall White, *Dark Caves, Bright Visions: Life in Ice Age Europe* (New York: American Museum of Natural History and W. W. Norton, 1986), offers a reasoned approach to the current state of information and theories about the life and art of the cave dwellers, with excellent illustrations. In *The Creative Explosion* (Ithaca: Cornell University Press, 1985), John E. Pfeiffer presents provocative theories about Paleolithic life and art in comparison with the previous Neanderthal era. Ann Sieveking, *The Cave Artists* (London: Thames and Hudson, 1979), discusses the cave paintings in France and Spain in some detail, with stylistic analysis and many good reproductions.

There are two fine studies of early Chinese art. Jessica Rawson, *Ancient China: Art and Archaeology* (New York: Harper and Row, 1980), begins with a chapter on Neolithic art and then moves through major early Chinese periods until the fall of the Han dynasty in 220 A.D. More specifically, Kwang-chih Chang, *The Archaeology of Ancient China*, 4th ed. (New Haven: Yale University Press, 1986), begins with the Paleolithic period and ends in 1,000 B.C., providing a very scholarly look at Chinese culture of the Neolithic period.

For a study of early American Indian petroglyphs, *Rock Art of the American Indian* (Golden, Colo.: Outbooks, 1981) by Campbell Gault provides a good beginning survey, with an extensive bibliography. More specifically, *New Light on Chaco Canyon* (Santa Fe: School of American Research Press, 1984) contains a number of interesting essays edited by David Grant Noble. The finest exhibition to date of traditional American Indian art was accompanied by Ralph T. Coe's catalog, *Sacred Circles* (London: Arts Council of Great Britain, 1977). It has a number of good color illustrations, essays on pertinent topics, and individual entries with black-and-white photographs for each of the 732 works of art in the exhibition.

Chapter 2: Traditional Views of Art

For the study of Western art theory, there are a number of good books, including Moshe Barasch's *Theories of Art from Plato to Winkelmann* (New York: New York University Press, 1985), which covers a wide range of approaches. The two volumes of *Readings in Art History* (New York: Charles Scribner's Sons, 1976), edited by Harold Spencer, contain a total of forty studies ranging from ancient Egypt to motion pictures. A recent survey of Western art that includes literature and music is Jack A. Hobbs and Robert L. Duncan, *Arts, Ideas and Civilization* (Englewood Cliffs, N.J.: Prentice Hall, 1989). For another view, Arnold Hauser's two-volume *Social History of Art* (New York: Vintage Books, 1951) offers a broad cultural approach based upon social history.

More specifically on Greek art and theory, several books by J. J. Pollitt are very useful. *The Ancient View of Greek Art: Criticism, History, and Terminology* (New Haven: Yale University Press, 1974) gives examples of important terms used by Greek writers about art, while *Art and Experience in Classical Greece* (London: Cambridge University Press, 1972) is a historical study centering upon the sculpture and architecture of the classical period.

As more and more scholars take up the field, Chinese art is well represented by books in English. The most popular survey is Michael Sullivan, *The Arts of China* (Berkeley: University of California Press, 1984), which covers many forms of art over several thousand years. One of the leading scholars of Chinese painting is James Cahill, who has published a number of fine volumes in the past three decades. His survey text *Chinese Painting* (Geneva and Cleveland: Skira, 1960) remains the finest introduction to the field, with lively prose and good color illustrations.

For the study of Chinese art theory, there are no less than five books that give translations and explanations of Chinese writings. Earliest was Chiang Yee, *The Chinese Eye: An Interpretation of Chinese Painting* (1935; Bloomington: Indiana University Press, 1964), which offers a general explanation of traditional views of art in China. Next came Osvald Siren, *The Chinese on the Art of Painting* (New York: Shocken Books, 1963), which combines translations of early texts with valuable commentary. Four years later, the novelist, biographer, and philosopher Lin Yutang published *The Chinese Theory of Art* (New York: G. Putnam's Sons, 1967), with excerpts from twenty-three Chinese writers about art from the sixth century B.C. to the eighteenth century A.D. Susan Bush, *The Chinese Literati on Painting: Su Shih (1037–1101) to Tung Ch'i-ch'ang (1555–1636)* (Cambridge: Harvard University Press, 1971), represents one important time period more fully. The same author joined with

Hsio-yen Shih for *Early Chinese Texts on Painting* (Cambridge: Harvard University Press, 1985), which covers theoretical writings from the earliest texts through the fourteenth century.

There are several fine books on the traditional arts of India, the most recent being Susan Huntington, *The Arts of Ancient India* (New York: Weatherhill, 1985). Older but still useful is Benjamin Rowland, *Art and Architecture of India* (Baltimore: Penguin Books, 1963). Three earlier books, all with the same title, *The Art of India*, were published within six years of each other. The first was by Stella Kramrisch (New York: Phaidon, 1954); the second, by Hermann Goetz (New York: Crown, 1959), and the third, a translation of the French original by Louis Frederic (New York: Phaidon, 1960). All three are well illustrated.

The most prolific writer on the art theory of India has been Ananda K. Coomeraswamy. His many publications are always of interest, although some were printed in India and are now difficult to locate. Two of the most fascinating books of his essays are *Christian and Oriental Philosophy of Art* and *The Transformation of Nature in Art* (both republished in New York by Dover in 1956). Coomaraswamy's writings were republished in 1977 in three volumes by Princeton University Press under the title *Coomaraswamy*.

For the study of European art, so many fine books have been published that it is almost useless to try to list them. Nevertheless, Kenneth Clark, *Civilisation* (New York: Harper and Row, 1969), written to complement Clark's television series, offers a traditional point of view with a good deal of cross-cultural discussion. On more specific periods, Henry Adams, *Mont-Saint-Michel and Chartres* (New York: Mentor Books, 1961), remains outstanding for its wide-ranging understanding of the medieval period. For the Italian Renaissance, there are a number of books by Bernard Berenson still in print; *Italian Painters of the Renaissance* (London: Phaidon Books, 1956) is one of the most outstanding.

There are many books on the art and poetry of Blake. One of the best is *The Portable Blake*, ed. Alfred Kazin (New York: Penguin Books, 1978), which is primarily made up of Blake's various writings, including many comments on art. Three of Blake's superb illustrated books have been issued in low-cost facsimile editions. These are *Songs of Innocence* (New York: Dover, 1971), *Songs of Experience* (New York: Dover, 1984), and *The Marriage of Heaven and Hell* (New York: Oxford University Press, 1988); the latter includes a useful commentary by Geoffrey Keynes.

For folk and primitive art, one of the finest books representing an international collection is Henry Glassie, *The Spirit of Folk Art* (New York: Harry N. Abrams, 1989). For American folk art, two beautifully illustrated volumes are Roger Ricco and Frank Maresca, *American Primitive: Discoveries in Folk Sculpture* (New York: Alfred A. Knopf, 1988), and Robert Bishop, *American Folk Sculpture* (New York: Bonanza Books, 1985). Gregg N. Blasdel, *Symbols and Images: Contemporary Primitive Artists* (New York: American Federation of Arts, 1970), explores current artists, while the conception of "outsider art" as personal rather than traditional is analyzed in Roger Manley, *Signs and Wonders: Outsider Art inside North Carolina* (Raleigh: North Carolina Museum of Art, 1989).

Chapter 3: Twentieth-Century Methodologies in Art History

The most fundamental book from which to study the theories of Heinrich Woelfflin is his *Principles of Art History; The Problem of the Development of Style in Later Art* (New York: Dover, 1932). Erwin Panofsky has written many fine books; perhaps the most broadly based is *Meaning in the Visual Arts* (Garden City, N.Y.: Doubleday Anchor Books, 1955). More specifically focused is *Studies in Iconology: Humanistic Themes in the Art of the Renaissance* (New York: Harper and Row, 1962).

A number of books of economic and social (often called Marxist) art history have been published in the past half century. One early treatise was Herbert Read, *Art and Society* (1936; London: Faber and Faber, 1967). Beginning his chapters with quotes from such diverse sources as Marx, Hegel, and Baudelaire, Read approaches art in relation to magic, mysticism, religion, secularism, the unconscious, and education, ending with a chapter on modern art in transition. A more recent book with one of the most purely Marxist approaches is Nicos Hadjinicolaou, *Art History and Class Struggle* (London: Pluto Press, 1973). While some of his ideas may be startling to those nurtured on traditional art history, the clarity of Hadjinicolaou's writing makes his book an excellent source for studying the influence of economic factors and class ideology on the work of European artists. A variation of this approach is taken by Vytautas Kavolis in *Artistic Expression: A Sociological Analysis* (Ithaca: Cornell University Press, 1968). Kavolis divides his book into sections on sociological and cultural influences on artistic expression, stressing class structures and values.

Many more books have taken social, economic, and political approaches to individual periods or artists. Among the fine studies in this group are three by T. J. Clark: *Images of the People: Gustave Courbet and the 1848 Revolution* (London: Thames and Hudson, 1973); *The Absolute Bourgeois: Artists and Politics in France, 1848–1851* (London: Thames and Hudson,

1973); and *The Painting of Modern Life: Paris in the Art of Manet and His Followers* (New York: Alfred A. Knopf, 1985). Among the most sophisticated views of art through particular periods of social history are those of Albert Boime in *Art in an Age of Revolution* (Chicago: University of Chicago Press, 1987), and of Robert L. Herbert in *Impressionism: Art, Leisure, and Parisian Society* (New Haven: Yale University Press, 1988).

For the study of women in art, a number of useful books have been published in the past two decades. Focusing upon biographical information and stylistic descriptions are Wendy Slatkin, *Women Artists in History* (Englewood Cliffs, N.J.: Prentice Hall, 1985); Elsa Honig Fine, *Women and Art* (Montclair, N.J.: Abner Schram, 1978); Karen Peterson and J. J. Wilson, *Women Artists: Recognition and Re-Appraisal from the Early Middle Ages to the Twentieth Century* (New York: Harper Colophon Books, 1976); and Ann Sutherland Harris and Linda Nochlin, *Women Artists: 1550–1950* (New York: Alfred A. Knopf, 1976). Germaine Greer, *The Obstacle Race: The Fortunes of Women Painters and Their Work* (New York: Farrar, Straus and Giroux, 1979), discusses the obstacles that have deterred the success of women artists. Perhaps the most influential book from a methodological standpoint has been Rozsika Parker and Griselda Pollock, *Old Mistresses: Women, Art, and Ideology* (London: Routledge & Kegan Paul, 1981), which challenges the traditional male conceptions of art history. Griselda Pollock followed up this book with *Vision and Difference: Femininity, Feminism and the Histories of Art* (New York and London: Routledge, 1988).

Two recent pioneering exhibitions on women artists in East Asia have been accompanied by catalogs: Patricia Fister, *Japanese Women Artists, 1600–1900* (Lawrence, Kans.: Spencer Museum of Art; and New York: Harper and Row, 1988); and Marsha Weidner, et al., *Views from the Jade Terrace: Chinese Women Artists, 1300–1912* (Indianapolis: Indianapolis Museum of Art; and New York: Rizzoli, 1988). Marsha Weidner, ed., *Flowering in the Shadows: Women in the History of Chinese and Japanese Painting* (Honolulu: University of Hawaii Press, 1990), carries the subject further.

Rudolf Arnheim's studies of how we perceive forms and colors through our eyes have been published in his *Art and Visual Perception: A Psychology of the Creative Eye* (Berkeley: University of California Press, 1974). Although not easy reading, *The Critical Writings of Adrian Stokes*, ed. Lawrence Gowing (London: Thames and Hudson, 1978) offers serious essays into art from a psychoanalytic perspective. One of the most provocative books on all the arts, including music, is Morse Peckham, *Man's Rage for Chaos* (Philadelphia: Chilton Books, 1965).

For further study of new approaches, a fairly recent compendium of articles, *The New Art History* (London: Camden, 1986), edited by A. L. Rees and F. Borzello, contains a short historical review of new trends as well as articles from various nonestablishment points of view. Another new book of articles is Norman Bryson, ed., *Calligram: Essays in New Art History from France* (New York: Cambridge University Press, 1988). Most of the essays in this volume are less clearly written and do not prove easy reading for those not versed in theory. Other works, also rather abstruse, by Bryson include *Word and Image: French Painting of the Ancien Régime* (New York: Cambridge University Press, 1981) and *Vision and Painting: The Logic of the Gaze* (New Haven: Yale University Press, 1983).

Most of the books by new art historians are more complex than those of the past and may be less appealing to those who prefer to study the biographies of artists and to understand form and style. There is no doubt that much contemporary art history has become a good deal more theoretical, and the writing has in some cases become more dense and less lucid. Nevertheless, some understanding of new methodologies is useful to those who wish to do art-historical research. The insights gained from these new approaches are valuable additions to the process of art history.

Chapter 4: How Art Historians Work

Because much of this chapter, including *Art History Resources*, concerns bibliography, readers are referred directly to the works cited in the chapter.

Chapter 5: Traditions of Teaching Art History

Frederick Logan, *Growth of Art in American Schools* (New York: Harper and Brothers, 1955), remains a historically significant volume in chronicling the development of art education in the United States. Logan's history traces developments in art education from the Common School movement of the nineteenth century to the child-centered philosophy that dominated art education in the middle of the twentieth century. Stuart Macdonald, *The History and Philosophy of Art Education* (New York: Elsevier, 1970), which appeared fifteen years after Logan, is a much more comprehensive history of art education, addressing art education in classical Greece, the Middle Ages, the Renaissance, and up through the 1960s. Though Macdonald makes some mention of art education in the United States, his history focuses on developments in Great Britain. Arthur D. Efland, *A History of Art Education: Intellectual and Social*

Currents in Teaching the Visual Arts (New York: Teachers College Press, 1990), has the scope of Macdonald's history and the American focus of Logan's. Efland not only presents the reader with the tremendous complexity and diversity of art education history, he also places that history within the broader contexts of changing ideas about art and evolving cultural circumstances. Foster Wygant, *Art in American Schools in the Nineteenth Century* (Cincinnati, Ohio: Interwood Press, 1983), is a comprehensive examination of a period in which art education emerged and developed as a separate discipline. Wygant focuses on such well-known artists as Rembrandt Peale, Elizabeth Peabody, and Walter Smith. His survey ranges topographically from the upper Midwest to Boston and thematically from Normal Art School curricula to manual training. *Framing the Past: Essays on Art Education* (Reston, Va.: National Art Education Association, 1990), edited by Donald Soucy and Mary Ann Stankiewicz, is a collection of articles that examines the nineteenth and twentieth century from a variety of perspectives. A number of articles consider cultural and moral issues in the history of art education.

The History of Art Education: Proceedings from the Penn State Conference (Reston, Va.: National Art Education Association, 1985), edited by Brent Wilson and Harlan Hoffa, collects the papers presented at the university's School of Visual Arts in November 1985. This collection of nearly fifty papers delves into the history of art education from many points of view, from analyses of instructional materials to biographies of prominent art educators.

Discipline-based Art Education: Origins, Meaning, and Development (Urbana: University of Illinois Press, 1987), edited by Ralph A. Smith, is a reprint of a special issue of the *Journal of Aesthetic Education* (21, no. 2 [Summer 1987]). The volume begins with four papers by Smith, Evan J. Kern, Arthur D. Efland, and Maurice J. Sevigny that chronicle the antecedents of DBAE. The central article, by Michael Day, Gilbert Clark, and W. Dwaine Greer, presents a framework for defining DBAE. There follows four articles, one each by an art critic (Howard Risatti), an art historian (W. Eugene Kleinbauer), an artist (Frederick Spratt), and an aesthetician (Donald W. Crawford). Each writer presents basic tenets of one discipline and reflects on relationships of that discipline to the other three. The final article, by David Henry Feldman, argues for the need to balance views of universal child development with an understanding of individual development.

In *Instant Art, Instant Culture: The Unspoken Policy for American Schools* (New York: Teachers College Press, 1982), Laura Chapman presents her explanation of art's marginal position in general education and the cultural factors that have placed it in that position. She also outlines her guidelines for developing sound art education curricula for elementary and secondary schools.

Chapter 6: The Nature and Educational Uses of Art History

Mark Roskill, *What Is Art History?* (New York: Harper and Row, 1976), was one of the first of several reexaminations of art-historical methodology in the last decade and a half. He proposed to demonstrate principles and techniques of art history. In his examination of specific artists and paintings such as Giorgione, Raphael's Sistine Chapel tapestries, De La Tour, and Picasso's *Guernica*, Roskill does not radically reinterpret the masterworks. Rather, he relies on critical consensus precisely to prove that art history is a workable, revealing, and empirical discipline. In *The End of the History of Art?* (Chicago: University of Chicago Press, 1987), Hans Belting concerns himself not with the demise of a discipline (as the title might suggest) but instead with the consequences of a paradigm shift from the mode of art-historical inquiry that has dominated since Vasari published *Lives of the Artists* in the mid-1500s. In two brief essays, Belting analyzes the historical circumstances surrounding the break between art-historical scholarship and contemporary artistic practice and the consequences of this break. In part a response to many of the issues raised by art historians such as Belting, *The New Art History* (Atlantic Highlands, N.J.: Humanities Press International, 1988), edited by A. L. Rees and F. Borzello, concentrates on exposing the hidden conservative ideology that structures the agenda of art history. By taking into account various contemporary theoretical models such as Marxism, feminism, psychoanalysis, and structuralism, this anthology of sixteen short articles serves as a radical critique of traditional art-historical inquiry.

The summer 1990 special issue of *Studies in Art Education* (published quarterly by the National Art Education Association) focuses on interdisciplinary relations among art education and anthropology, sociology, social theory, and history in an attempt to contextualize certain tacit assumptions and "truths" within the discipline. Such broad interdisciplinary focus was brought strongly into the field of art education through June King McFee and Rogena Degge's *Art, Culture, and Environment: A Catalyst* (Belmont, Calif.: Wadsworth, 1977). *Art and Democracy* (New York: Teachers College Press, 1987), an anthology edited by Doug Blandy and Kristin Congdon, contributes to the widening focus of art education by raising issues of diversity and broadening definitions of art. Alan Gowans, *Learning to See: Historical Perspectives on Modern Popular/ Commercial Arts* (Bowling Green: Bowling Green University Popular Press, 1981) argues that the popular and commercial arts in contemporary American society fulfill the same function that the "arts" have in a traditional, historical sense. Applying some of Gowans's notions, Penny Sparke, in her introduction to *Design and Culture in the Twentieth Century* (New York: Icon-Harper and Row, 1986), combines social history and material culture with formal principles of design to study the transformation of modern design through the past century. She examines the movement from the technological revolutions of the late nineteenth century through the "protodesign" of the early twentieth century through the latest trends in "antidesign." Thomas Schlereth, *Material Cultural Studies in America* (Nashville, Tenn.: American Association for State and Local History, 1982), collects research findings about American cultural artifacts ranging from folk art and photography to the Coke bottle. Containing theoretical essays and applied studies, this compilation is comprehensive and insightful. Henry Glassie, *The Spirit of Folk Art* (New York: Harry N. Abrams, 1989), is a beautifully illustrated analysis of folk art as it relates to people, art, and traditional concepts such as fine art, popular art, and primitive art. Wendy Slatkin, *Women Artists in History from Antiquity to the 20th Century*, 2d ed. (Englewood Cliffs, N.J.: Prentice Hall, 1990), delineates the contributions of more than sixty women artists to painting, sculpture, photography, and performance art. Whitney Chadwick, *Women, Art and Society* (New York: Thames and Hudson, 1990), presents an alternative view of women and the history of art.

Chapter 7: Art History and Educational Levels

Developmental Perspectives on the Social Studies (Washington, D.C.: National Council for the Social Studies, 1982), edited by Linda W. Rosenzweig, is a collection of articles by social studies educators addressing development theoretically and practically. Developmental issues of elementary, middle, and high school levels are addressed. Of particular interest is Christian Laville and Linda Rosenzweig's chapter on "Teaching and Learning History." Howard Gardner, *Art, Mind and Brain: A Cognitive Approach to Creativity* (New York: Basic Books, 1982) explores the psychology of art through a thorough scrutiny of artistic creativity. Beginning with a historical survey of the work of Piaget, Chomsky, Lévi-Strauss, Cassirer, Langer, and Gombrich, Gardner extends his analysis into education, media, and mental deficiencies. Like Gardner's studies, Michael J. Parsons, *How We Understand Art: A Cognitive Developmental Account of Aesthetic Experience* (New York: Cambridge University Press, 1987), derives its perspective in part from Piaget and Kohlberg but grapples specifically with the notion of aesthetic experience rather than artistic creativity. Patricia Miller, *Theories of Developmental Psychology* (New York: W. H. Freeman, 1989), is a well-structured, readable presentation of six very different theories of development that have dominated thinking and research in the field in this century.

Chapter 8: Curriculum

Michael McCarthy, *Introducing Art History: A Guide for Teachers* (Toronto: Ontario Institute for Studies in Education, 1978), advocates that art educators provide all students with a strong introduction to the visual arts. McCarthy suggests a comprehensive four-year program through which students are made familiar with at least Western art history prior to their first "pyramids to Picasso" survey course in college. While McCarthy's model might benefit by the inclusion of non-Western source material, it is nevertheless a detailed model that middle and high schools could use to structure existing curricula. Marcia Pointon, *History of Art: A Students' Handbook* (London: George Allen and Unwin, 1980), is an introductory study of the discipline. Extremely accessible for the relatively uninformed, Pointon's text tackles the nature, methodology, language, and literature of the art history discipline. As a "nuts and bolts" aside, the teachers' guide to Gerald F. Brommer, *Discovering Art History*, 2d ed. (Worchester, Mass.: Davis Publications, 1989), in addition to serving as a valuable consolidation of Brommer's text, contains both an invaluable source list of films, filmstrips, microfiches, prints, and slides and an inclusive bibliography for each chapter. Brommer's recommendations will prove invaluable to the art educator in planning a thorough course in Western art history from prehistoric through pop art, as well as in acknowledging non-Western art and such contemporary issues as gender and ethnicity. Jack Hobbs and Richard Salome's new text, *The Visual Experience* (Worchester, Mass.: Davis Publications, 1992), is accompanied by an extensive and useful teacher's manual. Seventeen model art history lessons for elementary through high school levels are available in Mary Erickson, ed., *Integrating Art History and History Learning* (Bloomington, Ind.: ERICArt, 1992).

Chapter 9: Integration

Laura H. Chapman, *Approaches to Art in Education* (New York: Harcourt Brace Jovanovich, 1978) is a standard text that serves to broaden the scope of art teaching in American elementary and junior high schools. Demanding that art is essential rather than supplementary to education, Chapman suggests a three-part curriculum framework by which children can heighten personal artistic expression and response, increase their awareness of artistic heritage, and develop an understanding of the relations of art to society. Integral to her model is the inclusion of interdisciplinary perspectives, especially those of art production, art criticism, art history, and anthropology. In *Research Readings for Discipline-based Art Education: A Journey beyond Creating* (Reston, Va.: National Art Education Association, 1988), editor Stephen Mark Dobbs gathers a variety of articles published in art education journals during the past two decades that trace the development of the discipline as it becomes increasingly pluralistic and questions many of its basic assumptions. Selected articles attempt to lend perspective to a variety of philosophical, empirical, curricular, and historical debates that have transformed art education into an arena of critical activity. Marcia Muelder Eaton, *Basic Issues in Aesthetics* (Belmont, Calif.: Wadsworth Publishing Company, 1988), analyzes various problems in contemporary aesthetics and relations to other branches of philosophy such as semiotics, epistemology, and ethics. Ranging from Plato to Derrida, Eaton's prose is remarkably free of the jargon that limits accessibility to many of the current debates within aesthetics. Finally, *Calliope's Sisters: A Comparative Study of Philosophies of Art* (Englewood Cliffs, N.J.: Prentice Hall, 1987) is Richard L. Anderson's challenge to the domination of Western philosophical principles in aesthetic experience. Implicit in his extended discussions of San, Eskimo, aboriginal, Sepik, Navajo, Yoruba, Aztec, early Indian, and Japanese aesthetics and in his relegation of Western aesthetics to a single chapter are a deprivileging of our metaphysical heritage and a revision of the very concept of aesthetics and its relation to a particular culture. Anderson's final chapters on comparative and cross-cultural aesthetics and the function of art as meaning within culture are particularly important and suggest the further broadening of perspective that art educators, historians, and aestheticians might adopt.

Index